Upon The Tented Field

Edited By

Bernard A. Olsen

Contributions By

Thomas L. Waterman

Foreword By

James M. McPherson

Historic Projects, Inc.
1993
Red Bank, New Jersey

Published by Historic Projects Inc.
Red Bank, New Jersey

Copyright © 1993 by Historic Projects Inc.
ISBN# 0-9638729-0-7

Published November 15, 1993

Book Jacket Design, Regan Graphic Design; Archival
Photography, Ken Corbran Photography and T.J.
McMahon; Public Relations, Mary Ann Matlock
Writing & Public Relations; Music Art Consultant, Dr.
John Olsen, Eastern New Mexico University; Research
Assistance, Bernard J. Olsen. Copy Editing, Heather
McCulloch, Karen McGlincy, Diane Miller.

*Book Jacket Photo: Three officers of an
unidentified New York Regiment at Camp Marsh
— from the Publisher's collection.*

Contents

To Kathleen, Louise,
B.J., Chris, Andrew, Ted,
Eric and Evan

Foreword

*by **James M. McPherson***
Princeton, 1993

"The real war will never get in the books." So wrote
the poet Walt Whitman, who had seen the real war close up as
a volunteer nurse in Union army hospitals. He also saw it
through the eyes of his brother George, an officer in the 51st
New York Volunteer Infantry, whose wounds at the battle of
Fredericksburg brought Walt into the hospitals where he
observed the reality of carnage and suffering. Whitman talked
with hundreds of wounded soldiers; it was their stories, the
inside story of the war, that he said would never get in the
books.

But this did not prevent Whitman from writing about
the Civil War. Indeed, he wrote a great deal, and the trauma
and nobility he described so eloquently go far to belie his own
assertion. Nor has it stopped others from trying to describe the
real war. In fact, the Civil War is by far the most written-about
event in American history. Some fifty thousand publications
about it have appeared in the past 130 years. The flood of
books shows no sign of abating. This should scarcely be surprising. The Civil War was the most devastating war in our
history. The 620,000 soldiers, Union and Confederate, who lost
their lives in the conflict almost equal the number of American
soldiers killed in all the rest of the wars this country has
fought combined. If the same percentage of Americans killed in
the Civil War were to die in a war fought today, the number of
American war dead would be five million.

But the impact of the Civil War involved much more
than loss of life. As Mark Twain wrote a few years after the
war, it had "uprooted institutions that were centuries old,
changed the politics of a people, transformed the social life of
half the country, and wrought so profoundly upon the entire
national character that the influence cannot be measured short
of two or three generations." More than any other part of our
past — more even than the Revolution that gave birth to the
United States — the Civil War shaped and defined the kind of
nation we would become. It resolved two fundamental, fester-
ing questions left unresolved by the Revolution of 1776:
whether that precarious experiment of a democratic republic
federated in a union of states would survive; and whether
slavery would continue to mock the ideals of this boasted land

of liberty. Northern victory in 1865 ensured that the nation did not perish from the earth but experienced a new birth of freedom. They were replaced by the institutions and ideology of free-labor entrepreneurial capitalism. For better or for worse, the flames of the Civil War forged the framework of modern America.

Little wonder so much has been written about that war. Many books focus on the social, economic, and political transformations it wrought. An even larger number deal with military strategy, leadership, campaigns, and battles. But none of these things was the "real war" as Whitman meant it. The real war was experienced every day by those who fought it and by their families at home. That experience was especially poignant for the families of the one-fifth of the soldiers who never came home. This was the war that can never get in the books.

But much of it did get into the letters that soldiers wrote home. Civil War armies were the most literate in history to that time. More than 90 percent of white Union soldiers and more than 80 percent of Confederate soldiers could read and write. And write they did — several letters each per week to family members and friends back home. These letters, unlike soldier letters in twentieth-century wars, were not subject to censorship. Their authors belonged to a letter-writing culture. There were no telephones, no radio or television, no way to communicate with loved ones except by words on paper. These

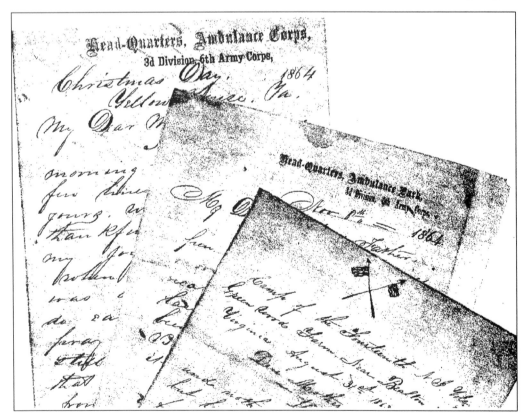

letters, therefore, written during the immediacy of their experience by most of the three million men who fought in the Civil War came as close as we will ever come to the story of the "real war."

And much of this story has gotten into books. Many collections of Civil War soldiers' letters have been published. Of all such collections I have read, **Upon the Tented Field** is one of the best. It includes the

letters of not just one soldier, but six, whose descriptions of
their experiences together provide a gripping narrative of the
14th New Jersey Volunteer Infantry.

Recruited mostly in Monmouth County in the summer
of 1862, the men of the 14th New Jersey became one of the best
regiments in one of the best fighting corps in the Union army
— the 6th Corps of the Army of the Potomac. After spending
most of their first year in bridge-defense and garrison duty
behind the lines in Maryland, the 14th linked up with the
Army of the Potomac during the pursuit of Lee after Gettysburg. They received their baptism of fire in the battle of Locust
Grove near Culpeper, Virginia, on November 27, 1863. From
there they never looked back, fighting with the 6th Corps in all
of its battles: The Wilderness; Spotsylvania; Cold Harbor;
Petersburg; Monocacy; Sheridan's Shenandoah Valley campaign; then back to Petersburg and on to the triumphant end
at Appomattox. The 14th was one of the "fighting regiments" of
the Civil War, as defined by the casualties it suffered — 147
men killed or mortally wounded in action, which put it in the
top 10 percent of Union regiments in that respect.

Four of the six members of the 14th whose letters home
are published here did not come home. The six ranged in rank
from Major Peter Vredenburgh, son of one of Freehold's most
prominent citizens, a private promoted to sergeant-major then
to lieutenant (William Burroughs Ross), a lieutenant (Marcus
Stults), another sergeant (Albert C. Harrison), and two privates (Jacob R. Wolcott and Edward Jones). Most of the letters
are from Harrison and Vredenburgh. They are also the best
letters in their descriptive power and penetration of insight.

The real war — the tragedy of suffering and loss —
does get into this book. Peter Vredenburgh writes to his parents urging them to discourage his youngest brother, aged 18,
from enlisting, for "if he could see as much of camp life even as
I have & if he with his spirit enlists — he will curse the day he
does it. If he expects fun and excitement (which between us is
at the bottom of his patriotism) he will be most emphatically
mistaken....Let him come here [a field hospital after the battle
of Antietam] and see the thousands with their arms and legs
off, or if that won't do, let him go as I did the other day through
the Frederick hospitals and see how little a man's life and
limbs are held in by others and what little return he gets in
reputation or money for the risk and privations of enlisting and
his ideas of the fun of the thing will vanish in thin air." On
another occasion, during the pursuit of Lee after Gettysburg,
Vredenburgh described "confusion, fighting, swearing and
stealing all the time. Scenes which would harrow up your inner
soul in ordinary times become so familiar that you scarcely
give them a second thought. The whole road is jammed up,
with men & teams for miles — men and animals dying along
the roadside are common sights." The fought-over regions of

*Regimental colors of the 14th
(above) and the Regiment's "Battle"
flag (below).*

New Jersey Archives, Trenton, NJ

Virginia were marked by "fields of overgrown weeds, fences down, plantations deserted.... the farms and even the gardens utterly void of cultivation or care.... If you could only see it, connected with the abuse, cruelty, extravagance, and demoralization of the army you would pray harder than ever for this 'Cruel War' to end."

But the real war was not only destruction and demoralization. It was also the dedication and determination of these volunteer soldiers who had enlisted for a great cause: the survival of the United States and its institutions of democracy, liberty, and majority rule. These convictions are voiced most articulately here by Sergeant Albert C. Harrison of Red Bank. "You wanted to know if I was home sick," he wrote his mother in July 1863. "Not a once Mother. I have something to do besides getting home sick. I didn't come down here to play. I came to save the Union, and it shall be saved.... It is true we see some hardship but what of that. That is nothing. I am willing to suffer anything to save and restore our old Union." Three months later he informed his mother that "if I was out of my time today I should enlist again. Remember our ForeFathers, how they suffered for the cause of Freedom. Must we not fight manfully with the help of the most High God to maintain it." As he waited for the orders to attack formidable Confederate defenses at Petersburg in April 1865 (where he would have part of his finger shot off), he asserted that the small remnant of the regiment was determined to vindicate the sacrifices of friends who had been killed during the past year. "The boys are all joyful and ready at all times to do their duty like men, remembering our old Revolutionary Fathers, of the hardships, privations and difficulties they encountered before they accomplished their Just and Glorious Cause." After Appomattox, Harrison wrote his mother that the enemy had surrendered "and thanks be unto God for bringing a stronger and I trust a better people. The great curse of slavery no longer hangs above the heads of the American People. It now may be called a Free Nation."

It was men such as Sergeant Harrison and his comrades in the 14th New Jersey who helped make it so. Here is their story, in all its tragedy as well as final triumph. Here is the real war.

Tenting on the Old Camp Ground

Tenting on the Old Camp Ground by Walter Kittridge; Published by Oliver Ditson Company - Boston, 1863. Source: The Free Library of Philadelphia, Music Department.

1 Introduction

By 1860, the North had developed a dynamic way of life, laced with a diversified economy of manufacturing, banking, shipping, and agriculture. The population of about twenty-two million was growing and immigration added strength and cultural diversity.

The South, on the other hand, evolved quite differently. Twelve million people lived south of the Mason-Dixon Line by 1860, four million of whom were enslaved black Africans. Predominately agricultural, it remained a poor region of small yeoman farmers dominated politically and socially by a planter aristocracy. Slavery, the South's "peculiar institution," had become ingrained in the social fabric of its society by the 1840's. Perhaps the industrial revolution and the invention of the cotton gin contributed most to the South maintaining this institution. There were sound arguments, however, that called for its abolishment in favor of a more diversified economy.

Price, Birch & Co. — slave dealers in Alexandria, VA.

Nevertheless, on the eve of the Civil War, slavery came to be considered a positive good and was doggedly supported by most of white southern society. Poor whites, whose economic circumstances precluded any chance of their owning slaves, supported the system which invariably placed them socially and politically, although not always economically, above the bondsman.

By mid-century, the South had clearly fallen behind the North in wealth and political power and became increasingly more dependent on the North's banking and shipping facilities. The political center in the Congress had also shifted from the old system whereby a tenuous equilibrium had more or less maintained itself in the Senate despite the North's numerical advantage in the House of Representatives.

U.S. Army Military History Institute

With the election of Abraham Lincoln in 1860, the South seceded from the Union and formed the Confederate States of America. They perceived Lincoln as a wily abolitionist bent upon destroying their way of life. They justified secession by a "compact theory of states' rights" which held that the state entities were superior to the central authority. They believed they could righteously nullify Federal law and, indeed, abrogate the Constitution. This clash of federal and state authority had been seen earlier in the Republic's history. Jefferson's and Madison's Kentucky and Virginia Resolutions and John C. Calhoun's Nullification Proclamation were examples. Perhaps the difference in 1860 was that the spirit of compromise and thus the ability to do so seemed to have vanished. The answer may lie, in part, to the passing of those great statesmen that had seen the country through earlier crises.

The North had quite a different concept of what had been accomplished at Philadelphia in 1787. It believed that the Union as established by the Constitution was the solemn will of the people. The laws which were passed by the Federal government as established by the Constitution were the laws of the people, and the states had no right to disregard them.

It is clear that both sections would have preferred a peaceful solution if it could have been arranged on their own terms. The South wanted independence; the North wanted preservation of the Union. It is also probably true that neither side would have opted for war had it realized the cost. The South would ultimately be vanquished and lose its entire way of life. The North would gain victory but at the cost of 360,000 of its young men. Both sides were confident of a quick victory. Senator John J. Crittenden of Kentucky introduced an amendment which would have allowed slavery in the territories south of the line thirty six degrees-thirty minutes and, in effect, guarantee its existence in the slave states. Lincoln, perhaps mistakenly, refused to consider it. Thus, the compromise failed, and the disparate political, social, and economic forces that had been at work for decades erupted in the early morning hours of April 12, 1861, when Confederate guns opened fire upon Fort

Fort Sumter, South Carolina

U.S. Army Military History Institute

Sumter. This action abruptly ended more than seventy years of delicate compromises which had somehow held the Union together. The Civil War had begun.

The first Battle of Bull Run shattered the illusion that the war was a glorious pageant of colorful uniforms, martial music, and chivalry. Federal General McDowell won some early success against the Confederates under General P.G.T. Beauregard but was repulsed by "Stonewall" Thomas J. Jackson. The retreat became a disgraceful route as picnicking civilian observers were overrun by fleeing Union troops. The South's morale rose as the somber realization of the enormity of the conflict settled over the North.

The Northern strategy by midsummer 1862 was three-fold: blockade the Southern coastline, cut the Confederacy by way of the Mississippi River, and take the Southern capital at Richmond. Lincoln entrusted the task to George B. McClellan. While highly qualified, McClellan lacked the decisive resolve to move quickly. The South had merely to hold out to win. In the meantime, it made the colossal blunder of withholding its cotton from Europe in hopes that the economic impact on the textile mills would compel England and France to grant diplomatic recognition. By the time the Confederate government reversed this policy of "King Cotton Diplomacy," it was too late; the Federal blockade had tightened.

As early 1862 approached, the eastern theatre became stagnated by McClellan's preparations against Richmond. In the West, General Ulysses S. Grant invaded Tennessee from Illinois, capturing Forts Henry and Donelson and from there moving to Corinth, Mississippi. At the Battle of Shiloh in early April, 1862, Grant was surprised by Confederate General Albert Sidney Johnston and only with the timely arrival of reinforcements managed to check the rebel advance and avoid disaster. Grant was removed from command as a result of the staggering losses at Shiloh. Meanwhile, McClellan's Peninsula campaign was stalemated at Seven Pines. When the Confederate general Joseph E. Johnston was wounded, command passed to Robert E. Lee of Virginia. To relieve pressure on Richmond, Lee sent Stonewall Jackson toward the Shenandoah Valley. Confederates under Jackson occupied Frederick, Maryland on September 6, 1862, and were poised for the great Battle of Antietam.

As these momentous events were taking place, each state reacted accordingly. The subject of this work concerns New Jersey, the population of which in the spring of 1861 was about 675,000 with about 100,000 potential soldiers. On April 15, 1861, President Lincoln called for 75,000 volunteers. New Jersey's quota was four regiments of about 800 men each. Within a short time over 10,000 men volunteered for service.

Authorities took other measures to enhance the state's preparedness. For example, communications were improved

Abraham Lincoln

Jefferson Davis

Photos: U.S. Army Military History Institute

when the telegraph line to Cape May was continued at state expense, and a maritime guard was established along the coast. Despite the patriotic turnout in support of the war, there were large numbers of people in New Jersey who had Southern sympathies. For example, New Jersey was one of the few states to vote for the Democratic candidate, George McClellan in 1864. The Democratic platform in that year called for peace even if it meant granting Southern independence. The activities of the so-called copperheads and pro-Southern sympathies held by some at home were a source of great anxiety and resentment for the soldiers in the field.

On August 26, 1862, in response to Lincoln's call for 300,000 additional troops, a new force of Federal soldiers was mustered at Camp Vredenburgh, outside of Freehold, New Jersey on the old site of the Battle of Monmouth. It was named the 14th New Jersey Volunteers, was commanded by William Truex, an experienced West Pointer, and consisted of mostly Monmouth County men. It left its home base on September 2, 1862. After reaching Baltimore, Maryland, the Regiment was sent to Frederick Junction to protect the strategic Monocacy Bridge, an artery of the Baltimore and Ohio Railroad. Shortly upon its arrival, news came of the advance of General Robert E. Lee's Army of Northern Virginia against Frederick, Maryland. Because of the far superior numbers of the rebel forces, the 14th N.J. Volunteers were ordered to fall back and shift their command to Elysville, about twenty miles from Baltimore. The Confederate forces burned the Monocacy Bridge and wasted much of the adjacent countryside before they were driven back across the Potomac after their defeat at South Mountain and Antietam on September 18, 1862. With the climax of these events, the 14th N.J. Volunteers were ordered to return to Monocacy and make repairs. They bivouacked along the Monocacy River until more permanent quarters were established at Camp Hooker.

Accordingly, this work is the actual story of six members of this regiment as told through their original correspondence. They include Albert C. Harrison, Edward C. Jones, William B. Ross, Marcus A. Stults, Peter Vredenburgh Jr., and Jacob R. Wolcott. These letters have preserved for all time the purest and unaltered moments in these men's lives as they struggled to endure the hardships of our nation's greatest upheaval. The unique perspective offered by each man's personal background, education, financial status, rank etc., gives the most thorough picture possible. The reader becomes encapsulated in time as the present fades into the past, and the events of more than one hundred and thirty years ago appear to be just happening. One develops a sense of closeness to each of these soldiers as personal sentiments and inner-feelings stir heart-wrenching emotions.

Beyond attempting another history of the war or unit study, the thrust of this work is to coordinate these precious documents within the context of the people and places as they are preserved in original photographs.

Old wooden bridge over the Monocacy at Frederick Junction.

GRAFTED INTO THE ARMY

Grafted Into The Army, by Henry C. Work, Published by Root & Cady, 1862. Source: The Free Library of Philadelphia, Music Department.

2 Answering the Call

July 1862 — February 1863

The following description of events in and around Freehold, N.J. is an edited version of a story written by Ira K. Morris, published in the March, 1905 issue of the Monmouth Democrat. Mr. Morris was a boy in August, 1862, although his recollection of events at Camp Vredenburgh was remarkable.

On a typically hot Sunday afternoon in late August of 1862, the Fourteenth Regiment of New Jersey Volunteers having been mustered into the Federal service, found a large number of visitors mingling among the soldiers in Camp Vredenburgh. The camp was on the old Monmouth battleground, the place honoring the Revolutionary fathers who fought the strategically important Battle of Monmouth nearly one hundred years earlier.

Back of the long rows of clean, white tents, or to the west, more properly speaking, was a delightful strip of woodland, formed of oak and chestnut and hickory shade trees, still dressed in the deep green foliage of early summer. Between the grove and the camp proper, board seats had been arranged for the accommodation of those who wished to attend divine service, and before the time for Chaplain Rose to ascend the crude little platform, as the signal for the commencement, every seat was taken, and scores of soldiers and citizens were also resting upon the ground. The sun was sinking behind the rim of the massive shade trees, and the audience was completely protected from its scorching rays.

There was a delay of several moments in the commencement of the services, which was partially explained by the sudden appearance of the commanding officer — Colonel William

Camp Vredenburgh, just outside Freehold, NJ.

U.S. Army Military History Institute, Carlisle, PA/Monmouth County Historical Association, Freehold, NJ

Colonel William S. Truex pictured above left; Major Peter Vredenburgh, above right.

S. Truex, a superb soldier, who had studied the tactics at West Point, and served on the battlefields of the Mexican War. As civil war broke out in the Spring of 1861, Truex had served as Major of the Fifth Regiment (N.J.) and Lieutenant-Colonel of the Tenth Regiment (N.J.), and now assumed command of this newly formed Fourteenth Regiment.

A seat had been reserved for the Colonel. At his right sat Adjutant Lemuel Buckelew, while nearby were Lieutenant Colonel C.K. Hall and Major Peter Vredenburgh, Jr.

Captain Austin H. Patterson and Lieutenant William H. Craig were standing near the platform, at first earnestly conversing about something that appeared to be of very much importance. Suddenly the latter departed, and when about a hundred yards away, saluted Captain James W. Conover, who was serving as Officer-of-the-day, and presently the two came to the edge of the woodlands and attentively listened to the eloquent words of the Chaplain.

So seemingly relaxed was the atmosphere among the officers of the Fourteenth that afternoon that it hardly seemed possible that sixteen months had passed since the war of words between North and South had given way to the roar of cannons. It was a time when men from all walks of life gathered in the village of Freehold, New Jersey, in answer to President Lincoln's call for 300,000 men.

A few days later, Colonel Truex received orders for his regiment to be in readiness to move. It numbered nearly a thousand men, among whom were those who had seen service in other organizations and even in other wars. The Colonel had promised "the boys" that, as a regiment they should visit Freehold, before starting south, and he proceeded to arrange for this event.

On the night

Main Street, Freehold, N.J.

before the first march of the regiment, the rain came down in torrents, washing away the deep coating of red dust that covered every object, and it also purified the atmosphere. To many it was their first experience at marching, and rifles began to grow heavy before the three miles or so were covered; but as the long, blue line, fringed with glistening steel, turned into the main street of the village, the men kept the ranks closed up very creditably, the oft-repeated order to "cover your file leader" seeming to be well remembered. Indeed, it was a fine looking regiment, even then, and anyone who knew the men could easily predict that it would win credit and honor on many a battlefield of the South.

The regiment halted on Main Street, came to battalion front, the right resting close to the American Hotel. There Colonel Truex permitted his men to enjoy the company of friends and to rest. Fully an hour passed. Colonel Truex, a superb horseman, rode a handsome mottled, "watch-eyed" grey, which seemed as proud of its position at the head of the regiment as did its rider.

"Attention, battalion! Carry arms! Right face! Forward march!" Thus rang out the clear, clean cut words of the veteran Colonel, and almost a thousand rifles were lifted from the ground, the regiment filed by fours, and amid the cheers of the throng of spectators, "the Gallant Fourteenth" retraced its steps up Main Street, to Railroad Avenue, and from there wound its way back to Camp Vredenburgh.

Many citizens would remember that day — the long row of men, in the very prime of life, wearing the uniform of

Lt. Colonel Cadwell Kepple Hall

The American Hotel, Freehold, N.J.

Adjutant Lemuel Buckelew

Broad Street, Red Bank, N.J. Adlum & Cole's Grocery is the building on the left.

their country, each awaiting the hour to labor, to suffer, and to die, if fate should so decree, for the flag which their color-sergeant carried "steadily on the front and center."

One scene in particular is easily recalled — the group of field officers, dismounted, and standing in front of the old United States Hotel: Colonel Truex, Lieutenant-Colonel Hall, Major Vredenburgh, Adjutant Buckelew, Quartermaster Cowart and Chaplain Rose — while around them, shaking hands and uttering the kindest of farewells, were New Jersey Governor Joel Parker, Major James S. Yard, William H. Conover, Sr., Andrew Murray, Colonel William D. Davis, General Charles Haight, Dr. John R. Conover, Andrew Ross, and a hundred others.

This is the story of the men of the Fourteenth. Far beyond a regimental review, this is a history of human courage and suffering, triumph and grief. The story, as told by the men who lived, fought and died in the service of their country, is history in its purest form. The eloquent words of Sergeant Albert C. Harrison, Major Peter Vredenburgh, Jr., Lieutenant William B. Ross, Lieutenant Marcus Stults and Privates Jacob R. Wolcott and Edward C. Jones, offer a rare and unique perspective of what the nearly three million men under arms endured during America's most bloody episode.

Albert C. Harrison

Sergeant Albert C. Harrison, whose correspondence originally inspired this work, was a native of Red Bank, New Jersey, a small town on the Jersey Shore. Harrison was an only child and the descendant of English ancestors who were among the early settlers of America. He was the son of Robert and Cornelia Dennis Harrison. His father spent most of his life at Galveston, Texas, and died of yellow fever while making a voyage from Galveston to New York. Albert was born a few weeks later at Rumson Neck, New Jersey, where his mother made her home with relatives at the Dennis Homestead Farm. Anthony Dennis, Albert's grandfather, distinguished himself during the Revolutionary War by carrying dispatches to American headquarters. Although he died before Albert was born, the lad relished the stories of how his grandfather had eluded the British and delivered the dispatches. Stories of his grandfather's devotion to duty perhaps inspired similar patriotic values in the young boy which became evident when he grew to manhood.

As a boy Albert attended the public school at Little Silver, New Jersey. Later, he attended a

New York School and received his final education at Ocean Institute near Eatontown, New Jersey. Shortly before the war, Albert was employed as a clerk at a grocery store on Broad Street in Red Bank (Adlum & Cole's — see photo).

On August 14th, 1862, at the age of eighteen, Albert enlisted in the Fourteenth Regiment of New Jersey Infantry (Company G).

Peter Vredenburgh, Jr.

Major Peter Vredenburgh, Jr. was born on September 12, 1837 in Freehold, New Jersey. He was one of three sons born to Judge Peter Vredenburgh (1805-1873) and Eleanor Brinckerhoff Vredenburgh (1816-1884). Vredenburgh's brothers were William H. (1840-?) and James (1844-1915). After receiving a liberal arts education, he studied law in Poughkeepsie, New York (1856-1857), and later studied under Judge Bennington F. Randolph in Freehold. He was admitted to the New Jersey Bar in February, 1859. Settling in Eatontown, New Jersey, he practiced law for three years until commissioned into the United States Army, 14th Regiment New Jersey Volunteer Infantry as a Major (Staff) on August 25, 1862, shortly before his 26th birthday.

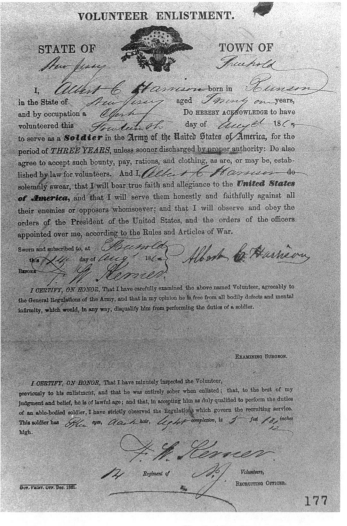

Harrison's enlistment document.

William Burroughs Ross

William Burroughs Ross

Lieutenant William Burroughs Ross enlisted in the 14th New Jersey Volunteer Infantry on July 28, 1862. Official records show that Ross enlisted as a private and was promoted to sergeant major on January 20, 1864, and was commissioned a First Lieutenant on September 14, 1864 (Company B). Being quite literate, Ross endeared himself to several officers as he was often assigned as a clerk early in his service. He was a native of Freehold, New Jersey, and was fond of playing the guitar. He regularly corresponded with his mother and father, as well as his sister Mimmie.

Portraits: U.S. Army Military History Institute/Monmouth County Historical Association/John Kuhl collection. Broad Street, Red Bank — T.J. McMahon collection. Enlistment document — N.J. State Archives.

Lt. Marcus A. Stults

Marcus Stults

Lieutenant Marcus Stults was from Prospect Plains, a village between Jamesburg and Hightstown, New Jersey, and the son of a farmer. He was commissioned a Lieutenant in the Fourteenth Regiment (Company H) in August, 1862. Little else is known about him, as he was not a very prolific letter writer.

Jacob R. Wolcott

Private Jacob R. Wolcott (Company B) was a native of Trenton, New Jersey. Wolcott's correspondence in this work are directed to C. Vance Powers, a prominent businessman in Trenton, who was his employer before the war.

Edward C. Jones

Little is known about Private Jones (Company C), except that he was a native of Plainfield, New Jersey, and served as a drummer in the Regimental Band. His correspondence are scattered, but as a private, his writings offer an interesting contrast to the very different life-style the enlisted man had as compared to that of an officer.

America was at a crossroads in 1860, and the direction it took would shake the very foundation of a nation. The men of the Fourteenth chose Freehold as their crossroads, and the direction they chose took them through the hell known as the Civil War.....

Vredenburgh family estate, located in what is today, Colts Neck, N.J., circa 1870.

The correspondence are opened by Peter Vredenburgh, Jr., with a letter to his parents, who it seems are vacationing. Presently, young Vredenburgh is at his home in Eatontown, NJ, about 16 miles east of Freehold, where the Vredenburgh homestead was located. The correspondence follow in chronological order, interrupted only by brief editorial commentary to keep the reader informed of parallel events during the war, with priority given those events that would directly influence the 14th Regiment, New Jersey Volunteers.

The letters as they appear are exactly as written by the men, although, in some cases, edited to shortened versions. The editor chose to slightly alter such things as tense for the benefit of the reader. Where interpretation was necessary, the editor used brackets [ ] within the correspondence, rather than footnotes, for convenience.

Quartermaster Enoch Cowart

Vredenburgh

Eatontown, July 31, 1862

Dear Mother

I received your letter on Monday evening but as I had to escort Aunt Dora Mary to Uncle Peter's on Tuesday I could not answer it. Everything goes well at home. Henry and Will are at Sing Sing and expect to return home today. Will is coming here to stay a few days with me. I am sorry Father declined the offer of Truex for me because I could have had a chance to get well acquainted with military tactics and will never have such another chance. I am young yet and should like to see a little of military life particularly if I can get such a position. I should not be surprised if I went off in either Truex's or Rob Stockton's regiment as Major. Enoch Cowart accepted the appointment offered me. A great many in Freehold wanted me to have it. Hoping you will both continue to improve and with much love to Father.

I am your Affectionate Son
Peter

[The position that Vredenburgh refers to in this letter is that of Quartermaster of the 14th Regiment.]

Harrison

Freehold, Camp Vredenburgh
August 22, 1862

Dear Mother

I have the opportunity of writing you a few lines. I am in excellent health and have a first rate appetite and first rate spirits. I must go to dinner now so I will wait until afterwards and write a little more. (I have had my dinner so you may think that I feel a great deal better, and if you don't, I do.)

I hope this finds you well as I am. I commenced a letter to you this morning and was going to send it by mail but I had the happiness of seeing John [Harrison's stepfather]. I don't suppose I need have written but I thought I must tell just how I was getting along. We have a nice lot of boys in my tent all officers but two. I rank as second sergeant and it suits me first rate as it clears me of all guard duty. I retire at 9 o'clock, every light has to be put out at that hour. I like camp life first rate. We have a splendid regiment. We each take turns in reading. We read a chapter in the Testament and a prayer every night and morning, don't worry about me mother, I'll get along first rate. So I must close as my time is up for drill.

From your ever dear and affectionate son,
Albert

Wolcott

Camp Vredenburg near Freehold, New Jersey
August 24, 1862

Friend Powers

I suppose you would like to know what I think of camp life. It is harder work than I had any idea of. We have to drill 6 hours every day and then have 2 dress parades every day.

We are called in line at sunrise and answer to the roll — then march down to the spring to wash for breakfast. After breakfast, we drill 3 hours then march back to our tent, blacken our shoes and put on our dress coat — then we are marched on the parade ground and formed in line where we are inspected by the officer-of-the-day. We then wash for dinner, dinner of Forst & Taylor shoulders — which one has to have a good appetite to eat. I went one whole day without eating anything but I had to come to it. [Forst & Taylor — provision suppliers from Trenton, N.J.]

I expect we shall go to Washington next Friday. Colonel gave orders not to issue more furloughs to anyone as he wanted all in camp on that day and to be in readiness to move. I would come to Trenton once more before

Union Regiment on parade.

we left but it is rumored in camp that Jeff Davis is marching on to Washington with 7000 men.

Seven men have run away — 2 have been caught and put in the guardhouse and will be tried tomorrow morning at 10 o'clock. One will be shot — this being the third time.

The drums are calling roll and I must stop and get ready for dress drill. I have a desk to write on — a board on my knees. Remember me to all inquiring friends and hope to hear from you soon.

Yours respectfully,
J.R. Wolcott

Jones

Camp Vredenburgh
Sunday August 24, 1862

Dear Father & Mother

We arrived here safe and sound on Friday night — away behind time and did not arrive in camp until 7 o'clock at night but in time for a bully supper. I think we have as good a cook as can be scanned up anywhere in this part of the country (Joe Reeves Regimental cook).

I have just finished my breakfast and we had coffee with milk and sugar in it, roast beef and fried potatoes (hot) now that is just as good a breakfast as anyone can wish to have. We have better living here than half of the folks in Plainfield have.

I could have come home yesterday but I did not want to come home until I received my twenty-five dollars. We were to be mustered in the service yesterday but the mustering rolls were not made out and so we are to be mustered in on Tuesday morning at 9 o'clock in the morning and the Capt. told me yesterday as I was with him in his tent for two hours and he asked me if I wanted to go home. I told him not until Tuesday or Wednesday and he said I could go but there came an order out on dress parade that after today no more than 5 could have a furlough at a time but I am all right for one.

We had orders to leave here on Wednesday but it was countermanded and we will not leave here until the 1st of Sept. or a few days after and then we are going to Meridan Hill and take quarters for winter. They are putting up wooden barracks for the nine months men. We have the best tent in the

Union Regimental cook preparing meal at Relay House outside Baltimore, MD.

Photos: U.S. Army Military History Institute

company and the nicest men into it. We have singing and everything is as handy as can be.

I caught cold on Friday night on account of not having straw in our ticks but we got here so late that we could not get any and there was none sent here by the major so we went to a farmer and bought some. We gave 5 cents for each tick and had a good bed and I slept like a log from 1/2 past 8 until 1/2 past 6 this morning.

E.C. Jones

Harrison

Camp Vredenburgh
August 30, 1862

Dear Mother

As I have an opportunity of sending you a few lines personally, I will endeavor so to do. Mother, I am in excellent health and in excellent spirits. I expect we will leave here next Monday morning and we look forth with joy for its coming. We had a parade in Freehold yesterday and won approbation and praise from the public. I hear you are well and by the blessing of God long may you continue so. I have received my $25.00 and I send you 20 of it. I have 5 of the other left so $10.00 will be enough for me. Don't worry mother I will get along all right.

Hotel Belmont — Freehold, N.J.

Freehold Public Library

I thought of coming down this week but I couldn't for longer than 24 hours so it was best for me not to because I would be all the time going and coming.

I don't know where we shall go yet but I will write as soon as we encamp. I think it will be in Alexandria [VA]. Don't think that I don't like this life because I do, better than ever. I saw Mrs. Bergen yesterday. Red Bank must be deserted today I guess by the looks of things up here. There is a piece of everybody up here today ha ha ha. Remember me to John and give my love to Libbie, tell her to keep a good heart. I haven't time to say anything more.

From your ever dutiful son,
Albert C. Harrison

Harrison

Camp Wood, Maryland
September 4, 1862

Dear Mother

As I am off duty at present, I must scratch you a few lines to inform you that we have arrived at our destination. As you may see by the above. I suppose you know we started last Tuesday, well such was the fact. And we have arrived in the land of Secesh [Secessionists, Pro-Confederate sympathizers] and I thank God that I can say I am enjoying excellent health.

I will try and give the details of our trip. Well after leaving the Old Camp Vredenburgh, which was a day of pleasure to us all we arrived in Philadelphia at about six o'clock the same night. We were introduced to the Soldiers Relief Society [One of many societies formed to offer aid to soldiers] where we had a hearty supper. Then we repaired to the cars again, and started about 12 o'clock and arrived in Baltimore about 9 o'clock Wednesday morning, but before I go any farther I must speak a word about the citizens of Philadelphia. The streets were thronged with women and children to such an extent that we could scarcely make our way through the crowd, but I must commence where I left off with our journey as I have but little time to spare. Well we left Baltimore about 9 o'clock Wednesday night but before we left, there was quite an excitement. One Railroad station burned down. Some thought it was done by Secesh, as nearly one half the population of Baltimore are Secesh I think by their looks. The stars and stripes floats over every part of the city, but you know there are often wolves in sheeps clothing. I guess it is the case there. We arrived here this morning (Thursday) at about 6 o'clock. It is a beautiful place and I think a very healthy place. There is a small river runs near our camp. And a splendid railroad bridge crosses the river near the junction which is guarded by 3 pieces of union artillery which came today.

I haven't time Mother to

Pro-Confederate citizens assault Federal troops in Baltimore.

U.S. Army Military History Institute

General Thomas "Stonewall" Jackson CSA

Contemporary photo of the railroad bridge over the Monocacy River at Frederick Junction, MD.

write any more at present. I will give you further particulars next time I write which will be as soon as I can. I simply write to let you know where we are so you can write to me. Give my love to Libbie. Give my love to all, receive a portion for yourself. Write immediately will you mother, for I am anxious to hear from all.

Your Son,
Albert

General Stonewall Jackson's Advance Against Monocacy
September 1862

General Lee's decision to move north in September 1862 was predicated on a number of factors that historians have skillfully and thoroughly examined. Among these were the South's attempt at getting the border states to join the Confederacy, the need for a dramatic victory that would bring foreign recognition, and the strategic goal of cutting the vital railroad links that connected Washington to the western theatre.

The 14th New Jersey Volunteers, recently mustered at Freehold, New Jersey, were sent to defend these vital points of transshipment and specifically found themselves near Frederick, Maryland. They were entrusted with the task of defending the bridges, particularly the new iron artery of the Baltimore and Ohio

Railroad. When General Lee sent "Stonewall" Jackson and some 30,000 veteran Confederates toward Frederick in the late summer of 1862, it was the 14th New Jersey Volunteers, among other Federal units who briefly opposed them.

Vredenburgh

Alberton, Howard County, Maryland
September 6, 1862 — 5 1/2 P.M.

My Dear Mother

You see that we are now about 12 miles west of Baltimore. We were at Monocacy Station about 3 miles south of Frederick from which place I sent you a few lines and I have only time now to tell you that I am safe well through. I have slept in the open air on the ground for the last two nights. The people here are in a great excitement. The rebels, 5000 strong, have taken the same camp ground that we yesterday vacated. We left about an hour before they came. We are expecting a cavalry raid tonight. Tell my dear Father not to be afraid but that I will act gallantly for I have experienced the hour before the battle several times and can stand the test. I will write fully as soon as possible.

One meal a day and riding all day and sleeping in the open air agrees with me. The Colonel says you would not know me I am so brown. I have not arranged my things yet until we get settled because we expect the rebels all the time. I will write fully as soon as possible.

Your Affectionate Son
Peter

Ross

Elysville, Maryland
September 6, 1862

Dear friends at home

I wrote you one letter while at Monocacy and as we left there the same night I will have to write again to let you know where I am so you can send a letter to me. We had orders to move here as the rebels were advancing on the place which we were at. There were about 30,000 of them coming so General Wood thought it would be useless for us to stand against so many. And therefore ordered us away.

Elysville is 10 miles from the Relay House and 20 miles from Baltimore. This is a splendid spot I can tell you. We are all well but sleepy tonight. When we were at Monocacy we

---

Barbara Frietchie

Up from the meadows rich with corn,
Clear in the cool September morn.

The clustered spires of Frederick stand,
Green-walled by the hills of Maryland.

Round about them orchards sweep,
Apple and peach trees fruited deep,

Fair as a garden of the Lord,
To the eyes of the famished rebel horde,

On that pleasant morn of the early Fall,
When Lee marched over the mountain wall,

Over the mountains winding down,
Horse and foot, into Frederick town.

Forty flags with their silver stars,
Forty flags with their crimson bars,

Flapped in the morning wind: the sun
Of noon looked down, and saw not one.

Up rose old Barbara Frietchie then,
Bowed with her fourscore years and ten;

Bravest of all in Frederick town,
She took up the flag the men hauled down.

In her attic-window the staff she set,
To show that one heart was loyal yet.

Up the street came the rebel-tread,
Stonewall Jackson riding ahead.

Under his slouched hat left and right
He glanced: the old flag met his sight.

Halt!-the dust-brown ranks stood fast;
"Fire!"-out blazed the rifle-blast.

It shivered the window, pane and sash,
It rent the banner with seam and gash.

Quick, as it fell from the broken staff,
Dame Barbara snatched the silken scarf;

She leaned far out on the window-sill,
And shook it forth with a royal will.

"Shoot, if you must, this old gray head,
But spare your country's flag!" she said.

A shade of sadness, a blush of shame,
Over the face of the leader came;

The nobler nature within him stirred
To life at that woman's deed and word.

"Who touches a hair of yon gray head
Dies like a dog! March on!" he said.

All day long through Frederick street
Sounded the tread of marching feet;

All day long that free flag tossed
Over the heads of the rebel host.

Ever its torn folds rose and fell
On the loyal winds that loved it well;

And through the hill-gaps sunset light
Shone over it with a warm good-night.

Barbara Frietchie's work is o'er,
And the rebel rides on his raids no more.

Honor to her! and let a tear
Fall, for her sake, on Stonewall's bier.

Over Barbara Frietchie's grave,
Flag of Freedom and Union, wave!

Peace and order and beauty draw
Round thy symbol of light and law;

And ever the stars above look down
On thy stars below in Frederick town.

John Greenleaf Whittier

Photos: "Stonewall" Jackson — U.S. Army Military History Institute; Barbara Frietchie — National Archives

were out all night expecting to see the rebels but nary one did we see. We are on the railroad 40 miles from the old place and our duty will be to scout around the country from here to prevent the guerillas from committing any outrages. I believe this is all as I only want to let you know where we are. After we get settled I will let you know all the particulars.

Write soon as I want to hear from home. All the people here are Union. I slept in one of the houses last night and got my supper and breakfast and they would not take a cent for it. Remember me to all my friends and tell them I like this business better than anything I have ever been at yet. I believe this is all at present so goodbye and write soon.

Burroughs

Vredenburgh

Camp Wood, Elysville, Alberton County, Maryland
Sunday September 14, 1862

My Dear Father

How glad I am to know that you are apprised of our true situation and know that the many exciting rumors which have circulated in the Philadelphia press of disaster to our regiment are false. They were not entirely though, without foundation. The bridges over the Monocacy which we were sent to protect we have since learned from reliable authority have been blown up and we would have taken the same elevating tour if we had remained there. We heard heavy cannonading all day yesterday and understood last evening that our forces were shelling the rebels from Maryland Heights. We do not apprehend any sudden danger where we are now.

Lt. Col. Hall has just returned from Washington this morning and says that a great battle is expected near Frederick today. There is no use in my writing war news though, because you know from the New York papers, before we do. We arrest all travelers and make them give an account of

Confederate infantry on the march through Frederick, MD.

32

themselves, and thereby gain sometimes a little news in advance, but we can hardly ever depend upon what we gain from such a source. We are very pleasantly located a mile southeast of Elysville in a beautiful orchard. The greatest obstacle to our enjoyment being the difficulty of getting supplies. I feel so thankful Father, that I did not accept the Quartermaster appointment. Poor Mr. Cowart cannot complain about the monotony. He has to keep on the go all the time, and even then owing to the tremendous influx of soldiers into Baltimore he meets with poor success. The men have been without bread and fresh meat for two days. I would not be Q.M. for five thousand dollars a year. Don't trouble yourself Father about my wants. I really want nothing more. I have too much to take care of now especially if we should have to take French leave again. My horse has apparently recovered from his lameness and both are looking fine and fat.

[no signature]

Stults

Major General Thomas J. Wood USA

Elysville, Maryland
Sunday, September 14, 1862

Dear Pa & Ma

I hardly intended to write sooner but better sooner than never. Since leaving Freehold the 14th has traveled a good ways and have had a hard time of it. We landed at Monocacy Thursday morning (by the way Monocacy is on the Baltimore and Ohio Railroad, a distance of 60 miles from Baltimore) and pitched our tents and was calculating on a stay of a month or two. But at night we received word that a strong force of rebels was crossing the Potomac at Point of Rocks, a distance of 11 miles above us. Company H was thrown out on picket and during the night nearly all expected we would be attacked. The next morning we got a dispatch from General Wood ordering us to fall back to Elysville a distance of 20 miles from Baltimore. We got out of the way just in time for the rebels reached our camp within 3 1/2 hours after we left.

The health of the Regiment is good considering we have not had but one good nights sleep since we left Freehold. We have had plenty to eat but most of the time not of very good quality. All hands are in good spirits and looking ahead to better times which we will have when we get settled. I must not forget to add that I am very well, and I would like to hear from Grandpa and the rest of you.

Yours,
Marcus

P.S. Just as I finish a train from Frederick Junction brings the news that the rebels are in strong force in and around

Chaplain Frank B. Rose

General George B. McClellan USA

Monocacy and Frederick City.

Harrison

Alberton, Howard County, Maryland.
Sunday night 1/2 past 7 o'clock September 14, 1862

My Dear Mother

As I will have more time tonight I will commence scribbling you a few lines with my pokeberry ink, my own manufacture, in answer to your letter which I received this morning. I was glad to hear that you could say you were well, only a little nervous. But thank God you were well enough to write to me, and by his kind Providence may you continue so. Dear Mother I rejoice to think that I am a soldier not only in this glorious union army, but in the army of God, where there will be no fighting. And I thank God that there are some soldiers in this, our own Regiment, that feel their need of a savior. We have a great many members of Churches of different denominations in the Regiment. We hold Prayer meetings every successive night until the taps of the drum to turn in. There was a happy time last night among us for our chaplain had just arrived, a finer young man you don't often crop or a smarter one. His name is Rose, he is from Trenton. We held a meeting this afternoon before the Colonel's tent, and had a reviving time. The boys are all in good health and excellent spirits. They are all anxious to say a few words to the Rebels in the shape of bullets. But as things look in the land of Dixie, I don't think they will have a chance to satisfy their wishes. There has been an old fashioned battle fought since last Friday. You will see it likely in the papers before you receive my letter. But I will tell you all I know about it.

The Colonel sent 105 men yesterday to guard the provision train as far as Frederick Junction. When I wrote to Libbie the Rebels were 30,000 strong instead of 10,000 at that place, but three hearty cheers for the union. McClellan has given them Hail Columbia assisted by the Noble Burnside [Major Generals George McClellan and Ambrose Burnside]. They took 2000 Rebel Cavalry and 800 infantry, at one haul and have the remainder of them surrounded without a doubt. Our boys returned tonight and said the provisions went through all right. There were about 3000 wagons ready to take the supplies on to McClellan. The bridge I spoke about in Libbies letter that we guarded is blown up. The battle was fought on our old camp ground. They said it was a sorry old spot. Some of the boys brought back swords, pistols, bayonets and all quantities of rubbish. There was immense excitement in the camp tonight when the boys returned. We heard they were all taken prisoners. But they came in all sound and whole.

I suppose Libbie told you all the particulars of our leaving Frederick so I will only state to you that we are encamped in an apple orchard and a splendid position it is. The water is excellent. The trees are loaded down with fruit and we are in an enemy country and on a Secesh farm. The owners name is Dorcey and he is rank Secesh. He came over when we first came here, but had little to say as it was not well for him to say much.

Monday morning, September 15, 1862

I will commence again this morning and say a few words, as I have a few minutes to spare before going to breakfast. It is a little cloudy this morning but will be a scorcher by and by. We have breakfast at seven o'clock, then get on our equipment at 9, drill until 11 o'clock, have dinner at 12 o'clock, equip ourselves again and drill from 2 until 4 o'clock, have a dress parade at 6 o'clock lasting half an hour. We drill well for the short time we have been in the field. The colonel is beloved by all and in fact all the officers. Major Vredenburgh is on hand all the while.

There were about fifty letters came yesterday morning for Company G, and you would have laughed to see the boys rush after me. Their faces were all pleasure. Some would receive 2, 3, 4 letters and turn away singing or whistling and some received none, they would turn away sad and dejected and wonder why there were none for them.

I haven't had a chance to find fault yet except when we skedadled from Frederick. Then we had nothing but paving stones, some may call them soda crackers but I think they came without calling. Without a joke mother, I have gained 4 lbs. since I enlisted. My health is better than it ever was in that store. I don't feel the least inclined to be there. When you write again Mother, let me know how the nine months men are getting along. I mean those men that were bought with a hundred dollars for fear of draft.

I am not sorry that I am one of Uncle Sams sons. He uses us well, even if we do have to sacrifice home ties, and feather beds and all such like. I would like to drop in and see you all this morning. You and Libbie especially. Give my love to her and tell her to be a good girl and I will come home and see her bye and bye. The Southern Confederacy is nearly played out mother. You may make up your mind to that for Mother, I can see more truth here than you can read in the paper in six months. There is only two cases of sickness in the regiment and they are in favorable circumstances of recovery.

Charley White sends his love to you mother. He hasn't any hair on the top of his head, the place where the Wool ought to grow. He has his head shaved and looks like a "what is it." We talk of sending him to Barnums [Phineas Taylor Barnum, American showman]. William Byram is getting bald. Thompson says he never was better in his life but would like to have a drink of apple. But I can't see it. George White says if it wasn't for Poke Berries it would cost me a pile for ink, but so be it, I am bound to write. The 12th NJ is within 3 miles of us, encamped at a place called Ellicotts Mills. I suppose you are

Major General Ambrose E. Burnside USA

Photos: U.S. Army Military History Institute/
Monmouth County Historical Association

General Robert E. Lee CSA

Major General Joseph Hooker USA

aware of our being in Wood's Division [Major General Thomas Jefferson Wood]. I think we will be Brigaded soon. Write when you have a chance. I must come to a close as it is time for squad drill and I must get out my squad. I must bring my letter to a close.

From Your Ever Obedient and Affectionate Son,
Albert C. Harrison

The Battle of Antietam

The Battle of Antietam on September 17, 1862, was one of the decisive engagements of the Civil War. In order to gain vital European recognition, General Robert E. Lee had to bring the war to the North and demonstrate to the world that the South could win a major campaign. In August 1862, Lee moved into Maryland to accomplish this purpose. He was closely followed by the Army of the Potomac commanded by General George B. McClellan. Lee hoped to enlist recruits for the Army of Northern Virginia and stockpile military stores before a major showdown.

Realizing that McClellan was in pursuit, Lee crossed Antietam Creek and consolidated his position on the high ground near Sharpsburg. Federal forces attacked Lee at dawn on September 17, 1862. General Hooker's artillery pounded Confederate forces in the cornfields north of the town. The battle raged southward from the north woods, through the cornfield, past "Bloody Lane," the Dunkard Church, and Burnside Bridge to below Sharpsburg where it ended. Reinforcements of Confederate General A.P. Hill's "Light Division" from Harpers Ferry checked the final Federal assault, and the battle ended without a decisive victory for either side. Both sides suffered staggering losses. The North suffered about 12,000 killed and wounded to the South's 11,000. Perhaps the most significant results of the battle were twofold: first, anticipated European involvement was postponed; second, the stage for Lincoln's ingenious political ploy was set. He outlined a preliminary Emancipation Proclamation stating that slaves in the rebellious states would be freed on the first of the new year. Thus, the war now took on the dimension of freeing the slaves and greatly impacted Western Europe. The working classes in England and France were strongly opposed to slavery and pressured their governments to refrain from helping the South.

The 14th New Jersey Volunteers were not engaged at Antietam but were located nearby. The men who are the subjects of this work were eyewitnesses to the carnage inflicted by the two great armies and recorded the aftermath.

Vredenburgh

Camp Hooker, Monocacy Maryland
September 19, 1862

Dear Mother

We have moved about so much lately and have had so much to attend to in camp, that

I have not written as I ought to have done. We are now at the Monocacy where the Baltimore & Ohio Railroad crosses it, but I cannot tell how long we shall remain here because we are now in Hooker's Division and may be ordered off at any moment. I was very sorry to leave Elysville for Lt. Col. & myself got very intimate in a pleasant family, but the excitement & new sights here partially atone for the change. There are 800 rebel prisoners here within 100 yards from me. They came in last night from the front. I was at Frederick when they passed through. They only excite pity. They are too despicable to hate. Poor, emaciated, devils, I can only compare them to the most squalid of our New York beggars. They slept last night upon the cold wet ground, nothing over them except the few ragged garments they wore & most of them with nothing under them. They certainly have an advantage over us in that you cannot discern one a hundred yards off — they are so near the color of the ground. There has been terrible fighting to the south of us near or rather to the south of Boonsboro and Wednesday the roar of artillery was incessant.

Lt. Col. [Hall] and myself took a ride yesterday to Frederick and I assure you it was very exciting. Thousands and thousands of soldiers were passing either in regiments or straggling along the road; immense trains of baggage wagons, each drawn by six mules or horses, quantities of equestrians, artillery & all tended to make the ride long to be remembered. The men invariably carry revolvers, and many of them dirk knives besides, which reminds the beholder, if he be of a literary turn of mind, of the exciting

Antietam

scenes so graphically described in Jack Shepherd, Paul Pry, and other works of like character. We have had very conflicting rumors from McClellan's headquarters today. First came the news that McClellan had the enemy surrounded. He on the high ground while they were on the plain below. And that he had agreed to an armistice for twenty four hours and that they had finally surrendered. Today at noon (about 2 hours ago) two men were in my tent who said they left the front yesterday afternoon at one o'clock and that the rebels had Harpers Ferry, our forces not having recaptured it as reported, and that Jackson had been reinforced. It is hard to tell what is true & Lt. Col. and myself intend riding as far as we can towards the front this afternoon to find out what we can.

It is a terrible road from Frederick I hear, to the scene of Tuesday's battle. All along the road the odor arising from the dead men & horses is sickening. Even the dead men are

Photos: U.S. Army Military History Institute

Antietam

scarcely covered with dirt in many instances and as for horses and mules they don't think of burying them, even here where we are encamped, there were quantities of the latter lying about. As Henry very truly remarked once, "the school of the soldier is a hard one." The brutality Mother, is horrible, every man must look out for himself. I never think of moving outside of the camp after dark without my revolver. My humanity has come near getting me in difficulty twice, it having led me to interfere with teamsters who I have seen fearfully abusing their mules. I am almost afraid to look towards the place where the army wagons are stationed for I always see some of the wretched drivers apparently trying to kill their mules. I suppose I will have to do as others do, leave such things to the care of the Great Ruler of the Universe. Thousands of wounded Union prisoners late from Sharpsburg are ever now within 1/4 of a mile from me, waiting and having been waiting since this morning for transportation to some place but there is such a large business done on this road, that if they get away in a day or two they will be lucky.

It is now nine o'clock in the evening. The 800 rebel prisoners are still shivering on the bare ground within 100 yards of my tent. The wounded Union men are still moaning at the railroad not 1/4 of a mile off, and yet all this misery & suffering must be endured. You and I cannot help it. No one can help it. It is the higher law that it shall be so. All I can do is to stay in my tent and see and hear as little of it as possible. To refer to a more pleasant subject Mother, this country here is beautiful. Tell Henry, he would never get tired of scanning over the fields here, the country is so lovely and beautiful. The Monocacy reminds me a good deal of the Raritan as it appears between Uncle Van Dorn's & Sommerville. It is fordable in as

Contemporary photo of the Monocacy River near Frederick.

many places and Bill [Vredenburgh's servant] takes great pleasure in bathing and washing the horses in it every day. On each side of the river particularly on the westerly side, the fields are fertile and rise gradually till they are lost in the mountains which run between us and the Potomac — and as I like this side of the soldier's life very well and the regular exercise has had a perceptible effect upon my physical condition. I couldn't be better and as long as I hear good news from home will be very happy.

Don't let Jim [Vredenburgh's brother] enlist on any account as a private. You had better send him to the state's prison at once. He will have to sleep in his clothes, nestled close in with 10 or 12 dirty-lousy devils who probably have not washed or changed their clothing in a month or two. And then be subject to everybody's beck & call from the Col. down to the corporal. I would rather work for some farmer in Monmouth for $3 a month, eat in his kitchen & sleep in his barn, and be free, than to be a private soldier. Let me choose my own place, regiment & officers. Now Father, tell Jim that he would agree with me if he could see as much of camp life even as I have & if he with his spirit enlists — he will curse the day he does it. If he expects fun and excitement (which between us is at the bottom of all his patriotism) he will be most emphatically mistaken. It is too preposterous to think of.

From Your Ever Affectionate Son
Peter

PS: The grey, which you thought would not suit me, is now a beautiful riding animal, very much admired and suits me as well as any of the higher priced horses could have done. Do not think of purchasing a horse at home for me because I would rather purchase here, if I have to buy at all. I wrote to the Democrat [The Monmouth Democrat] last week a letter, and in such a hurry that I am sure it should not be published & regretted having sent it but I had promised to write so I sent it. I wish now you would suppress it if possible before publication. I am progressing very rapidly in my new profession and commanded the parade last evening to the perfect satisfaction of all concerned I believe. We study recreation along side of law. Nothing of an unpleasant nature has occurred between anyone & myself. The Col., Lt. Col. and myself go nearly every evening down to the village to a Mr Gary's — a very rich man (in fact the owner of nearly every person and thing in the village) who seems delighted with our company. He is extra fond of whiskey, checkers, music etc. and we contribute to the mutual enjoyment of each other very much.

Vredenburgh

Camp Hooker, Monocacy, Maryland
September 21, 1862

My Dear Father

I received your letter of the 18th inst. and as I wrote to you the other day concerning my horses, will leave that part of your epistle unanswered. We expect to move from here as soon as the bridge over the Monocacy is rendered passable, which will be in a day or two but as our destination is as yet unknown to us, it is impossible for me to tell you where or how to come and see us. But as soon as we are permanently located I will forthwith inform you, and then I hope you will not fail to gladden my heart with a visit.

I find Father, that the advice you gave me before starting has been of great benefit to me. I have regulated my conduct in such a manner that I have escaped all difficulty with both above and below me in rank and moreover I think I am progressing very rapidly in the science. I sometimes command at the dress parades, and am complemented by the Col. & others. I have really enjoyed myself very much since we left. There are so many around me whom I have been accustomed to see at home that it is hard to believe that I am in a hostile country. The field and staff officers all mess together at the sutlers, and many a jolly hour I've spent there. Mr. Cowart bears it bravely and looks about as he did when he left home except that his beard is grown. I am afraid the practice will be too sharp for him. The Quartermaster's labors are incessant and I think it will require a younger and more active man. Lt. Col. Hall is very friendly and clever, and seems to think a good deal of me.

Yesterday afternoon Capt. Alstrom and myself took a ride to Frederick and while passing through I heard some one call out my name. On pulling up I saw it was a man by the name of Lung, from Eatontown. He left home last Monday and had been out here on a pleasure trip and was then on his way home. He said he had just then returned from Boonsboro where he had been in hopes he could get to the battlefield. He gave such a graphic description of the scenes along the road that left myself determined to ride out in the direction of Middletown (which you will see is on the road there) as far as we had time. So after sending a few messages to Will we bade adieu to Lung and started onward.

The scene defies description. Thousands of wagons, horsemen, and straggling soldiers filled up the road — some going onward, others coming from the battlefield. The atmosphere was decidedly bad from the immense number of dead horses, mules & cattle which in every state of putrefecation lay ignominiously around in the road and adjacent field. If it had not been for the interminable travel, the dust and wounded soldiers, the ride would have been delightful. There were many points along the road from which we had splendid views of the surrounding country. I could gaze for hours on the Monocacy Valley. The soil is similar to ours around Holmdel and the river is nearly hidden from the view by the trees and foliage which grow luxuriously upon the banks. The stream is clear and shallow, making very apparent the crystal quality and clean sand & gravel which compose the bed. As we reached the crest of the mountain we had a view of Middletown and I even imme-

Antietam Bridge — September, 1862.

diately struck the apparent similarity of the village to our own Middletown as it appears from the hill before entering the deep gully. It is just such a quiet little village (at least it appeared so from when we saw it). And so modestly buried in the shrubbery below us, that but for the present excitement there, its existence would hardly be known. From where we stood we could distinctly see Frog's Gap, the place where Reno was killed last Sunday and a man who we saw sitting near us on the fence said he lived in a house nearby and had seen the fight there — pointed out to us the relative position of the armies and the manner in which the battle was carried on. I give credit to a good deal of his story and whether true or not it increased considerably our interest in the premises.

I don't intend to write any more for the paper and wish I had not written the other. I guess Yard [Publisher of the Monmouth Democrat] found a shorter letter which suited him better for he has not published it. And I am glad of it. Give my sincere love to Mother and write as soon as convenient.

Your affectionate Son
Peter

Vredenburgh

Camp Hooker
September 23, 1862

My Dear Father

Mr. Casner has just handed me your letter of the 22nd inst. I wrote to you a day or two ago and I suppose you have received it by this time. We must certainly move from here soon because there is no use in our remaining. I would like to see you dearly, but do not think it safe for you to venture for you may miss us entirely.

Horace Greeley, publisher of the N.Y. Tribune (above); N.Y. Herald Field Office (below).

I am enjoying excellent health and feel elastic and vigorous in body and mind. I wish Father when very convenient sometime you would send me a New York paper (the Tribune) as I do not get mine though I have written to Greeley [Horace Greeley] to send it here. The Tribune is worth all the other papers put together out of New York City.

I wrote to Mother a day or two ago. I will keep you posted upon our movements and myself. You needn't be afraid of my gam-

Photos: Horace Greeley — National Archives. Field Office — U.S. Army Military History Institute

bling or drinking to excess.

Your Affectionate Son
Peter

Stults

Frederick Junction, Maryland
September 24, 1862

Pa & Ma

We are at Frederick Junction yet, but do not know how long we will stay here. The chances are we will stay some time, to guard the Monocacy Bridge on the B&O R.R. The bridge I spoke of, I told you in my former letter the rebels had burned, but a new one has been erected. The bridge is 400 feet long and 60 feet above the water. It was rebuilt in about four days — quick work.

Frederick Junction has been a busy place since the bridge was burned for all army stores intended for Harpers Ferry have been transported by wagons from here. You can form no estimate and I but a poor estimate of the number of wagons employed. The road was filled with them and hundreds of ambulances were constantly employed in carrying the wounded off the battlefield bringing them here, to be sent home and to hospitals in different parts of the country.

About 8000 muskets from the battlefield were brought here. You tell me that since my departure from home I have been remembered in your prayers, both in private and from the pulpit on the Sabbath. To my sorrow I must say I have never truly appreciated the true benefit of prayer, but I am convinced that the happiest life one can live is that of a Christian. But I must say a large part of our soldiers lead a different life. We have a good many Christian men in our regiment and their influence over the unruly is not small. We have a worthy chaplain in our Regt. He lectures us very smartly every Sabbath. Since our Regt. has left home we have made several moves, and have passed a good many hardships, but as yet we have had no engagements.

The first of this week nearly all the able men of our Regt. left camp, for a brush somewhere as they supposed, but with our usual hard luck (as the boys seem to think)

Fort Delaware

they were sent to Alexandria for guard duty, while the Regts. belonging there were sent on to Fairfax. The day after our troops had taken possession of the place, our Regt. was sent to escort a train of the wounded. It was an awful sight — thousands, shot & maimed in every possible manner. Some of them shot so badly one would think they could not live an hour. One man was shot between the eye and ear — the ball passing through the head and coming out in the same place on the opposite side. 1000 rebel prisoners were also sent here. We kept them a day and night, and then they were sent to Fort Delaware — three companies of the 14th being sent with them as guards. They were a rough looking set of men, and as strong on the secession question as ever.

Grub is poor — hard crackers and salt pork and coffee. Tom Newton & his brother-in-law Hank Lot ran away a few days ago. The Colonel says he is bound to have them. I pity them if he does get them.

Yours,
Marcus

Harrison

Camp Wood, Frederick Junction
September 25, 1862

My Dear Mother

I received your loving letter yesterday morning. I should have received it night before last, but I was Sergt. of the provost guard [detail of soldiers under the Provost Marshal], some distance from our camp. I received three papers also at the same time, a Herald from Harry Child, and two Advocates in one package, which I took to be Libbies directions, or rather her hand writing. And a standard but who that was from, I know not. Mother, I wish you would tell those that send me papers to please send their compliments.

The boys are all well. Charley White and George send their best respects to you. You said you were glad to hear I enjoyed myself if I meant what I said. I shouldn't have told you so if I hadn't meant it. There is no one that is true to his glorious country, but what can enjoy himself even if he meets with hardships. There are no hardships when God is near to bear us up, as for being back in that store, I don't feel the least inclined to be there, neither could I be hired, even if Uncle Sam would consent to it. He takes good care of me, gives me a plenty to eat. Hayo, what was that? Why its the call for dinner, so I will go down to the cook house and see what Joe Reeves [Regimental Cook] has got for us and then I can tell you what we have got. So here goes, with my haver sack.

Well mother I will now tell you what I had. Why pork and beans. What better do I want for you know yourself I never liked beans ha, ha. We have them three or four times a week

Camp Scene: Officers and non-Commissioned Officers; note the officer standing with a book, presumably the Bible.

and just as many as we can eat, but there will be one once in a while who will growl. You know there are some folks never know when they are well off, but as for me, I am always satisfied if I get enough, no matter what it is. I am getting right smart down yer (taken from or at least quoted from the Marylanders, ahem) You spoke about the nine months boys [nine-month enlistees], I think they must be getting along slowly.

I had to leave my old tent where the Red Bank boys all were, and go in another, they had to put a Sergt. in each tent to see if the boys or at least men I should call them, done their duty. Kept everything clean and so forth. But I thank God it was so, I have broken up all swearing and gambling and have set them a good example, by praying and reading the Testament regularly every night and morning. And if a soldier happens to come in our tent from another one and happens to swear, they order him out and tell him he is no company for them until he stops all profane swearing. May God help me to accomplish my object in view, He is my only strength, in Him I put my trust.

I have turned a shade darker and if I don't get shaved very soon I am afraid I won't know myself (ahem). Eseck Howland is in my tent. George Howland's brother and a fine fellow he is. He sends his best respects. I have all the popular boys in my tent, Abram Medzgar, Elliott Fields and they are all good boys. But mother I must close my letter as it is time for drill, so good bye, give my love to all receiving a share for yourself,

From your ever dear and affectionate son,
Albert

P.S. I have received my warrant as 2nd Sergt.

Ross

Camp Hooker, Frederick Junction, Monocacy Bridge
Thursday September 25, 1862

Dear Cousin

As Mr. Buckman is going home this afternoon and has kindly volunteered to take our mail to Trenton, I will avail myself of the opportunity by writing to you.

We are encamped on a hill alongside of Monocacy Creek. We have a splendid view from where we lay and it is very healthy here so far. This is the same place we had to skedadle from when we first entered Dixie. I can tell you things were changed somewhat from what they were before we left. We were only two hours ahead of the rebels. We could see their scouts on the hills when we left. So you may know it was a pretty close shave but we got away without being caught that time. They blew up the iron bridge which we were guarding and burned the government property around here so when we came back we hardly knew the place.

We were ordered back here just as our army was going after them. I can tell you it was a grand sight to see so many soldiers, all in motion. I saw several baggage wagons with "A of P" marked on them [Army of the Potomac]. I also saw Gen. Hooker and staff. We hear this morning that the rebels are crossing over again into Maryland, but as to the truth of the report I cannot say. There are encamped around us two of the regiments of infantry and some artillery and if the Secesh come again I don't think we will skedadle quite as fast as we did before.

I have heard from home several times since I have been soldiering. I like the business very much so far and think I shall like it, at least I hope so. I was sorry I could not get up to see you before I left. I am having my carte de visites taken in Frederick City and will send you one so you can see how I look dressed as a soldier. Tell Mimmie I often think of her and some day maybe I will come back and walk to church again with her. I believe this is all at present. Only remember me to all at home. I would love dearly to hear from you if you have time to write. When you write or send any word down to Freehold, tell them I am well and happy.

Burroughs

Vredenburgh

Camp Hooker, Monocacy
September 28, 1862

Dear Mother

Mr. Rose is going to Freehold in the morning and I take the opportunity of sending home a few things. My letters that I cannot accommodate, some caps for Henry, etc. etc. I will want the small carpetbag back again and would like you to enclose in it a piece of Buddington's best brown soap, the kind I used to buy off him for 2 cts a cake. One box of Brown's Trochees, and that large carpetbag I used to have. I think Aunt Sarah has it. I only thought I would like to have it in case I have to leave my trunk. I could fasten that on my horse's back.

I left at Elysville with a Mrs. Chord my epaulets, saddle cloth, pistol holsters, and a number of other things which you should attend to in case I never have a chance to myself. Mr. Cowart, Adjt. Buckelew, Mr. Rose our surgeon and myself drove over to the battlefield of Antietam last Thursday. It is a wonderful sight but I have not time to dilate. I saw the spot where Hooker was wounded. Bill is the best servant in the regiment. I give him $15.00 per month and would rather give him $30.00 than to part with him. I suppose Mr. Rose would bring the large carpetbag back if you can spare it. He can put the little bag inside.

Give my love to Aunt Sarah and all the rest and write soon to your affectionate son

Peter

Wolcott

Frederick Junction, Camp Hooker
September 28th 1862

Friend Powers

Sunday morning is the only time we have to ourselves. I take the time in writing to my friends. I received a letter from Nick last night. It does me good to hear from Trenton. It seems like an age since I left Jersey and when I look ahead for the time to expire — so we can take a look at old Trenton once more. Not that I am tired of this life. I like it except the fare is mighty poor. All we have is hard crackers and fat pork and that one half of it is spoiled. When we were on three days march all we had was 5 crackers. The rebels would not give us time to get anything more.

We caught three rebel spies the other day — one of them made a confession — if it is true what he told the Colonel — we made a very narrow escape. Longstreet was within a 1/2 mile of us when we left our camp. One of his officers disguised in a citizens clothes came in our camp and was talking to one of our men. Soon as he saw us preparing to retreat he reported to Longstreet. He sent two Regts. to cut off our retreat — two miles above us by tearing up the railroad track — but we were 1/2 mile ahead of them — they followed a mile or so then gave up thinking the cars could go faster than their horses.

3 o'clock AM

Colonel received a dispatch just now — between 12 & 14000 rebels had crossed at Point of Rocks 12 miles from Frederick and 10 from Harpers Ferry. We are ready to receive them. We have 10 cannons & 4000 men within 1/2 mile from us — and 3 Regts. at Frederick Junction. I think we can hold them till reinforced from the rear. We are upon a high hill and on the other side of the turnpike is the river. We have every advantage of them and can hold twice our number for three hours — so says the Colonel. He has full confidence in his men.

He says he knows that every man will fight like devils. Colonel is on his gray horse riding from one end of the camp to the other — he just passed me and said I better get my gun in good order as I would have an occasion to use it before morning.

I know I did not tell you what fine piece of work we had after the battle at Frederick (or skirmish I suppose you might term it). They blew up the large iron railroad bridge that crosses the Monocacy River. When we came back the next week after we had crossed it — seems that no human hand could make such a destruction. They were three days in doing it. The man who blew it had one half of his head knocked off by a piece of iron. They tried to burn the Turnpike Bridge but Burnside was closer on their heels than they thought for they ran in all directions leaving their dead upon the field for the 14th to bury.

Some of them smelt so bad it made me sick. It is a task I do not want again. I have seen more wounded soldiers since the last battle than I ever want to see again. The next day after the big battle I was standing on the corner of the street. I counted over two hundred wagons with wounded men pass. It was a heart rendering scene. It almost sickened me of soldiering — some with arms and legs off. I saw one poor fellow with his right arm off and left leg off. He was cut to pieces. I heard afterwards he died. I must close this — the order is to dig trenches. I am going to sneak out of it if I can. Good many of our boys are taken suddenly sick — but the Colonel is a little too sharp for them — his advice — a lead pill.

Yours truly,
J.R.Wolcott

Vredenburgh

Camp Hooker, Monocacy
September 30, 1862

Dear Mother

Since writing to you yesterday I have come to the conclusion that Mr. Rose had better not bring either Dash [Vredenburgh's hunting dog] or any of my shooting accoutrements. It looks now as if we would have larger game than quail shooting here or near here soon. A good many troops are arriving here and there is some talk that the rebels may attack Frederick to get the stores there, and if we have to move I am afraid the dog would bother me. I might leave him here at a gentleman's by the name of Thomas with whom I have become intimate, but Henry will want one dog this fall & I guess I had better leave him. There are so many quail here and other game that I thought I might have some huge sport in the afternoons, but I guess it will hardly pay to encumber myself. If Mr. Rose has started before you get this it will be too late of course but if you get it in time to prevent his bringing them do so.

I visited the Sharpsburg battlefield the other day but as I understand Enoch Cowart has written to the Democrat an account of our trip I will forbear saying more of this.

We have a large fire in front of the Col.'s tent every night at sundown, and then we all bring out our camp stools and pipes and sit around telling stories and cracking jokes till late in the evening. The Col. appreciates a good joke and can tell his share of them and we really have delightful times. There is something so old fashioned and comfortable about the large hickory fire, blazing 10 or 12 feet high and snapping such a cheerful accompaniment to our exuberant feelings, that I often think of Auld Lang Syne.

With unabated love I am your affectionate Son
Peter

Vredenburgh

Camp Hooker, Monocacy
October 1, 1862 — 9 P.M.

Dear Mother

I have just returned from an afternoon hunt — today the law expired against killing quail and I rode over to see if Mr. Thomas intended to shoot. He said he could not go himself but insisted upon my taking his dog and gun and going myself, but unfortunately he only had two loads of powder and I only killed one dove.

There is a rebel prisoner staying at his home by the name of "Lee." He is a nephew of General Lee of the Rebel Army and has been in the rebel army 15 months. During my absence his mother came & I had quite an interesting conversation with them. They are all of course, strongly in favor of the secessionists and talked freely of the rebels and the rebel generals. They don't like the proclamation [Lincoln's Emancipation Proclamation] much and say the South will have to be annihilated before there can be peace. Mrs. Lee looks like you except that she has black eyes. She is very ladylike and genteel. All is well.

Affectionately your Loving Son
Peter

Harrison

Camp Hooker, Frederick Junction
October 3, 1862

My Dear Mother

Last night was a happy time for me Mother, in receiving and reading over your dear letters. I was happy to hear
that God had spared all your lives. My health still continued
good. It will be better in about four hours, I think; for there
were two loads of splendid beef brought in this morning which
we will have for dinner. We have first rate bread now, fresh
every day. It is baked on the camp ground.

We are thirty five miles from Washington by turnpike
and southeast from there. There are troops passing through
almost constantly; within three days, there has been thirty
thousand troops passed here going on towards the Potomac. I
think that this will be made our winter quarters for we are
placed here to protect the Bridge which has been rebuilt. I
forget whether it was done when I wrote to you before or not
but I rather think not. I believe we don't receive any money
until the 14th of Nov., every two months.

Our Colonel has been in excellent health ever since we
have been away. He is acting Brigadier General. We guard
prisoners and take charge of all broken up regiments of the
army that come over this road. We have been favored very
much Mother, since we started out on our campaign. We
haven't had very long marches or done any very hard work.
But to God is the praise due. The Boys are getting along first
rate. The sun is warmer here today than I ever saw in that
state called Jersey, but my head is getting tough. I tell you I
am getting a rich color on.

There is nothing more I can say to you at present,
excuse the writing for I was pretty much hurried. May God
bless you and John and all my friends.

Albert C. Harrison

Stults

Camp Hooker, Monocacy
October 5, 1862

Dear Pa & Ma

I received your letter last night after looking a good
while for it. Pa, I want to know how you are getting along at
farming. I expect you are cutting corn by this time — the corn
around here is being cut, what little there was left by the
rebels. It is very dry here and so dusty we can hardly stand it.
We are encamped on a field that was ploughed for wheat, and
now the dust is about an inch deep. We have had no rain of any
account since we have been here, last night it rained some, but
not enough to lay the dust. We had a heavy frost some time
ago, enough to kill corn and buckwheat, but since then until
today it has been uncomfortably warm.

We got the boys to put us up a "patent" bed — my
patent, but still it won't sell in Jersey. It is made by driving
crutches in the ground for posts and instead of bedcord, we use

cross poles and then with a straw bedtick and four or five woolen blankets we sleep first rate. The grub is very poor but by spending two dollars a week apiece (that is Capt. Connolly, and myself) we could live middling good. Some of the officers with us live good but it is costing them, they say, $4.00 a week. We are not entitled to board by the government, but it pays us $36.00 a month instead.

There have been a great many troops passed through here the past few days bound for Harpers Ferry or the vicinity. Three or four Jersey Nine-Months, moved there, two Regts. passed by today. There doesn't appear to be any Sunday — there is no respect! Our duty is the same Sundays as other days with the exception we don't drill.

We have a smart Chaplain with us, he preached this afternoon and was very smart. He is liked by everyone — his name is Rose, of Methodist denomination.

Yours,
Marcus

P.S. Monday Morning 6 1/2. Very cold last night. The boys are around with overcoats this morning, and wondering how they will stand it this winter. The Col. says we will have to get stoves — he says they won't cost more than $3.00, the kind we want.

View of Harpers Ferry, from Maryland Heights.

Vredenburgh

Camp Hooker, Monocacy
October 7, 1862

Dear Father

I have paid strict attention to your suggestions in reference to my letting politics and superior officers take care of themselves, and have so far got along pleasantly enough. I find Col. Truex a much more intelligent and literary man than I supposed he was, and very easily gotten along with by a person who understands him.

A great many troops are continually passing here towards Harpers Ferry and Williamsport. What do you think will be done next? You can tell more about the aspect of affairs than I can because you get the New York papers. Don't you think the Emancipation Proclamation of the President's will have an injurious effect in every way? I do! You may depend upon it — we will have bitter fighting before the war is over. I am afraid it will have the effect of repelling the border states besides having a bad effect abroad.

You must be glad to have gotten clear of the 29th [evidently mustered in at Camp Vredenburgh recently]. I should think they would starve to death under such a Col. as Applegate. Our men even under the command of such an able and experienced Col. as Truex are sometimes pinched for necessaries and what will become of those Regts. who are commanded by elected officers with no experience or influence at headquarters.

It is a lovely moonlit night and the air is just cool enough to make a large open fire. We have in front of the Col.'s tent delightful times. Our camp is in a very lovely place, on a southeastern slope protected on the northwest and northeast by a beautiful wood. Every night as the "curfew tolls the knell of a parting day" our campfire is lit, and around its genial rays cluster the field staff and line officers of the Regt. and though beauty is absent, song and wit are there, flavored with the cracking of jokes and the cracking of hickory making one feel as if he was enjoying a clam bake or evening frolic at home instead of being here in the wilderness. I often think of you Father when I look into the cheerful, blazing fire, you enjoy one so much.

I am glad that Jim has not joined any Regt. and I hope he never will. I would not have him go for all my pay; it would be very improbable that we could both go through this war and come out unharmed. Let him come here and see the thousands with their arms and legs off, or if that won't do, let him go as I did the other day through the Frederick hospitals and see how little account a man's life and limbs are held in by others and what little return he gets in reputation or money for the risk and privations of enlisting and his ideas of the fun of the thing will vanish in thin air. I saw a man's leg taken off the other day at the hospital who had only been wounded by a mini ball,

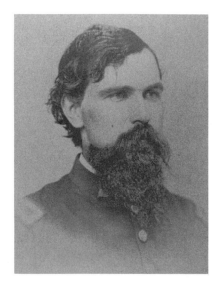

but the bullet had touched the bone & off the poor fellow's leg had to come. I would feel as if I was running a double risk all the time, if Jim should join the army and its enough as it is.

I wish Mother would send me my gun, shot pouch, powder flask, boxes of caps, washing apparatus for gun, box of cut wads, wad cutter and buffalo robe. If we have to move and I cannot carry all I can easily express them home. Tell Mother to pack them in a common wooden box and express them.

Ever Your Affectionate Son
Peter

Ross

Camp Hooker
October 9, 1862

Dear Mother

Tenadore Woodward pictured above. Ralph Goudy and wife, pictured below.

As I have nothing particular to do this afternoon I thought I could not improve my time better than by writing home. I am still in excellent health and spirits and hope I shall continue so until the end of my soldiering.

I just wish you could see the troops that pass here on their way to Harpers Ferry. I think there are at least five thousand pass every day and they have been going for more than a week now.

Capt. Goudy's wife is boarding at a farmhouse about a half a mile from camp. She came about a week ago with the Capt.'s brother and wife so the night before the Capt.'s brother and wife left, we decided to give them a serenade so Tenadore Woodward, myself, the Adjt., Sergt. Major and Lieut Tingley all went up. It was a most splendid night, almost as light as day. I had my guitar along and it made me think of days gone by when we used to serenade those lovely ladies of Freehold. We sang Lone Starry Hours first, but before we got through the Captain and gentleman of the house came out and invited us in, so we went in and stayed until eleven o'clock, it being only nine when we commenced. One of our number had a violin along so Capt. Goudy invited me to dance with his wife which I can assure you I did with the greatest of pleasure. If you remember, he was the gentleman who got married just before we left our camp at Freehold. His lady is a very fine woman indeed. I escorted her out to see the dress parade the other evening as the Capt. had to take charge of his company.

We have very warm weather here now and have not had any rain since we came. It is awful dusty and dry here now. Pop wished to know in his letter what I did every day. Well in the morning I make out a morning report. The orderlies of each company hand me in a report of their company and I make out a consolidated report of the whole, stating the number of sick, deserted, those on special duty etc. After I get that done, I copy the orders which were read on dress parade the evening before and after that, I commence on my descriptive book. In it I have to put the name, height, complexion, place of birth, age, and company affiliation, of every man in the Regt. I have been to work on that book ever since we left Freehold, but have not got it done yet. One reason is I don't write much in it for about the time it takes to describe a half a dozen men I have to stop and write a pass or some order from the Colonel.

I will send you some gun caps that the Adjt. picked up on the field of Antietam, when General Hooker was wounded for one of his aids showed the Adjt. exactly the spot where he stood when he was shot and he picked up the caps on the identical spot. I will also send you a Secesh letter found on the famous field of Monocacy Junction. I believe I have nothing more of importance to write, at present only remember me to all inquiring friends.

Your Affectionate Son
Burroughs

Vredenburgh

Camp Hooker, Monocacy
October 12, 1862

Dear Mother

It is Sunday afternoon and as I have just awakened from a refreshing slumber I will take the opportunity to tell you I am still well and also of a little adventure we had this morning.

Yesterday Lt. Col Hall and I were invited to dine at Col. Richardson's, a good Union man living at Buckeystown a distance of five miles from here and while there we heard that the rebels were moving in Maryland again, that Stewart's cavalry had entered Chambersburg in large numbers and later in the evening we heard that they had reached Harrisonburg. We of course, doubted the correctness of the rumor but this morning just as we had finished breakfast say 1/2 past 7 a horseman came up at full speed very pale and agitated and told the Col. that a large body of Stewart's were then at Urbana, which you will see is near four miles to the south of us. The Col. immediately ordered all the men (except two companies left under the charge of Lt. Col. to guard the camp) under arms and also ordered a section of battery consisting of two guns to accompany us. We were soon under way. The Col., taking charge of the artillery and I of the Regt. After we had reached the main road the men coming from the direction of Urbana verified the story of our guide but estimated their numbers variously from 250 to 5000. We pushed right on, the Regt. marching in quick time and in really lively spirits. As we reached near Urbana we saw where the cavalry had fed a few hours before in the road and had left in a hurry, a portion of their corn was still in the road and the stalks put out for their horses had not been touched. This was about 1/4 of a mile from Urbana and of course we continued on till we reached the honored place. There were a group of the citizens talking together and they with some few variations told us in substance that 250 of Stuart's cavalry had come in town about daylight that morning from the direction of New Market which lies off to the northward, that they had fed when I spoke of the corn lying in the road and had left an hour before we arrived there and taken the turnpike towards Leetown, and the U.S. cavalry 50 strong were in pursuit of them. We tarried but a short time and then faced homeward reaching here at noon. In camp there are all kind of rumors and only two hours ago an officer came from Col. Allen, commanding at Frederick, saying that 300 Rebel Cavalry had passed between Frederick and his scouts a few miles to the eastward. I suppose their forces must have been routed at Chambersburg or somewhere up there and are now returning in squads to the fords in the Potomac.

It will probably have the effect of keeping us here sometime longer to guard this bridge as in case of an attack by the rebels on our forces it would be necessary to break off the railroad connection with Washington. This railroad is the great artery which gives vitality to this part of the country. All the stores and troops are sent by government over it. As Bill Connolly says, "I would as leave drill it out as fight it out" but troops are still going towards Harpers Ferry & Sharpsburg all the time and I expect our turn to come every day. I am fixed quite nicely now. My horses are in excellent condition, very fat & frisky and work just to suit me. Bill is faithful and worth all the other servants in the Regt. put together. I give him $15 per month and anything else he wants. He has been sick for a few days and has not recovered yet though I think he is improving. I wish Mother, you and Father would not come now. I won't know what to do with you and though I would rather see you than all others on earth, it would be very disagreeable for you. Frederick is 3 miles off and the hotels are all taken up for hospitals. And you would be sure to be laid up for a day or two because it is such a long jaunt — then I have no accommodation for you at all at the camp nor anyway of transporting you.

[no signature]

Ross

Frederick, Maryland
October 13, 1862

Dear Sister

Union Artillery Battery.

I received your present which you sent by Lieut. Bedell and I can tell you those grapes went high. It seemed like home to be eating grapes once more. Serg. Major was pleased to death with his cake which you sent him. Tell little Mimmie I am very much obliged to her for those candy she sent me for the sight of candy out here is something strange. I suppose you heard of the cavalry raid into Pennsylvania. This morning a man came in and told us how near they were and you should have seen the men jump for their accoutrements and in less than fifteen minutes we were on the road to the place where the rebels were supposed to be. A section of the fifth regular battery which lies alongside of us went up the road with us but when we got to the place we found the birds had flown and therefore missed the chance of having a brush with them. We could see where they had been for the road was strewn with corn husks and such like.

I believe this is all I have to say only remember me to all my friends. I would like you to send me some carte de visites of some of the ladies around Freehold if you have got any. Write soon to your brother

Will

Harrison

Camp Hooker, Monocacy Creek, MD
Saturday evening, October 18, 1862

My Dear Mother

I want to amuse myself in some way so I shall take hold of my pen and write you a few lines. Although I don't think I shall have time to finish a letter tonight but I can do so in the morning if we don't have to turn out again tomorrow in search of the enemy, which I think will be rather doubtful for the rebels are not going to show themselves where the 14th NJ is if they know it before hand (ahem). The news from the west mother, looks very encouraging. It may not look so to you Mother but it does to us. The rebel army will soon be extinct in the southwest, also in the south, that is without a doubt. We have troops enough in the field to sweep the whole rebellion out of existence, and the movement will soon be made. Harpers Ferry is alive with Union troops. There are about five hundred thousand in the vicinity of that place. There was a New York Regiment went through here today on their way to that point, but about a week ago there would be regiments going through constantly, but we are left behind in our old position and likely to be I think because the bridge across Monocacy Creek must be guarded, and it so happened to fall to our lot to be the guards of said bridge. Some of our boys have been called out tonight to guard a provision train across the bridge that came in about dark and it will proceed to Harpers Ferry in the morning. I have heard from the 29th Boys two or three times, and they seem from all accounts to be having rather a rough time of it. They say they don't get enough to eat.

Some of the nine month's boys seem to be a little jealous of us and call us General Wood's candy regiment ha, ha, they have need perhaps of being jealous though. I have no objection. Ah, there goes the taps and the lights must go out but not before I read a chapter so good night.

Sabbath Morning October 19, 1862

Dear Mother as I said in the commencement of my letter, that I didn't think I could finish this letter before this morning, such proved to be the case. But I shall try and do so this morning. It is now nine o'clock. We have had an inspection of arms and knapsacks this morning. As I am not on guard today I will not have anything to do before dress parade tonight.

I don't think much of our Chaplain for I don't think he thinks enough of our spiritual welfare. When he does preach to us he has very short sermons. He never visits the tents to talk to us or no way appears sociable. But I suppose it is kind of a way he has got into.

Ah Mother, we have a colonel that is showing himself a man and one that every man in the Regiment loves and respects. The Bank boys are all well now.

Albert

Vredenburgh

Camp Hooker, Monocacy
October 19, 1862

Dear Father

I received your letter of the 11th inst. in due season and should have answered it sooner, but for some reason or other I have put it off from day to day until I am ashamed to think how undutiful I am acting. A number of the officers have ridden over to Sugarloaf Mountain (which is only 8 miles from here) today, but I stayed home determined to make up for lost time.

My time as you will see is fully occupied. At reveille about sunrise I attend the roll calls of the companies of my wing to see that the company officers are present and then return to my tent to dress which I complete by the time breakfast is ready. At 8 o'clock we have guard mounting and at nine drill. I drill with the rest of the officers till near 11, when recitation commences. The Lt. Col. hearing the right wing and I the left. Dinner is ready by one and at two we have Battalion drill which lasts till 4. At 5 we have dress parade till 6 and then tea. After tea I have to myself. So you see Father, a soldier's life is not so very easy even when we view it on its brightest side. Our Regt. is improving very fast and the Col. says the people can't tell us from regulars, if we are only left alone for two months longer. Our life is not so monotonous as you might think for there is some excitement daily. Last Sunday we all marched to capture Stewart's cavalry, but reached Urbana just as they had left. The Col. had charge of the artillery and I of the Regt., Col. Hall remaining at camp.

Last Thursday night the Col, having received information that three horsemen had put up in a woods 2 1/2 miles from our camp and the sentinels having seen a horseman near our camp two or three times recently in the night, evidently a spy, the Col. gave me permission to take some men over and search this house. The men having told one of our men that they were McClellan's mail carriers looked to me suspicious and therefore I took Capt. Harris of Co. C and 30 men to surround the house and started. The guide, a man of the same Co. who shoots game for the Col. took us through woods and meadows and over cornfields till he finally brought us in sight of the house. It was pitch dark, so that we had no difficulty in getting near the house without being seen. I halted the men about 150 yards from the house and then went forward with the pride to see how I had best proceed and soon determined to surround the house at a distance of 60 yards and then go to it. But I had hardly commenced my arrangements before a tremendous large dog gave notice to those within the house of our approach. The door was soon filled with women and negroes so the Capt. and I stepped immediately up and walked in. The man who owned the house laid on the bed making believe he was asleep but soon got up. I took him outside and examined him first and afterwards his wife and then the darkies and as they all told about one story which was very simple I let them be. The three men had been there representing themselves as mail carriers for a division at Sharpsburg. They had a bag with them like a mail bag — and two of them had left the day before, while the third had left only an hour before our arrival. The man who had departed last had left his horse in the barn saying he would be back the next day for him. I brought the horse to camp and told the man to send his owner for him when he returned. He has not been here yet and I guess my first suspicions of their being rebel mail carriers were correct.

I wish you would come here Father. I wrote to Mother that I could not accommodate her, nor can I, but you I could get

Captain Chauncey Harris

along with very well. If you come I will take you to Harpers Ferry or Sharpsburg, where you can see the battlefield you know. I cannot give you any idea on paper of the "points of the argument" as you asked me to. I could not even pretend the strategy. I couldn't judge of the theatre of the war. It is not much of a trip here. You can leave Freehold one day and get here the next. I wish you would come while it is feasible. Give my love to Mother and think of me often as your devoted and affectionate son.

Peter

Vredenburgh

Camp Hooker, Monocacy
October 20, 1862

Dear Father

As you see by the date I am taking advantage of Sunday afternoon to write you a letter. It is storming violently and consequently we are all confined to our tents, which are as comfortable under our present arrangement as a house. Some of the officers having brick fireplaces and chimneys while others, I amongst the latter, have stoves. I have a neat little cast iron one and Bill always keeps on hand a bountiful supply of hickory wood, so that it is really quite cheerful and cozy. I also, with the Chaplain and the Surgeon use the stove to toast bread for breakfast and tea.

If it had not rained today we contemplated going to Sugarloaf Mountain. Those who did not go last Sunday, but will probably go on Wednesday.

We are enjoying sweets of soldiers life here now. Our camp is as clean as a harbor and the country and climate delightful. Just think, this is only the second rain of any consequence we have had since our departure from Freehold. I took a short tramp after quail yesterday and if I had only had Dash here, might have gotten 20 or 30.

The Quartermaster, Capt. A.H. Patterson and Lt. Havens intend on going home tomorrow and I may send this letter by one of them. Havens is sick and has resigned his position. The Quartermaster will bring Dash back with him and I will write to Mother to that effect. Patterson's business is involved in some way is what takes him off. I wish you would come back with the Quartermaster and see us Father. I think you would like the trip besides delighting me.

Ever Your Affectionate Son,
Peter

Captain Austin Patterson

Photo: U.S. Army Military History Institute/
Monmouth County Historical Association

Wolcott

Camp Hooker
October 26, 1862

Friend Powers

I received your letter in good season, and have made several attempts to answer it and failed as often. This being Sunday and a rainy one at that, and no excitement to wile away the time, I thought I would take this opportunity of writing to you. Things are quiet on the Monocacy this morning but it is uncertain how long it will remain so. It is the talk in the camp we are to move to Harpers Ferry this afternoon. I want to go somewhere where we can have something to do besides guarding the Baltimore and Ohio RR. Last Sunday we had a fine chase after some rebels. They were a little too fast for us. We went four miles from camp and returned in time to eat hard crackers and pork which was devoured by us like so many dogs eating bricks. One of the gunners belonging to the 5th US Battery stationed with us was shot this morning while out on inspection and thought to be fatal. I was on the next post to him — he ran about 10 yards before he fell. There was great excitement to find the one who dare to do such a thing in daylight.

Last I thought how nice it would be to have hay to sleep in. The guards have it hard at night. They are not allowed to leave their post til nine o'clock in the morning. The four hours they have to sleep, they have to sleep on the ground wrapped in their blankets.

I had a flat stone for a pillow last night. There have been several of our men court martialed. You would laugh to see the punishment some get. One boy stole a gun — the punishment was his hands tied behind him with a large placard on his back — written on was the word — thief — then marched around the camp — guarded by the sentries.

Our boys are all right — they are a little sharp once in a while, it surprises Colonel Truex who says that Co. B. is the best drilled Co. in the Rgt. and the biggest Devils — there is no devilleting but what they have a hand in.

I must close — my fingers are getting cold. Remember me to Mrs. Powers and your little darling. I would like to be in Trenton one day and night.

Yours Truly,
J.R. Wolcott

Captain John Alstrom

George Patterson

Photos: U.S. Army Military History Institute/Monmouth County Historical Association

Harrison

Camp Hooker, Monocacy Bridge MD
Early Friday morning, October 31, 1862

My Dear Mother

I am happy to write you a few lines this morning to assure you that, that wonderful box was received by me last night (Thursday) and it came safe and sound. Everything was just as nice as it was when it started. And I can give great credit to the packers for it was the nicest box that has been in Camp Hooker. And such another time as we had over that box would fully have paid you for your trouble without a doubt if you could have seen us.

I didn't forget to call Joe Reeves in my tent to share a portion with me. The old darkey was pleased I can tell you.

If the rebels had come last night, I think I would have fought hard over that box. The captain [Captain John V. Alstrom] wanted to trade boots with me as soon as he saw mine but I couldn't see it. But I shall have to bring my letter to a close Mother, as my time is up. Hoping you will excuse this poor writing and accept the love and sincere thanks of your only son.

Albert C. Harrison

Ross

Frederick City
November 4, 1862

Dear Mother

I am in excellent health and spirits, though there are a great many sick now in the Regiment. I was in hopes we would be paid off this week but I hardly think my hopes will be realized by present appearances. I am entirely out of postage stamps and everything else in the money line so if you will send me a few they will come very handy. The weather is getting cooler down here now but it don't affect me much for I have enough clothes to keep warm.

The Sergt. Major and I have 4 heavy blankets to cover us up at night so you can imagine we keep pretty warm. We have some fun here with our Quartermaster. Last night the Chaplain & Adjt. went behind his tent and put a box over his chimney and in a little while, they had the old gentleman smoked out. He did not know what was the matter for some time until he thought someone might have been playing tricks on him and when he went to examine his chimney he found one of his dry goods boxes on top shutting off all the draft.

The other day George Patterson ran against the

Major's horse for a hundred yards. They bet ten dollars and the best one win. George came out in his shirt sleeves and stockings, so off they started. George beat the Major going but coming back the Major beat him, thereby winning George's ten dollars.

I believe this is all now. My love to all from your affectionate son

Burroughs

Vredenburgh

Camp Hooker, Monocacy
November 7, 1862

Dear Mother

Henry arrived here yesterday and left this afternoon for Washington. He looked well and I guess enjoyed himself. Of course I was delighted with the dog and I have one more request to ask and that is I want some good powder and I think I left a tin canister of it at Henry's when I came away. It is about 10 inches long — marked "Eagles and Hazzards Kentucky Rifle Powder." Will must have it if you can't find it but I think you have it. If it has so little in that it won't pay to send it, then get Uncle William to send over another and send it by Quartermaster but if it is say 1/2 or 1/3 full then send that. The price is about $1.50. You have to engage it the day before you want it at 89 Wall Street. Don't take any particular trouble or expense out, if convenient I should like to have it.

With love to Father and Uncle and Will and Aunt Sarah. I am your loving Son
Peter

Vredenburgh

Camp Hooker, Monocacy
November 8, 1862

Dear Henry

As I had good sport yesterday I thought I would tell you of it. It snowed the day after you left so that I stayed in camp but Saturday morning the snow was about 4 inches deep and at 10 o'clock I rode over to Mr. Thomas' to get him to go with me but he persuaded me that there would be no sport so I came back to camp but after waiting a while I thought I would try it anyhow and went out behind our camp and shot 14 by noon. At 2 in the afternoon Lt. Col. thought he would like to see me shoot so I started out in the cornfield behind the camp and found a flock scattered in the woods and shot 7 more without

William Foster

missing a shot, making in all 21 quails which considering the short time I was engaged in the sport was doing very well. Dash stood one quail with another in his mouth. If you have any good days sport let me know and where you shoot them.

Your Aff. Nephew
Peter

Harrison

Camp Hooker Monocacy Bridge, MD
Sunday, November 9, 1862

My Dear Mother

Your dear letter was received by me last night and pursued with the greatest pleasure imaginable, and this being my best opportunity I shall endeavor to give you an answer. The first thing I suppose you will want to know is about my health, which I can tell is very good, thank God for the blessing. Eseck is sitting on one end of my box before the fireplace mending his coat, or least sewing in the sleeve lining. His health is good as well as the rest of the boys, for it is good healthy weather. We have had a happy snow storm Mother. It commenced snowing Friday morning and snowed off and on until the next morning (Saturday) and cleared away by Saturday afternoon. Sergt. Foster and myself procured a pass and went to Frederick City, for the purpose of going to the express office to see if my box was there that Harry sent last Monday, week ago. But there was no such box there. We traveled around awhile until we got hungry and then we set out for home.

It is something quite uncommon to have snow in this part of the country so early. I guess the snow was about five inches deep when it stopped snowing.

I have some tongues left yet, some pickles and some cheese also some cigars. I am very saving of them as they are very scarce down "yer." It is almost certain that we will stay here all winter. We will cart logs I think tomorrow for the purpose of building kitchens, also to finish our guard house. The colonel intends to have the church and guard house together. The building is forty feet by sixty. It will be a right smart building. If we stay here all winter I expect we will be so lazy we cannot move by spring. The boys wish to be remembered to you and John.

I expect you are glad the election is over. I hear the Democrats have carried the day throughout the state, so I expect the war will soon be brought to a close if that is the case. Remember me to your neighbors.

I shall have to bring my letter to a close Dear Mother as I can find nothing more to say at present. Receive the love

Photo: U.S. Army Military History Institute/Monmouth County Historical Association

and affection of your son and may God bless you. Give my love
to Libbie.

From my mother's son,
Sergeant Albert C. Harrison

Ross

Frederick City, Maryland
November 13, 1862

Dear Sister Mimmie

Your kind letter I received from Capt. Patterson who
arrived here a day or two since. We are preparing winter
quarters here expecting to sojourn in this vicinity during the
winter months. All the companies have log kitchens put up at
the end of their row of tents and now the men are engaged
erecting a guard house, two stories high — upstairs will be all
one room — will hold five hundred men, which will be used as
a concert room for darkey performances, theatricals etc. and I
suppose on Sunday will be used for preaching.

I am getting fat down here having gained nine pounds
since leaving Old Monmouth. I have an invitation to a Ball to
be held at Frederick tomorrow night, but as I am rather short
of the needful I hardly think any of the dark eyed beauties of
Maryland will see me on that occasion. Four of our men have
died since we have been down here. I don't know whether I
mentioned it in any of my previous letters or not. The Adjt's
brother was down to see him a few days ago and a young
gentleman accompanied him by the name, Harvey Holmes,
who lived near Jamesburgh. They left here on last Saturday for
Washington and on Monday night he died. He was quite well
when he left. I believe he died of some kind of fever.

Capt. Patterson has sent in his resignation so I suppose
he will return to Old Monmouth again in a short time. I
haven't heard direct from my adorable Emma, as you call her,
in some time. I believe I have nothing of importance to communicate now only I am still in good health and spirits. We seem
to think down here that it is a good thing McClellan has been
removed for now we will be doing something in the way of
moving.

From Your Brother
Will

Wolcott

Camp Hooker, Monocacy Bridge
November 16, 1862

Dear Friend

I received your kind favor last night and devoured the contents like so many hungry dogs. You will see by the heading of this brief note we are still at Monocacy yet and I think it looks very much like our staying here this winter. Your humble servant J.R.W. assisted to build 2 bake ovens and sheds to cover them. Time I get home, I will be able to build houses, dig ditches, cut wood, carry brick-stone, etc. which I have had a hand in last week — building log houses and stables. Captain Craig has been sick 6 weeks and it is the opinion of some that he will not get well unless they grant him a leave of absence as this is not a fit place for anyone that is sick. He looks more like a dying man than a living one. It is like drawing teeth now to get a furlough. Lieut. Bodine got leave of absence for 96 hours to go to Trenton partly on some business for the Regt. but when he got to Baltimore, Gen. Wood sent him back to his Regt. again in double quick. Some of the officers are sending in the resignation but they take no notice of them. Those fellows that came out for the money has to stand the blunt now.

We have 2 officers — one Capt. and the other one 1st Lt. in this Rgt. was very bold and to hear them talk you would think they were anxious for a brush with the rebel devils, but yesterday morning a report came in camp that there were 300 hundred rebel horseman had crossed and were going over into Penn. The Colonel ordered 8 companies out to cut them off. These officers were not to be found — then when found, they were in the woods — hid away. The Colonel thought they would do that.

I shall call you fellows to account for the conduct of your behavior on the 4th of the month. When I left, I left the little state in your care with the full confidence but I have learned with sorrow that my confidences was misplaced. She has gone to the D-headlong [Democrats]. Gone so far that salt won't save it.

J.R. Wolcott

Pictured left to right: James W. Conover, Henry J. Conine and William H. Craig — officers of Company D.

Photo: U.S. Army Military History Institute/Monmouth County Historical Association

Vredenburgh

Camp Hooker
Monocacy November 16, 1862

Dear Mother

I received yours of the 13th inst. Do not take the
trouble of sending me any powder without there is enough left
in the large can. I had to make it worthwhile. You need not
fear that I will be indiscreet in my shooting as I only go when I
have nothing else to do. I did read the tract you refer to for
your sake. Has Father seen McClellan yet? Tell me what he
thinks of him.

I guess there is general rejoicing in the army that he is
removed. I for one am very glad and would much rather be
under Burnside or Hooker.

I herewith send my photograph. They are very poor I
think as they make me look sleepy and course, while really I
never felt better or more wide awake.

Theodosia is engaged to a Lieutenant in Co. A. She is to
be married soon. Don't let it go any farther but she will miss it
if she marries him for he is a consummate humbug.

Ever Your Affectionate Son
Peter

Harrison

Camp Hooker, Monocacy Bridge, MD
Tuesday Morning, November 18, 1862

My Dear Mother

I sit myself down upon my bed this morning to write an
answer to your dear letter which I received last evening. I have
just finished my breakfast and a hearty one it was on roast
beef, fresh bread and coffee.

Our cook house is finished and you can hardly touch
Joe Reeves with a ten foot pole now. He is as happy as any
lord, although he is in a log cabin.

I intended to have written to you Sunday but as luck
would have it I had to go on guard. That was the first time I
have been on guard of a Sunday since I have been in service.
They happened to fasten me that time. Three months is a
pretty long stretch to go without being on guard of a Sunday
but once. It was a very nice day but it began to rain Sunday
night about dusk and rained nearly all night. You know a
sergt. of the guard isn't exposed any to the weather. He has to
call out the reliefs and form them, and then give them in
charge of the corporal and he sets them. We have two sets of
guards; one is the camp guard and the other the provost

guards. The latter have to cross over the bridge to the junction to guard the cars etc., but there are only twelve men on that guard besides the corporal and sergeant. Four men to a relief. It happened that I was sergt. of said guards and I was not sorry for over there I could do just as I pleased. I was sergt. of the guard and officer of the guard and a little of everything. I had a good coal fire to sit by and every two hours I could call out my reliefs and set off and read my Testament.

Mother, I am very careful of my health. Don't worry about that mother. We have everything as comfortable as heart can wish and our Colonel is bound to have everything just so. There is not a man in the Regiment I don't think but what can say they love him and he knows how to gain the admiration and love of his men. It rained the best part of yesterday so that it was impossible for us to drill. When it held up in the afternoon the colonel set the men at work carrying slate stone to macadamize our avenues. But the men hadn't carried long before it commenced raining again like fun and then away they went for their tents, giving three cheers for the rain. ha, ha. The work was to give them exercise more than anything else but after we get that job done it will be a good thing for us because it will keep us from tracking so much mud in our tents. Eseck sends his love to you and John.

We have got a big fire in our fireplace this morning to dry our tent. Goodbye for the present and accept the love of your dear son.

Sergt. Albert C. Harrison

Vredenburgh

Camp Hooker, Monocacy
November 19, 1862

My Dear Father

Do not forget me nor think that I have forgotten you when I fail to write regularly, because news being as a general thing scarce here. When I write to Mother her letter contains about all I have to say. I received your letter dated at Trenton, a few days ago.

Dash seems to like camp life well enough and is already quite fat. I would almost as soon part with a horse as with him for it reminds me so forcibly of home to see him lying by the fire. Of course he is a favorite with all his acquaintances. I shot a wild duck the other day in the river and Dash went right in and brought him out by the head. I do not shoot so much as you may suppose; never when I have anything else to do.

Last Monday evening Sam Taylor, Joe Burrows and Wm Story (all from Middletown) came here to see us and yesterday I went with them to Harpers Ferry. We arrived there at 11 A.M. and immediately walked across the pontoon bridge from the village (on the Virginia side) to Maryland Heights. It was almost impossible to get along, the ascent was so very abrupt and slippery, from the previous hours rain. After we had ascended 1200 feet we found ourselves in the midst of the clouds which totally obstructed the view and enveloped us in apparently a drizzle. We then descended some 300 feet and the world was apparent again. Loudon Heights on the "left oblique"

Bolivar Heights

their dark crest then on a level with us — Bolivar Heights and Harpers Ferry and the Shenandoah Valley in front and Slocums Division, 18,000 strong on our "right oblique". They were resting on the south bank of the Potomac which formed the most interesting point of observation. The letter in the Tribune of the 15th inst. is correct but slightly overdrawn. Very few men should have held Maryland Heights against the world, while if they are in the hands of the enemy, Harpers Ferry and Bolivar Heights are helpless. We are preparing for winter quarters here as we may stay all winter. Write to me again soon Father and don't be afraid of giving advice as you have given me many a seasonable hint.

Your Affectionate & Devoted Son
Peter

Harrison

Camp Hooker, Monocacy Bridge, MD
Sunday evening November 24, 1862

My Dearest Mother,

I shall make another effort tonight to write you a letter for I commenced one last night and hadn't time to finish it, so I shall write a little faster. I expected to have finished it this morning but the first thing I knew was the order given to fall in, and go to work. This is the first time we have worked on a Sabbath since we have been out. But it was a case of necessity as you may imagine for our Colonel wouldn't compel us to work otherwise. We have worked all day long stockading our tents. We cut logs five feet in length, then dug a trench around our tents two feet deep, leaving three feet above ground. We then chucked up the cracks and dabbed it with mud, that is as far as we could get with it. So God willing we will commence again in the morning and take down our tent and set it on the stockade, so you see it will give us more room. But the worst of all, we will have to tear down our chimney as it will come too far in the center of our tent, but we can soon stick it up again and then we can live like folks if Uncle Sam lets us stay here long enough to pay us for our trouble.

There are three of us sitting here writing on my old box; Elliott Fields, Asher Pearce and myself. The pens are awfully walking over the paper, I can tell you. I suppose you remember Elliott, don't you? He says he can remember you, he sends his love to you. Eseck is sitting before the fireplace toasting his shins. He wishes to be remembered to you and John. He wants to know which is the worst, to mend coats on Sundays, or carry logs and dig trenches etc. Tell John he says he would rather be home in a marl pit than to drill. He likes soldiering well enough, all but the drilling part.

My health is as good as ever I knew it to be. Take away your grocery stores for me; I am a soldier, it agrees with me right smart. I hope this will find you enjoying the best of health. The Red Bank boys are all well. I had to send one of my men to the hospital. He has got the measles. His name is Charles Springstein. He caught a heavy cold while on guard. I shouldn't have sent him to the hospital but I couldn't get him to take any medicine. The boys say it was a hard time to get him to take any medicine when he was home. I heard from him today; he is getting better.

I must bring my letter to a close as it is nearly nine o'clock. I hope to have a letter from you the first of the coming week. Please answer this soon and receive the love of your son in the army.

May God be with you and bless you all,
Albert

Harrison

Camp Hooker, Monocacy Bridge, MD
Thursday, November 27, 1862

My Dear Mother

This Thanksgiving day evening I shall devote in answering your letter which was duly received by me. I hope dear Mother you have enjoyed yourselves, but you could have enjoyed yourselves better no doubt if I had been in your midst. But it was not so to be. But God grant before another Thanksgiving Day shall pass around again these wars may be brought to an end and we may again return to our friends and once happy home but made unhappy by war's wide desolation. You must not worry about me Mother, for let us remember that all things work together for good to them that love God. It has been almost like a Sunday with us this afternoon. This morning we had to drill, but I didn't drill as the captain wanted me to do some writing in some of Uncle Sam's books. But this afternoon he gave me clear and as there was to be a lecture delivered by our chaplain at 3 o'clock, the most of the Regiment was in attendance. The lecture was a short one but it was to the point. It was held outdoors and it was rather chilly, was one reason he didn't make a very lengthy speech.

We are prepared now for the coming winter. I don't see anything of the paymaster yet. The Red Bank boys keep remarkable well. God grant that we may keep so. There are three of us seated around my box writing to their friends. I hope Dear Mother this will find you in better health. I must close Mother, bidding you a good night and a happy Thanksgiving. Give my love to John and all enquiring friends.

Albert

Harrison

Camp Hooker, Monocacy Bridge, Maryland
Monday evening December 1, 1862

My Dear Mother

I must write you a few lines tonight in answer to your dear letter which was received by me this afternoon. But I shall have to stop writing I believe, and stuff something in my ears for they are making such a noise in the next company that I can hardly think of anything. They have a violin and a banjo and they are singing at a great rate. I can thank you very much for sending me that money Mother, although I could have got along well enough without it, but I believe I will not send it back, ha, ha. I hope Uncle Sam will let me have some soon so that I can return it though. But the longer we have to wait, the bigger pile we will have when it does come. God grant that we may both be spared to meet again Mother. I hope you will be better when this reaches you. Let us put our trust in God dear Mother for He doeth all things well.

I think you must be having a hard time with a sore finger and a sore toe besides. Mrs. White thinks I had better come home. Well I reckon it will be a right smart time before that happens. I came forth to serve my country and share with my fellow soldiers the hardships and privations of a soldier's life. But may God grant that this wicked war may soon be brought to a close.

Eseck says he will keep up his spirits as long as he can, but he wouldn't want to wait until the Democrats settled the War. Yesterday was general inspection. It took one hour. But as luck would have it we had the rest of the Lord's Day for rest.

[no signature]

Wolcott

Monocacy Bridge, Camp Hooker
December 3rd, 1862

My Friend Powers

I received your letter of the 30th last evening and was glad to hear you were all well. We have some pretty exciting times here now every night we have reports that the enemy are near us. They go in small parties for the purpose to plunder. The other night, night before last, they were at a small place called Urbana — 3 miles off — and entered a store — killed the clerk and committed rape on the proprietor's wife and took him prisoner. We had word of it before a half hour after they had done the deed and gone to parts unknown. Col. Truex is using every effort to capture them. Every night he sends out two companies, but there are so many damned Rebel citizens around.

They watch every movement of ours and can carry the news to them before we can get near enough. If I was the Colonel, I would make every man around here take the oath of allegiance or send him to the headquarters of Gen. Wood.

I was out on last Sunday night with the scouting party and the officer commanding stationed me in a thicket next to an open field. The pickets were about 200 yards apart. I saw 10 rebels about 15 feet from me but before I could fire the signal one of the pickets coughed — they being on horseback put spur to their horses and was soon from us. I can tell you the Com. officer was mad. If this fellow had kept quiet for 5 minutes we would have had a fine bag of game to have taken in camp the next day.

Today I have been putting a floor in the Col.'s tent and he treated me twice to good brandy, the first I have had since I left old Jersey. I could not very well refuse it coming from such a source.

J.R. Wolcott

Wolcott

Monocacy Bridge, Camp Hooker
December 4, 1862

I had a long trip last night through the mud, 100 men (picked) were sent out to a place called Buckeystown — 3 miles off, where there was said to be 20 Rebel horsemen, but when we got there at one o'clock they had retreated. We followed their trail for 2 miles, when it turned off in the woods and we lost it. We turned homeward with a heavy heart caused by our unsuccessful expedition.

A man came in camp this morning and told the Col.

where they kept themselves in the daytime, it is on the Sugarloaf mountain. The Col. has sent to Baltimore 500 cavalry and three pieces of cannon — then he is going to send all the men he can get and capture them if he has to follow them to the Potomac. This party is a portion of the raid came over some two months ago and got strayed off from the main body and with the river so high they cannot get back again. I must close this and go to bed. Write soon and remember me to all inquiring friends.

J.R.Wolcott

1st Lt. Frederick W. Kerner

Vredenburgh

Monocacy
December 6, 1862

My Dear Mother

I received your loving letter of the 28th inst. all right. I hope you have not repeated or hinted to anyone what I said about Lt. Kerner. He is positively engaged to Theodosia so that the more said the better she will like him. I wish Henry would send me that whiskey, for it would be very acceptable now. You need not be afraid that I will ever drink to excess Mother. I can get some here but it is rye whiskey and $3.00 a gallon.

The country around here is infested with guerillas or rather robbers and are near our vicinity every night. Tell Henry that we had another musical party at Thomas' the other night and towards midnight the darkies who had had a frisky frolic came in and after partaking of a supper squared themselves for dancing. Henry would have enjoyed it exceedingly. It was real plantation.

Your Affectionate & Devoted Son
Peter

Harrison

Camp Hooker, Monocacy Bridge, MD
Monday, December 8, 1862

My Dear Mother

I sit myself down on my knapsack this evening to write an immediate answer to your letter which was received by me this afternoon. I was glad to hear you were a little better, thanks to the Lord. I hope you may still continue to gain. My health still continues excellent. Our regiment is not quite so sickly as of late although we have already lost fourteen men by sickness since we have been here. But I am thankful there are no more.

U.S. Army Military History Institute/
Monmouth County Historical
Association

I received those two standards this afternoon also. I haven't had time to look at them yet but I will as soon as I finish your letter. We have got a roaring fire in our fireplace tonight. The weather has been fair today. We had quite a snowstorm day before yesterday. The snow lays about 3 inches deep in some places. You say that Grandmother has sold her cow so you need not send me any butter, as I can do without it just as well as not.

I must now bring my letter to a close as I want to read Uncle Abe's Proclamation so I bid you good night. Please write soon.

From your son Albert in the Army

Vredenburgh

Camp Hooker, Monocacy
December 12, 1862 — 8 P.M.

My Dear Mother

I recd your letter of the 6th inst. a day or two ago. Do not be surprised or disappointed if I fail to write as often as you would like to receive letters because I have nothing in particular to say sometimes and do not feel in a humor for writing.

The regiments in our vicinity have all been ordered off and I expect it will be our turn next, though the government may consider it necessary to defend the bridge here and in that case I suppose we will remain. I shall regret very much to

Fredericksburg, VA —
December, 1862.

move now for I am so comfortably fixed. I have fitted a board frame over my cot which keeps the straw and blankets on and prevents the cold wind from penetrating as it used to before I had it so fixed. About 11 or 12 at night Dash finds it too cold for him on the bricks by the stove and so he very quietly and gently gets upon my bed and immediately lies down on my feet and so we mutually warm each other. I will find him of great benefit if we have to march this winter.

I have shot quails considerably this fall, with pretty good success. Thomas and I get better friends every day.

Everything goes on well and I am getting quite fat. I think I will soon be able to wear Father's old clothes. Mr. Rose delighted me the other day by saying that Father looked better than he had ever seen him. Give my love to him, Henry and Aunt Sarah and think of me as your affectionate and devoted son.

Peter

Battle of Fredericksburg
December, 1862

As the 14th Regiment rested comfortably in winter quarters at Monocacy, events were unfolding to the south that would do little more than further the image of Robert E. Lee's invincibility. General Ambrose E. Burnside, who had replaced McClellan after Antietam, planned an aggressive attack on Lee's strongly fortified positions in and around Fredericksburg, Virginia. In the middle of December, 1862, he crossed the Rappahannock at Fredericksburg. The Confederates were solidly entrenched behind formidable defenses. Burnside, as if showing disdain for the reluctance and timidity of his predecessor,

The "Stone Wall" at Fredericksburg, VA — December, 1862.

engaged the Army of the Potomac in frontal attacks against the rebels. Huge gaps were torn in the blue lines as wave after wave of Federal soldiers was repulsed. There were particularly heavy losses at the stone wall before Marye's Heights. Casualties that day amounted to over 12,000 dead, wounded, or missing for the North and some 5000 for the South. The results at Freder-

U.S. Army Military History Institute

icksburg fell nothing short of another Federal military disaster. President Lincoln, still looking for the able commander, replaced Burnside with General Joseph Hooker.

Ross

Frederick City, Maryland
December 13, 1862

Dear Mother

Your dear letter I received from Mr. Rose in due season. Your letter had the most news in it of any I have yet received. I do so like to hear what is going on in the old place. So Mimmie is going to leave you pretty soon. I am sorry it is coming off before pay day or I should come home and witness the grand event. Don't forget to send me some of the wedding cake. When it comes off, you must tell me who all was there and all the particulars thereof.

The weather is very warm here now, but a few days since we had some very cold weather. It was so cold that it froze the Monocacy over and we had a good time skating.

Capt. Conover's company went up to Urbana which is about five miles from here, with the expectation of seeing some Rebs and I only went along to see the fun, but we came back without seeing a Reb. It was the only time I have been out and only went there for a little excitement. For it nearly gives one the blues to stay here doing nothing.

Our first performance of the season comes off next Tuesday evening at 7 o'clock. We have some star performers in our Regt. so I suppose it will be something grand. I believe this is all I know to write. My love to all from

Your Affectionate Son
Burroughs

Harrison

Camp Hooker, Monocacy Bridge, Maryland
Thursday, December 18, 1862

My Dear Mother

I have received your letter tonight and now I shall sit down and answer it immediately. And before I proceed farther let me tell you that I am enjoying excellent health as usual. I am not the pale clerk you saw some four months and five days ago, but a hearty and rugged soldier. So you see Mother, that you need not worry on account of my health. And I believe it was all for the best that I gave up clerking. I am in far better health than while doing such. The health of the Regiment is far better at present than it has been a time back. The weather has been quite cold now for two or three days. The Red Bank boys are all well with the exception of George H. Mount who is not able to do duty but he is not very sick.

The 29th Regt. has been taken to the front. But we still hang around old Camp Hooker and to tell the truth I don't think we will leave here this winter. But come what will we are prepared for the worst.

I must draw my letter to a close, that I may read a little while. Give my love to John and all the neighbors accepting a large portion for yourself. So I bid you good night, hoping this may find you in good health. Write soon and remember me your son Albert. May God bless you, all my friends. You are always in my prayers.

Sergeant Albert C. Harrison

Wolcott

Camp Hooker, Monocacy Bridge
December 18, 1862

Dear Old Friend Powers

I received your letter this afternoon, and I hasten to answer it. Friend Wright arrived here on yesterday afternoon. He was well pleased with his visit to Jersey and gave a good account of his reception in Trenton. I am going to try and see if I can't get a furlough for 48 hours in January. The Col. thinks a good deal of me. I will test how strong his love is.

I must tell you about our expedition on Monday night. Co. A & B started at 7 o'clock for Urbana — 5 miles distance — arrived 9 o'clock and surrounded the town and sent 11 men in town to look about and report if any game should be in place. They came back on the reserve without finding anything worth noticing. The officers concluded to stay until morning. At 3 o'clock it rained like thunder for 15 minutes — drops large as ten cent pieces. I had on three coats and three shirts and in the 15 minutes I was soaked through and I had to remain in that position until 6 1/2 o'clock and laying on my back at that for we dare not move or stand for the officers were watching very close to us in a log cabin. Then we took up our line of march for Camp Hooker, where we arrived at 9 o'clock of a quick march 2 1/2 hours through mud knee deep and forded creeks that had raised higher than we had expected.

I should not be surprised if we should be ordered from here before spring to some place in Virginia. General Morrison was here today and inspected the Regiment. Companies G & B — the 2 skirmishing companies was brought out and put through the skirmish drill. Did you ever see a skirmish drill? It is a splendid drill. The command is given by the sound of the bugle. Its fun to see the boys going through the brush and cross creeks. The Gen said we could be best on the skirmish. The

Col. says Co. B is the best drilled, and further says he is not afraid to attack double number, and they are regular devils. Gen. Morrison says we are called, by the other Regts., Gen. Wood's band box Regiment. The boys got new suits yesterday and they look as though they came out of a band box.

Good night. Please write soon and I will try and have something interesting for you next time.

Yours truly,
J.R. Wolcott

Jones

Camp Hooker, Monocacy Bridge
Sunday Night December 21, 1862

Dear Father

Yours of the 18th was received yesterday and I was very happy to hear from you. I am now getting acquainted with all the good Union families. You ask what I think of Burnside now. I think just as much as ever I did "He is the man." You call it a blunder now I cannot see how you make it a blunder. I call it a good licking. He was beaten by a force greater than he had and fetched his whole army over the Rappahannock — wounded and sick you say.

If McClellan was there we would not have had the repulse. He would have laid in about of Fredericksburg until half of his army had died off. "Remember the Peninsula." I have my doubts if he had Burnside's place after the battle if he had read enough to have fetched the army over the river in as good an order as Birney did.

You ask me where our position is in battle. I think I told you once but only briefly. Our position is invariably in the rear. You know we are considered noncombatants. After the battle we carry off the wounded and a drummer getting shot is either done by a stray shot or he is so patriotic enough or fool enough to pick up a musket and go into the ranks but I am not quite so patriotic as all that. But there is not much danger of our seeing much fighting. I cannot tell when I shall be able to get home but I hope to before long. The Drum Major and I know a thing or two.

It has been very cold here for the past few days. Tell mother I am much obliged to her for the envelopes and to write. Give my love to all etc.

Ed

Vredenburgh

Monocacy
December 21, 1862

Dear Father

I recd. your letter of the 16th inst. a few days ago and I expected to see you here before this time, for Mr. Buckelew was here last week and said his son Isaac and you were coming together, but I suppose some good reason prevented you. Our camp life is not as monotonous as you would think, there is always some exciting rumor afloat and we have our scouting parties out all the time. I am afraid from present symptoms that if Burnside does not advance some way or another, to keep the rebels busy -- that we will have plenty of business attending to the guerillas in this part of the country. I should not call them guerrillas perhaps, for they deserve the name of robbers and murderers. The Col. talks of sending me with a couple of companies to Urbana, a small village four miles from here, to take up quarters there. Persons who have left there for the rebel army are constantly returning in force and robbing the stores and committing other outrages as they please.

Kerner has gone on to marry Theodosia Forman. I hope he will not succeed and measures have been taken to apprise her of his character, so that if she has him now, she will deserve what will follow.

I wish you would tell Henry that we have not recd. the whiskey and I wish he would let me know exactly how he sent it and where he had placed it. The future looks gloomy Father, but the tallest fellow gets the persimmon and we must whip the rebels yet.

Your Affectionate Son
Peter

Harrison

Camp Hooker, Monocacy Bridge, MD
Friday Evening December 26, 1862

My Dear Mother

I have just finished a good hearty supper and sit myself down to write an immediate answer to your letter which was received by me about 4 o'clock this afternoon. I was happy to hear from you all again and more happy to hear that you were well. Well Christmas has come and gone again and a happy time has it been at Camp Hooker. The Col. gave us two holidays, and yesterday he gave permission that all might go out of camp without a pass and stay until three o'clock PM if they didn't go to Frederick City. So I guess there wasn't over forty men left in camp beside the guards. You know I suppose that the military law prohibits all liquor dealers from selling intoxicating beverages in this state, but occasionally they will sell it on the sly. I guess if you had seen some of the men when they came in camp you would have thought that they had seen a little Christmas.

Well, now I will tell you Mother, how I spent my Christmas. I started out of camp about ten o'clock and walked about three miles, coming to a log house. I stopped and got up on a rail fence to rest but I hadn't sat there long before an old man presented himself in the door of said house and sung out to me, says he, Sergt. Harrison, "what are you doing there?" So by that, you will know that I was acquainted with the old gentleman before. Well, says I Mr. Kahn, I am only resting myself. By that I got off the fence and advanced towards the house and met the old man half way. Saluted him by shaking of hands we then repaired to the house. He said, he began to think I wasn't coming. It was getting so late in the morning. But thinks I to myself, old man I am not too late for I smelled something cooking, very much like turkey. It was about half past eleven when I arrived there for I walked very slow taking a good view of the surrounding country as I went. I went in with him and says he, take a seat and rest your hands and face ha, ha. Then I wanted to laugh but I dare not, for his wife and daughter came from the kitchen to welcome me. So I took the offered seat and conversed with the old man on different topics until dinner was ready. Welcome Sergt. says he. Lets partake of some dinner and we passed into the kitchen. And Mother, a more splendid table I never saw set. Didn't it put me in mind of home. Well I'll bet it did. There was roast turkey, roast lamb, sauce, tomatoes, potatoes, bread and butter, sour kraut, squince jelly, blackberry pie, apple pie (dutch to kill) and coffee. Now says the old man I want you to help yourself and do just as you would at home. Well I guess I did. How I did enjoy it. I was not at all backward for it was just like home. But you know Mother, I am not one that makes a hog of himself, so everything passed off well. The old man said he had been 29 Christmases married and hadn't had liquor in his house on a holiday. He is a very religious old man. So I left there about two o'clock and the women filled my pockets with cakes and apples to let the boys see that I had found Christmas. But I must tell you about their Christmas tree. It was a splendid one. I saw some nice ones in New York when I lived there but I saw none equal to that. They told me I must be sure and come over New Years Eve as they were going to hold a watch meeting in the school house close by. So I promised them I would if the Lord spared my life and I could get a pass from the Col. So the old man came nearly half way to the camp with me.

The boys are all well. Eseck is well and sends his love to you and John wishing you a Happy New Year. It is raining quite hard. It has been trying hard to rain for several days but has stayed off until tonight. It is quite warm. There is no signs of getting any shinplaster [small bills issued for denominations as small as three cents] yet as I can see. But I guess it is because we are not brigaded.

Monocacy Creek has been frozen over. Some of the officers have had a skating time. But it is all open now. It has been so warm.

Give my love to John and I must bring my letter to a close as it is getting rather late.

Sergt. Albert C. Harrison

Vredenburgh

Monocacy
December 27, 1862

Dear Mother

I recd. yours of the 25th inst. enclosing a draft for $15, and I assure you it was very unexpected for I little thought of getting my usual Christmas present this time. It is too bad Mother that Theodosia married that infernal rascal Kerner. How could she do it after all she has heard. He is not only nothing but a low ignorant Dutchman but a criminal and thief and a liar. He was connected with some swindley operation in New York and got off. He is the poorest officer in the Regt. and just before he left here he borrowed all the money he could and stole some letters out of the P.O. and the letter he told you I had written him was one in which I asked him to return to me the letter of mine he had taken. Don't trust so readily Mother. Theodosia will wish she was dead before long. His 50,000 florins [Dutch and other European currency] I think must be all moonshine. He lies about everything else so that I guess he is lying about his fortune and only circulated the report to get off.

I have just returned from Frederick where I went this morning to church. As I was standing on the sidewalk just outside of the church door after services were concluded, a lady stepped up to me and inquired if I was Major V etc. I told her "it were." She then said that her name was Drusilla Dorsey and that she knows you, Will, and any quantity of people in the north. She visited Dr. Conover in Freehold last summer and fall and stayed a good deal of her time in Red Bank where she frequently saw me. Of course I pitched right fast and displayed myself alongside of her as far as her house and finally entered and took dinner. She is rather antiquated, but on the whole a fair girl. I have just recd. a letter from Father dated Dec. 26 since beginning this. We intend extending our pickets along the line of the railroad from New Market to Adamsville. Lt. Col. Hall and I will have plenty to do then riding back and forth to see that things go on right.

Don't say anything about Kerner now as it is too late to prevent trouble. With love to all

Your Affectionate Son
Peter

Vredenburgh

Camp Hooker, Monocacy
December 28, 1862

Dear Father

I have just recd. your letter of the 26th inst. dated N.B. General Schenck sent us orders yesterday to picket the railroad from New Market to Adamsville. Col. Hall and I will have plenty of riding to do up and down the road to see that everything is right. I frequently drill the battalion now and feel competent to manage it anywhere. The officers frequently compliment me upon my success. What a humbug it is to talk of taking regiments of three months drilling in the field. We have drilled very steadily since we left home, and have only just arrived at tolerable proficiency.

Father, it is just as I told you about the President's Proclamation, it will ruin us. Men here, who were good Union sympathizers before are now on the other side. I have met a good many intelligent men here and they all say that to carry out the Proclamation will ruin them. The Border States will not submit to it. Strictly it may be right, but it was unwise to enforce it, because there are so many ignorant and prejudiced people who say, "well, if they are going to take our niggers away we won't stand it," etc.

That Fredericksburg battle showed the most puerile kind of strategy I think. Burnside ought to have been certain the pontoon bridges were already there before he moved his army from Warrenton and picketed in the mean time as the rebels do so closely that a hen couldn't get in to see what was going on. I will not be imprudent.

Your Affectionate Son
Peter

Ross

Frederick City, Maryland
December 30, 1862

Dear Mother

I received yours and Mimmie's letters combined a few days since and also an invitation to the home bringing, which I shall be compelled to most respectfully resign. I have entirely recovered from my slight cold, and am now in my usual good health. We haven't been paid a cent yet which makes it rather inconvenient, especially about Christmas and New Years, when a person always needs a little of the needful.

You ought to see our camp now, all trimmed up in greens, every avenue has an arch of greens over it with the letter of the company on it in evergreen. We had a twenty pound Turkey on Christmas and on New Years we will have another. The Col. came in our mess tent the other day to see how we fared. He was surprised to see the style we had things, and told us we lived better than he did himself. There is only six of us and we have a good cook just for us. Charley Bartruff is boarding with us at three dollars a week which keeps us in little delicacies. Austin Patterson wanted to board with us too but we haven't the room.

Union soldiers' dining hall at Christmas.

Next week our Regiment is to be cut up for picket duty. We are going to send out five companies at one time, ten miles above and ten below and then keep pickets out each way. This will be Headquarters still, so I shall remain at the old post.

New Years, we are going to have a burlesque parade. Nearly all the boys are going to turn out. They will have stick brooms and anything else they can get. We will elect a Col. from the ranks and have a grand time generally. I believe I have nothing more of importance to write only remember me to all my friends.

Your Dutiful Son
Burroughs

Vredenburgh

Monocacy
January 1, 1863

My Dear Mother

I recd. yesterday the letter mailed on the 30th inst. Did you get mine in which I spoke fully of Kerner. I mean to get the thief dismissed from the service as soon as I get the proof of his stealing the letter from me I spoke of.

I did not write to Mrs. Forman but I know who did. I did write to her but for certain reasons took the letter out again and destroyed it, but another wrote my sentiments and if Theodosia had not been the biggest fool in the world she would at least have waited long enough to investigate. I did not know Kerner at that time to be such an infernal rascal and I knew also if I wrote to Theodosia she would be fool enough to let Kerner know that I had written which would have involved me in a duel or some mess. And though I should not have hesitated to do my duty for her sake yet there was no use in it as long as the same purpose could be accomplished in a safer way. Kerner is one of those kind of villains who never will repent. Be careful to acknowledge all letters you get from me by their date and if I do not acknowledge yours write and tell me of it. If I can catch Kerner at any trick of the kind I mean to knock him in the head with a club.

We were all on the quiver again the other night waiting for "Stuart's Cavalry." Maj. Genl. Schenck telegraphed three times that they were crossing near us at Harrison's Island and we were all ready to receive them in the warmest possible manner. Give my especial love to Aunt Sarah and tell her not to think I have forgotten her because I don't write.

Your Affectionate Son
Peter

Harrison

Camp Hooker, Monocacy Bridge, Maryland
Thursday Eve. January 1, 1863

My Dear Mother

I seat myself upon my bed this first evening of a new year to write you my first letter of the present year. I wish firstly to let you know that I have received that small box you said at first you was going to send me but I find Mother, that it is nearly as large as the first. And everything was in perfect order. Let me sincerely thank you Mother for your trouble and expense.

I didn't open it until this morning but I tell you it was rather a hard task to go to bed without seeing the inside of that box. But most all of the boys were asleep when I came in and I didn't like to make any noise to awake them. The first thing I saw I believe when I opened the box was your letter, and read it of course before I took out any of the things.

The boys are all well and in good spirits tonight and some with intoxicating spirits. It is a lucky thing I think that we didn't get paid off before the holidays or some of the men would have been minus a few $. So you see they haven't got any money and of course they cannot spend any.

Well Mother, I believe I have nothing more to say this time so I will close and go get a piece of bread and butter. So give my love to John with a very happy New Year and best respects to all enquiring friends. So good night my dear Mother. Accept the love of your son in Uncle Sam's employ.

Sergeant Albert C. Harrison

Ross

Frederick City, Maryland
January 5, 1863

Dear Mother

Your welcome letter I received in due season. Tomorrow three of our companies leave to do picket duty fifteen miles down the railroad — everything is about the same as usual about here. We have got a football now and have fun playing matches — one half of the regiment against the other. Today all the officers had their photograph taken together.

We have had quite a snow storm today but it has cleared off now. You must excuse me from writing more as I am going visiting with Lt. Woodward and Capt. Alstrom to a gentleman's some three quarters of a mile from here. We are going to have some music. There is going to be a number of ladies present. Write soon to me mother and tell me all the news.

I Remain Your Affectionate Son
Burroughs

P.S. January 9th, Col. went to Washington today to see about our pay. I believe some of the boys say if they don't get paid this month they will desert and go home.

Wolcott

Camp in the Field, Va.
January 10, 1863

My Dear Old Friend Powers

Once more I take my pen in hand to write you a few lines. I have made an attempt to write you a few lines but I am afraid it will prove a failure as I have no news that would be of any interest to you, except that the talk is the Army of the Potomac has got some big work to do that soon we have been made to understand that we are to move. I hate the very thought of moving. We are so nicely fixed for the winter — good warm cabins and stove that cost us 15 dollars to roast our beef and turkey in and that will have to be left behind and the weather is so cold now that the wounded would freeze to death before they could be taken off the field.

I received a box last night — sent from the Trenton House. It was a treat to me — from Jersey sausage and mince pies. Although we have lived pretty well since we have been on this ground there is five of us in the mess — the Quartermaster takes mess with us and we get everything that we want from the commissary.

The rebs made a rush at our pickets the other day but they found that it was hot work for them and they went back. You can see the rebels encampment from our picket lines. They have log houses — same as ours and look very comfortable. I would give a dollar to be in Trenton today. I think I could enjoy myself. It is a dull life — this laying quiet. When we are on the move the time passes by without interruption. I shall have to close for the want of substance to write about. I remain your ever true friend.

J.R. Wolcott

Wolcott

Camp Hooker
January 11th 1863

Dear Friend Powers

I again have the pleasure of answering your most welcome letter and while twilight shadows have gathered around me and in the stillness of the evening hours as I sit alone in my tent, thoughts of bygone days come settling across my mind. I almost wish I was in good old Trenton again. We are situated in the same place as when I last wrote but I am in hopes that the day is not far distant when I will meet my friend once more.

We had quite a snow. It commenced yesterday morning and it continued until the evening when it commenced raining and it still rains. We have good news from Rosecrans and Grant, but it is learned that Sherman has met with a heavy loss and was driven back several miles. I sometimes think the war never will end. It looks mighty black. Where is the Army of the Potomac? I find the people are getting disheartened. I am tired of laying in camp. I want them to pay us or send us to the front. I would like to have a fight — laying in camp does not agree with me. I am getting so lazy. By the time the war is over I will not be good for anything.

We had quite an excitement the day before New Years. The Rebels tried to cross at Harpers Ferry but were driven away. Then part of them did cross at Poolesville and they were attacked by the 3rd Delaware and scattered through the woods — part of them are in Maryland now and trying to get back on the Virginia side. I must bring my epistle to a close.

Good night — write soon.
J.R. Wolcott

Harrison

Camp Hooker, Monocacy Bridge, MD

Major General W.S. Rosecrans

National Archives

Monday evening January 12, 1863
My Dear Mother

I take this present opportunity to pen you a few lines in answer to your dear letter which was received by me this afternoon. I was happy to hear from you again. And sorry to hear you complaining. I hope this may find you well.

I am enjoying the best of health as usual thank the Lord. I suppose you have received my letter before this to assure you that I received the box. There is no news in camp of any importance. The Regt. is in middling good health at present. Two of the companies have left us. They are guarding up the railroad about sixteen miles from here, on the road to Baltimore. I can hear of no news from the Armies today of any importance. Things seem to be at a standstill.

It is just as you say mother. If there are any girls around I am bound to find them. You want to know what that girl's name is; it is Marian. I haven't had a chance to get over to see the old man now in ten or twelve days. I started out yesterday for the purpose of going there, but changed my mind and went to the city and took dinner with another acquaintance of mine and had corn beef and cabbage and mince pie for desert. And as I started to come home I found a glass of peach jelly in my dress coat pocket. So you see Mother it don't make any difference where I go I am bound to get on the right side of girls. But I get on the right side of the old folks first.

I must now tell you, Mother, that the bridge has not been destroyed across the Monocacy yet nor will it be again while the Brave 14th are here. Without Jackson [Thomas Jonathan Jackson, General C.S.A.] comes upon us again with 80,000 men as he did before but he will never get here again with such an army as he brought before. So you need not think that we will have any fighting to do.

Please give my love to John and all enquiring friends, accept a portion for yourself and remember you son Albert in the army. Write as soon as convenient. May God bless you all.

Sergt. Albert C. Harrison

Vredenburgh

Camp Hooker, Monocacy
January 13, 1863

My Dear Mother

I received yours of the 9th inst. last evening. The letter I lost or rather which was stolen by Kerner was not from you or any of the family. Kerner said he found it and I could not prove otherwise. He knows that I think he stole it and keeps away from me. I would have him dismissed from the service if it were not for Theodosia. I did not recover the letter as Kerner said he destroyed it. Don't say anything more about it.

I should like very much to see Jim and if he will come and stay a few days. Therefore perhaps it would be best to pack a trunk and let Jim bring it as baggage. If Jim does come you had better pack the trunk with some of my best clothes, vest, best black pants and blue frock coat and best boots. For they may come in play here while at home they never can do anybody any good, being too small for Jim. You had better put in my best dress coat too, if there is room and what I don't want Jim can take back without any extra trouble.

Besides having a pleasant time here, he can ride all over and see the country to his hearts content. I wish you would urge him to come for I did not see him before I left you recollect. The expense need not be considered for I would willingly pay it three times over to see him.

Col. Hall and I have lately made several acquaintances among the ladies of Frederick. I wish Col. Hall and Sallie Taylor had "hit it" in Trenton, for he is one of the best fellows I every saw and I feel myself a better man from his intimacy. He smokes, drinks and swears a little, but a more honorable, high minded, and generous man never lived. He is just the kind of man I would like to marry one of my sisters if I had one. Tell Father I recd. his letter from New Brunswick and will obey his injunctions to the letter.

Your Affectionate Son
Peter

Vredenburgh

Monocacy
January 16, 1863

My Dear Father

I recd. your letter from New Brunswick and also heard from you through the Trentonian which gave an elaborate report of the judicial proceedings in that city.

I should not be much surprised if we did not have much more fighting. If the Northern Democrats whose sentiments are getting so fearfully popular, do not compel the administration to pursue a different course I am afraid our finances will, as in 1812, compel us to make peace. What can we hope for when our own state sends a man like Jim Wall to cooperate with the administration. A man whose feelings will not allow him to view with judgement or favor any acts of Mr. Lincoln. From present appearances we have been a very short time to do what can't be done at all — conquer the South.

Our Regt. has not been paid anything yet and there is a great deal of "croaking" on that account, and I understand most of the other Jersey regts. were just as fortunate — men will not fight without their pay.

When I get my pay which amounted to about $600. on the 1st. inst. what shall I do with it? I guess my best plan will be to send it to you and you use it or deposit it in the Freehold Bank and then get their bills for it and make a special deposit. I don't think Treasury Notes will be safe nor would I be much surprised if the Government repudiates.

I have made some very pleasant acquaintances here in Frederick, some few Union, but mostly Secesh. But I am so used to meeting persons who openly proclaim their sympathies for the rebels that I am quite used to it and talk the matter with them as I would any other political subject. The only Union people I have met here are General Cooper's and General Shriver's families. They are Brig. Genls. in our army. Lt. Col. and I were at Cooper's last evening to a soiree and there met two ladies from Falmouth by the name of Washington, as rebellious as they know how to be. They are related (grand-nieces) I understand to the immortal of that name. Col. Hall is quite a lady killer and popular with every lady. He and I are inseparable and I am proud of his friendship; he is the most high toned, honorable friend I ever had. The ink is so poor Father that I will stop here. Hoping you will be well when you receive this and write soon etc.

Your Affectionate Son
Peter

Ross

Frederick City Md.
January 16, 1863
Dear Mother

Capt. Conover has just arrived from home and handed me a letter from you and Mimmie. I am sorry to hear Pop is not very well. How I would like to see you all. I am going to try and get home after we are paid off but cannot tell whether I will be successful or not.

I have been in some high society lately down here. Last night Col. Hall, Major, Lt. Woodward, Alstrom, and myself went to Frederick in an ambulance and called on Miss Cooper, whose father is a General in the Union army. I took my guitar along. There was a Miss Shriver there whose father is also a Gen'l and a Miss Washington, from Fredericksburg. She is a descendent of Gen'l Washington and came here for safety. Miss Cooper told me she was strong Secesh though. There were several other ladies present and we had a glorious time singing, playing and dancing. You can't tell how we enjoy ourselves down here but I'm afraid it can't last long.

Do you know how so many of our Regt. get home, I will tell you. The Col. can only give them a furlough for forty-eight hours so he tells them if they will go on their own responsibility they can stay a day or two longer. In Baltimore they examine all soldier's passes and if not correct are sent back to their regiments so our men get a citizen's overcoat and hat and get through Baltimore in that manner. Write soon and give my love to our neighbors and to yourself and Pop.

From Your Affectionate Son
Burroughs

Ross

Frederick City, Maryland
January 22, 1863

Dear Sister Mimmie

As I have nothing to engage my mind tonight but thoughts of home and friends, I feel as I could not employ my time better than by writing to my dear sister Mimmie. This is the first time I have written to you I believe, since you became Mrs. Garrett Van Deveer. I was sorry I could not be present at the ceremony, but then my wishes for your happiness were nonetheless those miles intervened between us. Remember me to Garrett and tell him I will be happy to call him by the name of brother, and that he has my best wishes for his happiness and welfare.

I should like much to come on and see you all but I cannot tell when that happy day will be just at present. Do you ever hear from Julia Van Dorn now. I have her carte de visite you know. By the way when are you going to send me yours? I would like to see your facsimile very much as long as I cannot see the original.

I suppose Pop must feel lonesome sometimes now that we are all gone from home. I must close for there is nothing of importance to communicate. Remember me particularly to your new sister and tell Pop and Mother I am still in my usual good health.

Your Affectionate Brother
Will

Vredenburgh

Office Provost Marshall
Frederick City, Md.
January 28, 1863

Dear Mother

You see by the date of this letter that I have taken up my residence at Frederick City so that you will direct letters here and I will get them sooner than if sent to Camp. I begin to understand my duties now pretty well and think in a week I will be perfectly alright. They are much more responsible and multifarious than I at first presumed they would be. In the mornings I have a general jail delivery, i.e., all persons of high or low degree who have been confined during the preceding 24 hours in the city are brought before me and I either discharge them, sentence them to fine, prison, or turn them over to the civil authorities or — do just as I please.

I have completely remodeled the office. I have moved in to a fine large room with gas. I have taught the orderlies to take off their hats and pay proper respect and have really made a most perceptible and salubrious change. It used to be a noisy, dirty place, every one talking at once — hats on and some smoking. Now it is as much like a courtroom as a "place where justice is judicially administered." I have the sole power of granting transportation for the U.S. from this place according to my own discretion. I have the sole power of allowing passes, arresting rebels, seizing contraband goods or goods going South of the Potomac. Arresting stragglers and deserters and sending them to their regiments making orders, relative to the sale of liquors, seizing and confiscating liquors improperly sold and arresting and punishing the persons guilty. The charge of all the city guard and patrols, making the details and pointing out the location of the guards and patrols. And in general whatever is the matter they seem to come to me to get redress. Business has been incessant since I have been in office, but the young clerk with me says he never knew it to be so brisk before.

The only things that bothers me is having no prescribed limits and being governed by no particular instructions of precedents. For instance, a man left here with the rebels when they made their raid here and was appointed Capt. He afterwards was captured at Winchester and paroled and sent here to report daily to the Provost Marshall. Yesterday a deputy U.S. marshal came for him with a warrant issued by a U.S. Commander setting forth that he was arrested for treason. He then came to me for protection and it bothered me very much to determine whether he could be tried for treason, because if he could, he could be hung and if he could be hung, every prisoner could be, but I shirked the responsibility of deciding that I had no control over him if a U.S. marshal had a warrant because he was paroled and not in my custody. I suppose Father can appreciate my dilemma better than you, but you can show him this.

I can accommodate you or Father most beautifully and I would like very much to see you after it gets more pleasant out. I am sorry now that I did not urge Jim to stay, but I was so bothered when he was here that I did not want to think of anything else but my business, besides my horse was lame and I could not make it pleasant for him.

Ever Your Affectionate Son
Peter

Harrison

Camp Hooker Monocacy Bridge, MD
February 1, 1863

My Dear Mother

    I seat myself this Sabbath morning the first day of February to pen you a few lines. I expected a letter from you yesterday but I received none. I hope you are not sick again. This is the first chance I have had to write a letter in three or four days as I am acting Orderly Sergt.
    It is just the hardest office in the Co. to fill. Our late orderly has been promoted to a second Lieut. in Co H. Therefore it leaves a vacancy in our Company and one I don't wish to fill. Our next orderly has not been elected yet but I am in hopes he will be soon as I want to fall back to my old position as second Sergt.
    The weather is quite fair this morning but we had an awful snow storm. The largest snow we have had this winter and the deepest one.
    It is now Dinner time. I shall have to come to a close, give my love to all, write soon.

From your affectionate Son in the Army
Sergeant Albert C. Harrison

Wolcott

Camp Hooker
February 1, 1863

Dear Old Friend Powers

    I read your favor of the 22nd. I was glad to hear you were in the enjoyment of good health and sorry your little girl is ill but I am in hope she is in the enjoyment of good health.
    Things are very quiet along the Monocacy but we expect a battle soon on the Rappahannock. Soon as the roads are fit. We have a good man now at the head of our army — one the rebels do not like much — they call him fighting Joe Hooker. All I ask of him is he will not call on the 8th Army Corps. General Schenck is anxious for a fight — he wants to get a big name and he has a great confidence in the 14th. It has been very stormy for the last three weeks, and it is very disagreeable to us.
    The paymaster has not been around yet, and the devil only knows when he will be. When he does come we only get paid up to Oct. 31st. Our Colonel is acting Brig. General and he wants me to put off my visit home as he thinks he will have some use for me. Lt. Col. Hall is commanding — a big thing.

He makes a good officer but he is not Col. Truex. Good night and remember me to your family.

Yours truly
J.R. Wolcott

P.S.
I suppose New Jersey is in the Union yet? I hope Jeff Davis will be disappointed.

Vredenburgh

Office of Military Commandant
Frederick City, Md.
February 1, 1863

Dear Mother

Here I am waiting for a sergeant of the patrols, and as I have conveniences for writing will address a few lines to you. I recd. Jim's letter with yours yesterday afternoon. I wrote to Jim on the 29th inst. asking him to come on again, but as I see by his letter he left Freehold before the letter reached him.

I suppose you had better express the trunk to me if Sergeant Conover leaves without you're having a chance to send it by him. Brig. Genl. Schriver is a warm friend of mine and invited me tonight to bring his daughter (a very interesting young lady) down to Baltimore next Friday night to one of the Union assemblies and I expect to accept his invitation.

Everything goes on well and I am becoming well acquainted with the citizens of high and low degree of Frederick. My position brings me in contact with everyone and I am about as public a man as the mayor or chief of police of a city. Everybody that or thinks he knows anything mysterious seems to come to me and the quantity of memorandums that I have stored away is monstrous.

With much love to Father & hoping his indisposition is nothing serious I remain devoted to you all.

Peter

PS: Theodosia "Kerner" I see is in town but I have not seen her to speak to her though she has been here since Friday. I have parties watching Kerner at the P.O.

Harrison

Camp Hooker, Monocacy Bridge, MD
Friday, February 6th 1863

My Dear Mother

I am going to pen you a few lines this afternoon, but I don't think I can finish your letter before tomorrow, as it is now rather late in the afternoon.

The Paymaster has reached our Camp at long last we received pay up to the 31st of October. Therefore I received $29.20 cts. I think we will receive the remainder due us before a great while. I will send you $10.00 Mother in this letter and if this comes to you all right I will send you some more in the next letter I write you. Therefore I want you to write immediately Mother, if it is only a few lines to assure me that this was received by you safe. Don't you spend that ten dollars for anything, than to buy a dress Mother. Be sure you get your dress & then you can do as you like with the remainder if there is anything left.

I took my boots this morning to a shoemaker in Co B. They will be fixed by tomorrow night. I expect that will cost me about $2.00 if I had received all my pay I should have sent you about $80.00.

Well Mother Spring will soon be with us again. Eight more days will make six months for me in the Service. I expect It seems like a year to you Mother does it not?

May God watch over you & Bless you all.

Sergt Albert Harrison

Wolcott

Camp Hooker
February 18, 1863

Dear Old Powers

I was happy to hear from you and happy to hear you were in the enjoyment of good health — also to hear your little one was well and growing fat. You will see by the heading of my letter we are still on the old camp ground but it is not certain how long we will be allowed to stay, as we are under marching orders and I do not care how soon we are on the march for I am tired of this mud hole and the duty is very hard. I am guard the days and night — every week — one day Provost duty searching the cars for deserters and suspicious looking fellows. Most every day we bring some deserters to the guard house. Most of them are from the army of the Potomac. I tell you I feel for them and if I could I would let a good many of them go, but I am afraid I would be caught, then the devil would be to pay. One day I go five miles from camp and do picket duty 24 hours and the other camp ground. You can judge it is hard to lose the night's sleep in a week, especially if they send us to the front, where we expect to go when we leave here.

You say you were disappointed because I did not come to Jersey but you can not be more disappointed than I was for I had intended to have a big time but it is no use crying for it is all dry with furloughs. Gen. Schenck has issued orders that no furlough except to those are disabled or sick. I think it would be a good plan to shoot my finger off, don't you think that would pay. You think the war will be over before next August but the impression among our officers is there will be some hard fighting before it is ended soon as the roads are in condition for the army to move. I am afraid there will be but a few of the 14th that will get home alive, they will be so brave. We will have the best of the rest of the Jersey boys on a bayonet charge. We have learned the French Bayonet Exercise — only Regt. that has learned. We shoot at a target every morning and afternoon and the most of the men are good marksmen. The distance we shoot is 200 yards and I can hit the bull's eye 5 times out of 10.

A report just came in camp a few moments ago that the rebels are marching on to Frederick. They always come on rainy nights and we poor devils have to stand in line for 2 or 3 hours. I expect to hear the long roll every minute. It rains like thunder.

Good night
J.R. Wolcott

Ross

Hd Qrs. Military Commandant
Frederick City, Maryland
February 28, 1863

Dear Father

As I have nothing particular to do at present, I thought I could not employ my time better than by writing to you. I am now at Frederick with the Col. acting as Ass. Adj. Genl's Clerk, and have been here since Monday last. The Col. has a whole house to himself, and I have a room to myself upstairs which would seem like home. The Chaplain is appointed Post Chaplain and he has a room here also, and likewise the Major who is Provost Marshal.

I went out last evening with Major and called on some ladies who seemed much pleased with my performance on the guitar. I received a letter from Mimmie a few days since and also one from Let, with some good advice from her to the absent soldier.

I believe there is nothing more at this time that I have to communicate so will close hoping soon to hear from home again. My love to Mother and Sister I remain

Your Affectionate Son
Burroughs

All Quiet Along the Potomac To-Night

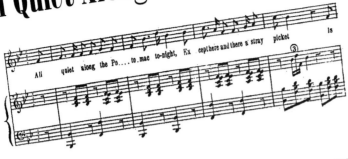

All Quiet Along the Potomac To-Night; Words by Lamar Fontaine, Music by J.H. Hewitt; Published by George Dunn & Company, 1864. Source: The Free Library of Philadelphia, Music Department.

3 Movement...at Last

March 1863 — September 1863

By early spring, 1863, the 14th New Jersey Volunteers were eager to move into combat. The winter had been hard on the regiment as some seventy-five men were lost to sickness. Those who remained were temporarily brigaded with the Third Delaware Regiment and the Purnell Legion.

Six companies of this regiment were sent to Martinsburg to reinforce General Milroy but returned six weeks later due to the lack of enemy action. This marked the end of the relative inactivity for the regiment. They were ordered to Maryland Heights near Harpers Ferry to counter Lee's move toward the Potomac after the Battle of Chancellorsville.

Harrison

Camp Hooker, Monocacy Bridge Md.
Saturday, March 7, 1863

My Dear Mother & Father

As Sergeant Joseph Chadwick starts for home at half past three tomorrow morning I cannot let the opportunity slip, and write you a few lines to send by him. I was very glad he received his furlough, as his family is sick, and besides I shall be sure to know how times are around the village of Red Bank. He has an eight day furlough. It commences next Monday, but I said he is going to start tomorrow morning, and going by the way of New York. He will be in New York tomorrow night if nothing happens to him. And will be in Red Bank by 10 o'clock Monday morning.

The Battery that has been stationed here with us all winter has moved to Murfreesborough. Some of the boys rather hated to leave their good quarters. We have

Union camp scene.

National Archives

taken one of their buildings for a guard house as it was far better than our old one. The boys have some chance for rest now, when they are off duty.

I don't think there are any signs of our leaving Maryland very soon. I heard a part of the Regt. were going to Frederick City and two companies were going to stay here. I don't know whether it will prove true or not.

The boys are sitting around the fireplace discussing old matters, talking about one thing or another. Their general conversation ranging between New York, New Jersey, and Maryland. Will Byram has come in and seated himself in our midst. He sends his love too. Cousin Elliott Fields of the Bank Boys sends his love. Charley White and Charley Wood and the rest of the Bank Boys are all well.

I am going to send you a Confederate bill. There is no war news of any importance. I think the war will soon come to a close for our armies have the Rebels pretty well penned in. One year will I think wind up the whole concern & peace & happiness once more reign in our much loved republic & the land of the Heroic Washington.

I must close now so I bid you good night & may God guard over you and bless you. Write soon & believe your ever affectionate soldier boy.

Sergt. Albert C. Harrison

Stults

Camp Hooker, Monocacy Bridge
Sunday March 8, 1863

Dear Pa & Ma

Yours of March 4th I received yesterday, and very glad to hear you are all well and hearty. You spoke of your not hearing from me since you sent that box of clothing. I wrote you a long letter I think you must have received by this time. At that time I said I was very well pleased with my clothing, but as usual I must find some fault. My pants were a little too short and not near loose enough in the leg, and if my coat had been a little better, I would have liked it just as well. I am very glad I got my dress coat at Frederick, for I have a splendid fitting coat I can tell you. The officers have purchased new hats — cost only $10.00 apiece. The style of the hat is the same as I used to wear excepting the crown is higher, and are black. The hat itself cost about $4.00, the trimmings costing $6.00, cord, eagle and bugle, you will think we are getting rather gay, well you don't miss it much — why shouldn't we be, times are good and money plenty. I hardly know what I want sent in my valise, a couple pair of white cotton gloves. I want very much, the boots you spoke of but I can get them in Frederick by paying about $1.00 more than they would cost at home and then I can get them to fit. I would like to have my valise sent on right away.

It is talked we will have to move before long, of course none knows for a certainty but there is a probability of it. We have quartered here a long time, and may stay all summer.

Kushler Lansen's cavalry and the 3rd Delaware have been sent away from Frederick, the Purnell Legion still remains. If we are sent from here, other regts. will take our place, for the Monocacy Bridge, and Frederick city are important points. At the latter place are stored immense quantities of government stores. The section of Battery L. 5th U.S. Regulars, which has lain here a long time, has been sent on to Winchester, Va. a distance of 50 miles. The boys are anxious to go. This battery enlisted a good many of the 14th, sometime back a bill was passed authorizing the regulars to enlist men from the volunteers, of course it could enlist only those who were willing to enlist, and at that only 10 men from a company. Comp. H did not lose any men, but several comp.'s did. The men, on getting angry at their officers would go right over to the Battery and enlist. I like the regular service very much, and if I hadn't held a commission I think I should have enlisted in the Battery. If I could get a 2nd Lieutenancy in the regulars I would accept it.

The weather continues very changeable, clear one day and stormy the next. Yesterday was very damp, today likewise. We have had one or two company drills, and dress parades the past week, but it is very muddy at present, and a right smart chance for more mud. But it is supposed there are but few regiments that can drill with the 14th. We will never drill better. After a regiment is put into active service it doesn't learn any fancy movements.

We still have a good many visitors from Jersey and elsewhere. I expect Pa, and Uncle Isaac on soon.

I spoke of Alexander Vendue. I did not think he would ever move off the farm. I suppose Dick routs Henry Stults. There was an auction sale Friday last, at one of our nearest neighbors. The old man, two daughters (young ladies) having died within the past two months. My health is good as usual, all the boys have grown fleshier and heavier than they ever were before. Fred Hagle is as fat as a bear, and is a very good

Frederick, MD

soldier I can tell you. You remember Fred. I suppose you often wonder how we keep supplied with fire wood. You would hardly believe the quantity it takes to keep us going. Throughout the regiment there are at least 125 fires kept burning near 20 hours a day. There is plenty of woodland near and we used to carry all our wood, but now we have it carted, government paying $5.00 per cord delivered at our camp. We cut it in the woods.

The boys appear well contented with their rations

just now, they have fresh beef and fresh bread — plenty of it. The sutler keeps his mess table well supplied. Tell Uncle Reed I would like to be at home for awhile to go ducking with him and J. Lelover & Vanderhoef. He had fair luck his last trip. I think I shall apply for leave of absence soon. Several of the officers have applied, only about half are successful. We apply to Gen. Schenk at Baltimore. Several of the enlisted men have been granted furloughs. Polk Higgens of our company is at home now. I wish I could send you a contraband or two, but they are awful lazy. If you want horses you should come out here and attend an auction of condemned government horses held at Frederick. They sell at all prices from $2. to 50. My Respects to all

Yours
Marcus

Harrison

Camp Hooker, Monocacy Creek, Maryland
Saturday, March 13, 1863

Dear Mother

Your letter of the 3rd. inst. was just received by me last evening and as I have my spitfire [Springfield rifle] and equipment all ready for tomorrow morning's inspection, I have nothing to do but sit down & pass the morning away by writing you a few lines, to assure you that I am well.

You said you were disappointed when you opened my letter you thought you would see my photograph. I went to the City this week for the purpose of getting some cards, but as the day was dark & stormy I didn't get them. But I shall go up again before long and try it over again as soon as it comes my turn to have a pass.

It will be seven months tomorrow since I put on Uncle Sam's dry goods. Time flies away fast, time and tide waits for no man.

I don't think we will move out of Maryland this Spring. I will be glad when we do make a move for I am tired of laying around loose. Hardly doing enough to keep the blood in circulation.

My boots cost me $1.00. I thought they

Sergeant Harrison's weapons.

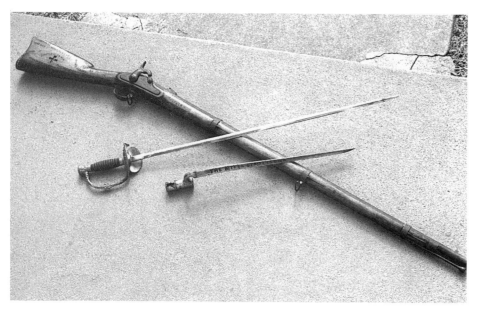

would cost me more. I believe I have nothing more to say at present so I close, with love to you and John.

Your Affectionate Son
Sergt. Albert C. Harrison

Stults

Officer of the Guard's Tent
Camp Hooker
March 15, 1863

Dear Pa & Ma

It is very strange to me that you don't write more often. News in camp is scarce, everyday alike nearly, once in awhile something turns up to give a person an idea to write of. Last Friday night, about 9 o'clock, news was brought in camp that a party of rebel cavalry had called at a house about 3 miles distant from camp. You remember how cold it was at that time and you may be sure the news was not welcomely received. The only dread the men had was at that time of night, nearly every one was in bed, thinking that they were lucky in enjoying such comfortable quarters. Companies G and B were called upon to go in search of them. And being short of Lieuts, Captain Alstrom of Co. G invited me to go with them and of course, I must be foolish enough to go and after a hasty preparation we started. And after walking three miles of the worst walking I ever found in my life, we reached the place where it was reported we would find at least 50 of the enemy. We heard that they had merely called and were right on. None knew where. We tracked them aways but losing all trace of them we gave up the search and posted ourselves on a bridge that crosses the Monocacy near Buckeystown. We waited for them to make their appearance, but 4 o'clock came and no rebels so we left for camp reaching it at daylight. This is the luck we usually have hunting mounted rebels for it is impossible to catch them if they see fit to keep away from us. We suppose that as soon as the traveling gets better we shall be sent on plenty of excursions of this kind for the rebels intend to annoy us as much as possible.

I am on duty today as officer of the guard, went on at 8 o'clock this morning and will be released at 8 tomorrow. As I write, 10 P.M. Sunday night, it is snowing fast, it is a hard night on the sentries, who are on duty two hours at a time — two on and two off for 24 hours.

My health is very good. Capt. has been suffering with the toothache a good deal of late, but that is not serious. The health of the Regt. is very good at present. We haven't heard of our moving from this place. Two month's pay is now due us,

Lt. H.G. Conover of Co. H.

but we hear the paymaster is sick, but as soon as able he intends to pay us off. No more at present.

My Respects to all
Marcus

P.S. Monday morning 7:30 Snowing — Plenty of snow for sleighriding. Enclosed you will find the Photograph of Lieut. H.G. Conover, Co. H.

Vredenburgh

Provost Marshal's Office, Frederick, Md.
March 16, 1863

My Dear Mother

I hope you have not been alarmed at not hearing from me for some time, but I have been rather busy and had nothing in particular to say and therefore my silence.

Since I began this letter we have had a fire here and I have just returned from it. A fire here is rather a serious affair where there are so many soldiers and I was present with the patrol, though not identified with it. I wish you and Father could come on soon for I am afraid if you do not come before the 1st. of April, that then Father, I will be busy til the last of April and we may have to move before that time.

Chaplain Rose goes to Burlington this week to the conference. I can go to Baltimore and Washington when I please now without charge, as I have to send convalescents there daily and I can either go myself or send whom I please with them. I have only been to Baltimore once though and not at all to Washington.

Tell Henry he should send on that barrel of potatoes soon. Mr. Thomas speaks of them occasionally. Tell Henry to tell T.C. Forman that I have been enjoying some fox hunts here lately. The farmers in this vicinity seem to take great delight in the sport. If you can not come here before April you must be sure to come the first opportunity afterwards. I can accommodate you elegantly now. I board at a private house in the city at $6 per week.

I felt rather ashamed, ahem, you spoke of Theodosia telling you that I had taken her out etc., for I treated her very shabbily. I only called on her once, but I detested her husband so much and her too for marrying him that I did not feel like seeing or having anything to do with her.

Col. Hall seems to be paying attention to Brig. Genl. Cooper's daughter. She is a very uninteresting young lady in my opinion but he does not see it in that light. I am very universal in my attentions and see no probability of my soon concentrating either my attentions or affections. With much love to all I remain

Your Affectionate Son
Peter

Ross

Hd Qrs. Military Commandant, Frederick Md.
March 19, 1863

Dear Mother

Your dear letter reached me today and I hasten to answer it, as I was under the impression that I had written last, or should have written before this.

Yes I have everything almost as comfortable here as at home. A good room and bed, and plenty to eat, to make me contented for it is entirely different from what I expected when I started. I remember often when I would ask you if I could not go to war, you would say I would soon get tired and wish I was back home. I am going to disappoint your expectations. When you thought I would wish myself back, to be sure there is no place like home! to me, but I don't feel a bit homesick as long as there are so many pretty ladies to pass away the evenings with.

Roland Ellis was down here yesterday to see us. I have nearly all the officers carte de visites and will send them to you the first opportunity. Mr. Rose is on home somewhere now, Mr. Chandler was very kind to remember me in his prayers. After this Conscription Act comes in force Col. says he will have the power to grant furloughs himself and then I can go home for a few days. I am writing with a new gold pen which the Adjutant presented me with. I have stopped smoking. Adjutant gives me a dollar a month for that. I will send you on a carte de visite of myself in my next so you can see how I look. I manage to keep up appearances very well. I got the new coat, pants, and boots and now I go to church every Sunday. Tell Mimmie she must write to me for I don't have time to write to all hands. Give my love to Pop, Aunt Jane, Garrett and Mimmie and write soon to

Your Affectionate Son
Burroughs

Ross

Hd Qrs. Military Commandant, Frederick, Md
March 20, 1863

Dear Sister,

I wrote a letter home to mother yesterday and now will send you a few lines. I should love to come on to see my new relative but it is impossible now. I should not wonder if our regiment moved pretty soon. The Gen'l commanding is coming on from Baltimore today to inspect our regiment. I think it is preparatory to sending us to the front. Are you going to farming in the spring or what do you and Garrett think of doing? How are the ladies coming on around Monmouth. When I want a wife I guess I will take one from Maryland, there are more pretty girls in Frederick than you could shake a stick at in a week. I am paying particular attention to a Miss Nelson. She is a very handsome lady. I think the Col. says he supposes he will have to give me a furlough to go on our wedding tour. I will send you my carte de visite so you can see what your soldier brother looks like. I believe I have nothing more of importance to communicate so will close. Remember me to Garrett, Lib, Rita, Aaron and all the rest of my friends. My love to Pop, Mother and Aunt Jane.

Your Affectionate Brother
Will

Wolcott

Camp Hooker
March 24, 1863

Friend Powers

I received your letter this afternoon and I can assure you it was received with pleasure, and one from John Dolton also. Tomorrow we will begin to make preparation to move but God only knows where. Different reports — some say to Frederick City — others to join Hooker's army. But I am certain that the orders are to move on the 28th, and I think likely it will be somewhere near Winchester as that is where the rest of our Brigade is stationed. It is reported that our Lieut. Col. has been offered Col. of the 10th Rgt. I am glad of it. We have had him long enough with us.

Last Saturday we were reviewed by Genl. Briggs and he spoke in good praise of the 14th. He said he thought he would take us for his body guard. There is great fear in Frederick City that the rebels will make another raid in Maryland before long. We have captured three spies within the last two weeks and it has been reported by the niggers that there is a party that meet every night at different places and drill but we have not been able to find them. The Col.'s scout is out every night but he has failed so far to find any clue of their whereabouts.

General Schenck telegraphed to Col. Truex that he had a dispatch this morning that the rebels were going to cross somewhere between Point of Rocks and Poolesville. But he thought that was too high, but he must have his eyes open and stick to the bridge. They can easily cross at the Point of Rocks as most all of the troops at the Point have been taken from there and sent to the front. 20,000 troops passed through here last night on their way to join Burnside's new command. Among them was the 27th N.J. Regt. One of the men jumped off the bridge last night and was very much injured. He had a long leap. The bridge is nearly as high from the water as the old Delaware Bridge. I tried to learn his name but in vain.

Have you seen Don Pierson lately? When you see him tell him he had better report to Major Jones before the 1st day of April. After the 1st day of April, General Schenck is going to send and arrest all deserters and make an example of the first one he gets, and if he is caught, I would not give a cent for his life and he is surely to be brought back sooner or later.

The weather for the last few days has been most like spring and the roads have dried up wonderful and I expect before many days the Army of the Potomac will soon make some move towards Richmond, but before Richmond is taken there will be thousands of poor fellows sent to their graves. The rebels here strongly fortified their positions and there are a great many masked battery and our men will run into them before they are aware of it. They will be sent from the earth. I hope I will not be one of them.

A person living in a quiet place like Trenton forms an idea of the horror of a battle. I seen enough of the effect of the battle of Antietam although I was ten miles from it but we had wounded and dead enough to fill a 2 acre lot full piled on top of one another, some with arms off, legs off and wounded in all shapes. I think I shall have to take a look at Trenton some time this summer if the rebels do not put a pound of lead through me and I do not intend to give them a chance if I can

Union Hospital at Point of Rocks.

help it. I had bullet to come within about 2 feet of my nose one night last summer when I was out on picket and I did not like the smell of it at that distance and the smell must be more disagreeable on a closer look.

Give all my inquiring — my regards and do not forget to write soon. Tell Nick I am waiting to hear from him. I am sorry Nick left you for I had not much confidence in the new firm from the first, their foundation is not sound. Remember me to Mrs. P. and

your little girl. I suppose she is getting big by this time.

Some of our boys got into the guard house tonight. They were at Frederick and they went to an eating saloon to get something to eat and a glass of beer. The Col. is very strict. He will not allow a man to drink or take or smell liquor. If he does, he is sure to be punished for it.

J.R. Wolcott

Vredenburgh

Provost Marshal's Office, Frederick, Md.
April 9, 1863

Dear Mother

I recd. both of your letters. The bill of Cooper's is all right and I would like to pay it. I sent Will a blank check about ten days ago and have not heard yet whether he recd. it. I herewith send you a paper containing an account of Genl. Cooper's obsequies. I am glad you enjoyed yourself here I am sure you could not have been as much pleased as I was.

I wish Father would come as soon as he can after court. Those potatoes have not arrived yet and if they do not reach me pretty soon I will take means to have them forwarded. I have been rather active since you left in arresting Southern sympathizers who find ways to vent their feelings in any manner, and I think I am not so popular with the secessionists as I was a week or two ago. I think I will get worse and worse all the time. The right way is to keep pressing these secessionists closer and closer to the wall all the time.

Schenck is pursuing the right method at Baltimore. I have no red tape or legal difficulties to contend with in dealing out justice to secessionists and liquor sellers.

Tell Father that I have kept McClellan's official report of the battles of South Mountain and Antietam and when he comes here we will take a few days and visit Harpers Ferry and the said battlefields.

Ever Your Affectionate Son
Peter

Vredenburgh

Metropolitan Hotel, Washington D.C.
April 12, 1863 — 4 P.M.

Dear Father

I have no doubt you will be surprised and perhaps startled to see my letter dated at this place, but I have not been ordered away from Frederick yet; only came down here on business. I ordered myself down here with some prisoners yesterday. I stopped last night at Willards, but was so disgusted with the place that I changed to this hotel. This morning I went to Alexandria to get some of our soldiers that are in the convalescent camp but found on arriving that the camp had been moved four miles from there so I came back to Washington intending to have gone out there this afternoon. I hired a horse and got to the long bridge when I saw there would be rain before I could get back so I turned around. I mean to go there in the morning and have engaged a horse for the insignificant sum of $4.

I am very well acquainted with one of General Abercrombie's daughters and mean to call on her tomorrow if I have time. The General lives at Arlington House now. I met the young lady at Brig. General Cooper's in Frederick and showed her moderate attention.

Hooker means to do something soon. The regiments that have been in this city have been ordered to march tomorrow morning. General Talburt I heard today, is hesitating whether to call for the 10th or 14th N.J. I hope he will take the 10th. I saw Dr. Taylor's son (from Trenton) last night at Willards. I also saw Alfred Forman who was engaged to John C. Forman's daughter, an old law student whom I met at Poughkeepsie, today.

There are a good many officers here yet but the number is growing beautifully less. I wish you and Gov. Parker would come down to see us as soon as you can and the Col. and I will take you to Antietam and Harpers Ferry, show you around generally. Can't you come as soon as court is over at Freehold? With love to all and Mother in particular I am

Your Affectionate Son
Peter

Harrison

Camp Hooker
April 13, 1863

Dear Mother

I must sit down this morning and scratch you a few lines to assure you that I am getting along finely and feel first rate again. I hope this may find you and John enjoying excellent health. Dan Thompson started for home this morning on a furlough of eight days. I thought I would send a note by him but he got off this morning before I saw him.

I don't think I shall apply for a furlough yet a while. I shall wait till summer I think. For the war may be at an end, in three or four months. It is my opinion, if the rebels do not gain the next battle. The Rebellion is at an end, but if they gain the next battle, they will try to make a raid in some of the Northern States. Maryland for instance. If they succeed in

New Jersey Governor Joel Parker.

such a case, it will prolong the War for a year longer, but they will have a hard road to hoe.

One half the rebels in the South want to come in the Union at this present time, for all accounts.

There is no news in Camp of any importance. The paymaster has been around at last and left us two months pay. So I shall send you fifteen dollars, and keep the remainder in case I make up my mind to drop up and see you. But I don't want you to expect me for I may not come yet awhile. There is some talk now that the Regiment will be split up and stationed along the railroad, where each company will be posted there will be a blockhouse built.

I believe I have nothing more to say this time. May God bless you all my friends.

[no signature]

Harrison

Camp Hooker, Near Frederick City, Maryland
Wednesday April 22, 1863

My Dear Mother

I must sit down this fine morning and scratch you a few lines to assure you that Albert feels first rate this morning. I heard the sad news of Uncle Charles' death before I received your letter, as I had a letter from Libbie.

I could hardly believe my own eyes when I saw it. I had written him a letter about a week ago. God moves in a mysterious way. His wonders to perform, let us look up to God, and trust that the spirit of the departed is rejoicing with its maker. The Book of Jeremiah tells us, "saith God, Leave thy Fatherless children. I will preserve them alive. And let thy widows trust in me. How good is the Lord. The Lord provideth for us. He is a father to the fatherless and a husband to the Widow." Remember me to Aunt Elisabeth, tell her to trust in God for He doeth all things well.

I have heard some of the greatest news lately. It is really laughable. I have heard that I was going to be discharged. And I heard again that I wouldn't live long if I stayed down here, and all that sort of thing, and it all comes from Jersey. I would like to know who tells such. They tell, and seem to know, more about me than I know myself.

It is no such thing. I have made no application for a discharge, and I do not intend to, so you see Mother whoever told that don't know anything about it. But folks will talk and I think once in awhile they raise things right out of the solid. I think if the Lord spares my life to be discharged from Service it will be when the Regt. is mustered out, for I love the Service too well to leave even if I could get my discharge. You must not think that I am deceiving you for I tell the truth and nothing but the truth.

I received the two "Standards", and I found among the deaths the name of one of my old school mates, Sydney Aumack. Let us be constantly on our guard, for we know not when the Son of Man Cometh. Let us keep our lamp trimmed and burning, that when the dark cloak of death shall be thrown around us our spirits may take their flight to the everlasting regions of bliss prepared for those that love and serve God, and keep his Commandments.

Your Son Albert with love

Harrison

Camp Hooker, Near Frederick City Md.
April 25, l863

Dear Mother

Your affectionate letter was received by me this afternoon, and as it is Saturday night my letter will not start before Monday. But I thought I must sit down tonight and scratch you a few lines in answer to your letter, dated April 23rd.

I feel first rate, and my health is as good as it ever was with the exception of my back, that bothers me considerable yet.

We have had a very severe storm, but the weather promises fair now for awhile again. There was such a freshet that it was feared the Bridge would be carried away, but trains were not allowed to pass over yesterday and day before. They depoted a train on the Bridge loaded with coal to keep her firm.

But the trains are going through all right now. There is not much news of importance about Camp. Our company presented a splendid sword to Captain Alstrom this afternoon and he made quite a speech over it. The sword cost some sixty odd dollars. He seemed very highly tickled.

Give my love to John, and bear me in sweet remembrance to all the neighbors and especially to Aunt Lib.

Your Son with love
Albert

Vredenburgh

Office of Provost Marshal,
Frederick Md.
April 27, l863 — 1 o'clock A.M.

Dear Mother

I have just returned from camp. We see a large number of camp fires burning on the Va. side of the Potomac off Point of

Rocks. The 151 N.Y. Vols. have bivouacked on our parade ground. Col. Truex recd. a telegram last night about 10 P.M., to have the 14th ready with two days rations to move at any time. I guess there is some fun at Winchester or in that vicinity. Troops have been ordered to Harpers Ferry from Washington and the Col. of the 151 N.Y. thinks that his Regt. and the 14th will be kept here as a reserve. For my part I should like to go for a few days.

Affectionately & very sleepy,
Your Son Peter

Ross

Frederick
April 28, 1863

Dear Mother

As I am doing nothing of importance today and thought you would like to hear the news I will write and send it home. Our Regiment received marching orders yesterday and in the afternoon started on the cars for Harpers Ferry. The mail boy came from there today and said they were occupied on Maryland Heights on the banks of the Potomac near Harpers Ferry. I believe the rebs made a raid on Cumberland, a small town on the Baltimore & Ohio Railroad and captured a train of cars loaded with cattle which was the cause of our moving. At least that is the supposition. The troops that were stationed where ours are now, went in pursuit of the Rebs and our regiment was ordered to stop where they were. So it is not likely they will see any fun, and will be ordered back to the old camp when the other regiments return. Lt. Col. Hall has command of the regiment. Old Col., Major, Adjutant, Lt. Woodward & myself were ordered to stay in Frederick and see to things. Quarter Master Cowart & Chaplain both went with the Regiment.

There is nothing more of importance to write but anything could occur. I will let you know in due time.

Your Affectionate Son
Burroughs

Barracks at Frederick, MD.

Battle of Chancellorsville — May 1863

In the spring of 1863, General Joseph Hooker ordered the Army of the Potomac to cross the Rappahannock and move toward Chancellorsville, Virginia, perhaps a dozen miles from Fredericksburg. Reminiscent of McClellan's indecisiveness, Hooker failed to take the initiative which allowed General Lee to send "Stonewall" Jackson to attack the Union flank. The Federals were thrown back with great losses. Other actions included clashes between Confederate forces under General Jubal Early and Federal troops commanded by John Sedgwick.

Casualties ranged from about 17,000 Federals to 13,000 Confederates. An irreparable blow to the South was the loss of General "Stonewall" Jackson who was accidently shot by one of his own pickets crossing the lines at twilight. Lee likened the loss of Jackson to losing "his right arm."

The deployment of the 14th Regiment in the spring of 1863 counteracted Confederate troop movements in Virginia and the expectation of an advance northward into Maryland.

The Battle of Chancellorsville.

Harrison

Camp Hooker, Near Frederick City, Md.
April 29, 1863

Dear Mother & Father

As I have an opportunity this morning, I must sit down and pen you a few lines, for I don't mind writing when I can find something to write about. My health has returned I can say that I feel first rate.

We received marching orders last Sunday. We were to be prepared for a light march with overcoats and blankets, at ten minutes notice. I tell you we were in high glee to think we were going to move.

Monday morning, the order came that we were to move, and such a time you never saw, giving three cheers, and a hubbub in general. Then the Colonel said two companies were to stay here, they must be the two left Companies G and B. Well if Captain Alstrom didn't rage its a caution. But it couldn't be helped, he said to some of the men, says he, go in your tents, and go to bed, and get sick. But yesterday he cooled down considerable, he said we had either got out of a scrape or into one he didn't know which.

The six companies, with the 151st Regiment New York from Baltimore, left here Monday afternoon, as they thought, for Harpers Ferry. But one of the men came back to camp yesterday and said they had arrived at their destination for the present on Maryland Heights, near Harpers Ferry. They don't know whether they will stay there, go on farther, or come back again, but I am in hopes they will not come back again. But send us on. We will know in a few days what they will do. We have our own fun here all alone. Capt. Alstrom is acting Colonel, Capt. Craig is Lt. Colonel and the privates are all corporals ha.ha.ha. We don't have any drilling to do. Nothing but guard duty. Well we have things our own way in general. The boys are all well. George White wishes to be remembered to you, write soon, and if anything more transpires I will write the first opportunity. I must now close my letter as I want to go a fishing, but I reckon I will have fisherman's luck.

Your Son Albert with love

Stults

Camp Briggs Maryland Heights
9 P.M. April 30, 1863

Maryland Heights, from Harpers Ferry.

Dear Pa & Ma

We still are encamped at the foot of Maryland Heights, but what is in store for us, I have no idea. Some think we will be sent back to Camp Hooker in a day or two. Some think we will never be sent back. I think it not likely that we will be sent back. A new and well drilled regiment is not likely to be sent to the rear, but don't understand me that we are near the front, we are in the rear yet. The 151st N.Y. which came with us has received marching orders, and this minute is just leaving camp. I have heard they go to Martinsburg, Virginia. I don't care where we go, if we could have our whole regiment together. We hardly know the cause of our being sent on here, some unfounded rumors regarding the rebels crossing into Maryland, I suppose is the cause of it.

We have just finished muster for pay. We are mustered every two months. I don't know when we will get paid. We haven't any shelter tents yet, but have constructed brush houses which shelter us a little. It has

been stormy the last 36 hours. The mail is just leaving. Direct as usual.

Harpers Ferry

Marcus

Stults

Martinsburg, Virginia
May 2, 1863

Dear Pa & Ma

I wrote you this morning but in such a hurry I could only tell you we were at Martinsburg, but no particulars. Said place is 30 miles distant from Harpers Ferry on the line of the Baltimore and Ohio R.R. It is quite a noted place, larger than Hightstown [in New Jersey, West of Freehold] somewhat. We received marching orders, or orders to hold ourselves in readiness to move at a moments notice yesterday afternoon at three o'clock. And at 11 at night we were rousted up. We moved in a few moments down to the R.R. depot, at Harpers Ferry, and at 2 this morning we started. We reached here at 4, and as soon as possible, companies H, C, and D were on the road according to orders, for Winchester 22 miles distant. There is a good turnpike road to said place and we were to foot it, which would have been the largest tramp we have had yet. We got about 2 miles on the road, when we received orders to go back, which we did and at present are quartered in the suburbs of town. A splendid place, far more pleasant than any camp we have

Photos: U.S. Army Military History Institute

occupied, yet, or at least could be made so. I say we are quartered there. Three companies are at this place — Companies D, A, and H. Companies I and C are quartered in the court house. Only six companies are in town. Companies E and K have not been with us for a long time, Companies B and G we left at camp. We are not at all suited that we cannot be together. If we could be we are ready to go anywhere.

We hear General Briggs is making an effort to get us to Baltimore. We are his favorite regiment, but I think we are too far in the wilderness to get to Baltimore. The 151st N.Y. has been pushed 100 miles ahead of us, large bodies of troops are being sent on. The rebels have been gathering up that way. The only extra clothing we have is our overcoats and blankets. While at Harpers Ferry we sent for our clothing. I suppose it will be sent on here. I have no idea how long we will be kept here. I think the chances are good for staying awhile. There is but few troops quartered here at present. The 12th Penn. cavalry left here this morning. The 14th Mass, and the 14th Penn passed through here yesterday so we hear. Have I sent you Floyd's map — you should have it. My health is first rate. I received a letter from you yesterday. That clothing you can make up. I will send for it if possible. I want it soon. No more at present — write soon.

Your Affectionate Son
Marcus

Vredenburgh

Office of Provost Marshal
Frederick, Md.
May 2, 1863 9 A.M.

Dear Mother

A change has come over the spirit of my dream and I am afraid I shall not have the pleasure of seeing Father here. I suppose you are aware that 6 companies went to Maryland Heights last Monday. 2 Companies stayed at camp and the Col., Adjutant, and I remained in Frederick. Last night Chaplain came down for the men's baggage, tents, etc. Just after he arrived a telegram came from Baltimore that the Col. should send shelter tents and cooking utensils, so that all our "sibleys" will have to be abandoned. This morning three of the 6 companies were ordered to Winchester and the other three (of the 6) to Martinsburg. So you see we are pretty well scattered. One company at Mt. Airy, one company at Monrovia, two at the camp and the other six as aforesaid.

The Col. said this morning that I had better go to Winchester or Martinsburg to take charge of the detachment there. I expect therefore to go at any moment. A great many of the citizens have dropped in to see me and the rumor for a week past has been that I was going. They seem to feel sorry that I am to be relieved.

The Secesh will be glad of my removal though, for I have been adopting Genl. Schenck's plan in Baltimore and have pressed the rebel sympathizers closer and closer till now they hardly dare breath a traitorous sentiment. I sent off nineteen the other day. I took Miss Abercrombie (Genl. Abercrombie's daughter) to Keefer Thomas' yesterday to dinner. I went to see if I could get a horse. My brown horse is getting so bad, that is pulling so hard that I mean to part with him. He is also lame most of the time. I was offered $150 for the grey mare, a day or so ago but I think I will keep her. Blooded stock is prized very much here and that sorry mare that Uncle William owned would bring 3 or $400.

I don't know what I will do yet so you can direct any letters here. I have everything all ready if I do move. Stephen is excellent. I give him $16 per month. He will have work enough to do if we move.

Ever Your Affectionate Son
Peter

Ross

Hd Qtrs. Military Comdt., Frederick, Md.
May 2, 1863

Dear Mother

Six of our companies have been ordered into Virginia. Three to Winchester and three to Martinsburg. Captain Conover, Captain Patterson and Captain Goudy's companies are among the number. Mrs. Goudy is here on a visit and she is nearly crazy she says she will never see her husband again. Col. is very angry at having his Regiment cut up so after taking so much pains to have them so well drilled in everything. They are scattered along over a hundred miles now. One company at Mt. Airy, one at Monrovia, two at Monocacy Junction. Col. & his staff at Frederick, three companies at Martinsburg and three at Winchester. Col. says we won't all get together again while the war lasts. I asked him when he thought we would all get together again. He said not till our three years are up and we are ordered home. It is likely we will stay in Frederick as long as the Regiment is separated. If Mrs. Cowart asks anything about the Qr. Master tell her he was at Maryland Heights with the regiment until they started, when he started for Frederick, so he will be here sometime this morning. I believe he is going to remain in Frederick. The Chaplain is here now but is going to Winchester tomorrow. No more at present. Love to all from

Your Affectionate Son
Burroughs

Vredenburgh

Office of Provost Marshal
Frederick, Md.
May 6, 1863 — 4 P.M.

Dear Mother

I have not moved from here yet, and there is no telling now when I will move. Our 6 companies did not divide as expected they would but all went to Martinsburg Va. and are now fixed very comfortably there. Col. Hall commands the post. Bill was here yesterday and he says, "Dare ish blenty lager bier & oyster saloons and more pooty wimins as ever he did see." So I suppose everything is lovely. I have sold my brown horse for $147. He pulled so hard that he became useless and I am afraid he is a little foundered besides. I bought another horse for $175 but as he was warranted to me & him, and the man paid my money back as he had agreed to do in case the horse was not perfectly sound. The horse stepped short when I got him so that I was careful to make the man agree to have the horse examined.

I sold my saddle cloth & epaulets to Dr. Ridjeh for $10. I gave $40 for them but they were worse than useless to me as I could not carry them. I bought a pair of large saddle bags from the Chaplain for $7.00. I wish you would tell Father that he ought to come here after the Tom's River Court. I think I will be here then and he will feel better for the exercise. I wanted to go to Antietam and we can have a very pleasant trip there. I wish you would send one of my photographs to Julia Dwight and Tilly Hendrickson.

Ever Your Affectionate Son
Peter

Vredenburgh

Office of Provost Marshal
Frederick, Md. May 23, 1863

Dear Mother

I have recd. two letters from you since I have written, but I supposed you were absent from home and as I had nothing in particular to say I have thus delayed. I recd. Sallie Taylor's cards and should like to have attended the wedding. I came near going to Cincinnati last week. I had convalescents to send there and could have gone if I wanted, but I did not like to leave the office for so long a time. Yesterday I went to Martinsburg and returned at three o'clock this morning. Our Regt. i.e., that portion that was there has been ordered back to Harpers Ferry and they are now there. I had a delightful time at Martinsburg and don't wonder that the men hate to leave there. I met Col. Smith of the 126 Ohio. He is the son of Horace Smith formerly of Trenton who used to shoot with Morcross Phillips and me. Of course we affiliated.

I also went to Mrs. Faulkner's who lives on the suburbs of the town. Faulkner you recollect was minister to France previous to Dayton and is now South of our lines. His wife and daughter are strongly Union though, and live in superb style. Col. Hall and I went up to the house in the afternoon and took the young ladies out riding (horseback). We had a lovely ride and I found the daughters very accomplished and vivacious, and well acquainted with the Roosevelts whom she had met at Long Branch and New York. After we returned from our ride they invited us very cordially to take tea, and then to call after tea. We accordingly went after tea and met several young ladies there. Of course, all of the F.F.V.'s [First Families of Virginia]. Col. Hall says he has been there twice a day for the last fortnight and remarked, in case he got a leave of absence at Harpers Ferry he wouldn't know which way to go. The ladies there think the Dayton's can't live on their salary and say that Mr. Faulkner spent $40,000 a year. The ladies at Martinsburg whom I saw said they had heard of me as I have helped so many there to get goods up from this city. I generally have to endorse their permits and in a few cases have interfered with the government detectives where they have assumed too much authority.

A Mrs. Washington called on me yesterday morning in company with some other ladies to get assistance in getting her goods through. She said she had seven children of her own and six orphans to take care of. I refused to give her a pass on account of her disloyalty. I learned at Martinsburg that the six orphans are the children of John A. Washington deceased. I left there at 2 o'clock and arrived here at 5 so I have been up all night.

I sold my brown horse and bought one off a Doctor here. I returned him because he was unsound and a couple of days ago bought a beautiful mare. I also bought a buggy wagon off the executors of Genl. Cooper's estate and drove out every evening. I have been keeping Col. Hall's horse since he has been absent and therefore have three horses to keep in exercise. I don't use all three of them as much as one should be used and wish I had help. Do tell me whether Father means to come. Now is the time for my relations to come here for I have time and facility for to make it pleasant. Ask Henry if he won't make another trip here. Rose or Kerner will soon leave these "diggins" — they don't affiliate. Write and tell me about the wedding as soon as convenient.

With much love to Father and all the rest I am your Affectionate Son

Peter

P.S. It looks as if the Penn. militia would take our place and we go with Hooker soon.

Vredenburgh

Office of the Provost Marshal
Frederick, Md. May 27, 1863

Dear Father

I have just recd. yours of the 25th inst. and I wrote to
Mother a few days ago in which I mentioned that I did not go
to Cincinnati, though I expected to.

I am very glad you will come the 2nd week in June and
will expect you. It is delightful here now. The Colonel, Q.
Master, Capt. Conover and Geo. Patterson's respective wives
came on today and I suppose we will have gay times for awhile.
The Col. was presented with a sword yesterday by the company
officers. A.H. Patterson made the presentation speech, which
would have been well enough if he had not repeated so much. I
bought a beautiful mare for $125 the other day from the Q.
Master, and I have a very pretty team now. I herewith send
you a check for $500 which I wish you would invest as you
please. Perhaps Will would like to have it to speculate on and if
so he can give me his note for it.

The Col. is acting Brig. General now and gives lots of
furloughs. I suppose I could get one but I think I had better not
ask for one till there is some necessity and then I will stand a
better chance of getting one.

I wouldn't let Jim study law with Throckmorton if he can
get in Bedle's office because Bedle's practice is that of an
attorney and is what Jim wants.

The mail is just closing and I will close in haste

Your Affectionate Son
Peter

Vredenburgh

Office of Provost Marshal
Frederick, Md. June 5, 1863

Dear Father

There are a great many rumors here of a second advance
of the rebels and every night there is some startling intelli-
gence of their proximity. But I have no apprehensions of another raid here. Genl. Briggs takes command at this post
tomorrow so that Col. Truex will be relieved and return to
camp. The Genl. says he wants me to stay here and continue
Provost till further orders. I like it here very much and am in
no hurry to return to camp without they move and then I
would insist upon it. Mrs. Cowart and Truex are here now.
Mrs. Truex returns today. Yesterday I had business at
Woodboro and drove there taking Mrs. Cowart and Truex

along. We had a delightful ride. I have bought a new horse you know and have now a very fine pair. I think I will buy a set of double harness and am only waiting to see what I am to do. If I move I will leave a number of things here.

I sent you a check for $500 a week ago. Have you recd. it yet? I have not heard from you since. We have been expecting Gov. Parker daily for the last week. I guess he don't mean to come at all.

Tell Henry that Mr. Thomas was very much pleased with those potatoes and would like to see him.

With much love to Mother and all
I am Your Affectionate Son
Peter

Harrison

Camp Hooker, Frederick Junction, Md.
Wednesday June 10, 1863

Dear Mother

I must take up my pen and drop you a few lines in answer to two of your letters received by me this afternoon. I was happy to hear from you again. There is no news in camp of any importance, the men are at work carrying away the dirt from around the stockades so as to white wash them tomorrow morning. We expect the Governor [Parker] of the little state of Jersey to pay us a visit tomorrow and we want to have things in trim. The boys are all well. Sergeant Chadwick is seated before me and is also writing.

I have just heard that the Governor has arrived in the train tonight. But he will not be in camp before tomorrow. I expect there are a great many frightened on account of the Draft. That reminds me of a Darkey that enlisted in one of the South Carolina Regiments. He said he wanted to get in out of the draft, ha.ha. As for myself Mother I fear no draft. I took a wise plan, I think. You say you wish this Rebellion was over, and there are not many but what does. I don't think it can hold out much longer than next winter. God grant it may not.

It is quite cool tonight, it is cool nights and warm days. Sergt. Chadwick is my bedfellow. We have to pull both our blankets over us before morning.

So you see it is very cool for summer nights. There is no signs of our moving away yet. I think it is probable we will stay here all summer, but I must close bidding you good night and keep you from all harm.

Your Son Albert with love

Ross

Frederick, Md.
June 11, 1863

Dear Sister

I suppose you think it is about time you heard from me so I will try and not keep you waiting any longer. I arrived here safe and sound with all my lady friends. Our most worthy Governor Parker is here today and is going to present our Regiment with a set of Colors which they have never had since we came out. Mrs. Parker and two other ladies are with him. The weather is growing pretty warm down this way and we have not had any rain since I came back and I don't know how long before. Mrs. Rose is here now and a lot of other officers' wives too numerous to mention. I have not received a letter from home since I came back. When you have your carte de visites taken don't forget your exiled brother. Remember me to Garrett and also to Mr. & Mrs. Schenck and write soon to your

Affectionate Brother
Will

Vredenburgh

Office of Provost Marshal
Frederick, Md.
June 14, 1863   11:45 P.M.

Dear Mother

I have again to write in haste that we are on the skedadle. Telegrams say that the rebels are advancing in force at Harpers Ferry, Nolans Ferry etc. Refugees from Martinsburg are here in force. They say the rebels are there. We have just recd. a telegram to go to the Relay House. It will be nearly morning before we can get off.

Ever Your Affectionate Son
Peter

P.S. Recd. a letter from you a day or two ago. My horses are all saddled snugly in front of our headquarters. The ladies are all in the flurry. I leave my trunk at Mrs. Hopkins and owe her $28 plus $2.50 - for whiskey. I leave a set of new double harness and set of single harness, buggy, wagon, two blankets here. Your Morgan knows where they are. I drew all my money out of the bank. I am now going to camp.

Ross

Relay House Md. nine miles from Baltimore
June 16, 1863

Dear Mother

We arrived here last night from Frederick, it is supposed
on our way to the Pennsylvania border. I suppose you know as
much about the Rebs as I do so it will be needless for me to
state the particulars. We are all here safe and sound. Col.,
Major (alias Provost Marshal), Qr. Master and all of our Regiment. We have about three thousand troops here and a battery
of artillery. We all seem to have the impression that we will
soon have a chance to distinguish ourselves. I have not time to
write more at present but if anything happens I will let you
know immediately.

The Quartermaster isn't very well. He fainted once or
twice yesterday afternoon. I suppose from the excessive heat
for it was awful warm. He is very much better this morning
though. My love to all from

Your Affectionate Son
Burroughs

Harrison

Camp Near Relay House Md.
June 16, 1863

Dear Mother

I will sit down this morning and drop you a few lines to
inform you that we have bid farewell to the fair banks of the
Monocacy. We expected to leave there last Sunday but as it
happened we did not leave until yesterday afternoon, at the
hour of two o'clock. We the 14th, are encamped about 150 yards
from the Relay, it is a splendid place.

I am sitting under a tree, beside my old bedfellow Sergt.
J.P. Chadwick. He is also writing to his family.

Oh my how glad we were to get away from the Junction
once again we had been there so long — I said we, I can speak
for all as they were all glad to be on a move once more, we
haven't put up our tents yet, but will get them up this morning. I don't think we will stay here for more than two or three
days, we cannot tell where we will go. But I will tell what I
think, and that is this, that we will go to Washington. We are
about a mile from the city of Baltimore. You have heard and
read enough in the papers I suppose to know just what kind of
a place the Relay House is and as I haven't any more time to
spare I cannot give you particulars. The boys are all well and
in jovial spirits, it is quite cool this morning. I tell you Mother,

the people of Frederick and in the vicinity of the Junction were sorry to see us go away. But we may get back there for aught I know. Give my love to John and all the neighbors and enquiring friends.

I remain your son with love
Albert

Harpers Ferry*

Harpers Ferry is located on a point of land at the confluence of the Potomac and Shenandoah Rivers and overlooked by the Blue Ridge Mountains. Peter Stephens set up a ferry service in 1733, and by the mid 1750's Robert Harper took over Stephens' business and established a mill. It was an ideal location with abundant water power. The next century saw the area grow from a small town to an early industrialized center. President George Washington convinced Congress to establish a national armory on the Potomac. The armory became the area's chief economic base which sustained other forms of business and industry. The Chesapeake and Ohio Canal and later the Baltimore and Ohio Railroad assured the area's prosperity by the middle of the 19th century.

This congenial beginning abruptly ended with John Brown's raid. A radical abolitionist intent upon freeing the slaves, Brown took over the federal arsenal in October 1859. He was ultimately overpow-

Harpers Ferry, Maryland Heights and Loudon Heights where the Shenandoah and Potomac Rivers merge.

*From information provided by the Harpers Ferry National Historical Park, WV.

ered by troops led, ironically, by Robert E. Lee. Subsequently, he was
tried for treason and hanged. The war which followed a year and a
half later saw the destruction of the armory and arsenal by Federal
forces intent on depriving the advancing Confederates of these
resources. Because of the town's geographical significance and splendid railroad facilities, both armies occupied it throughout the war.
The most spectacular event during the war occurred just prior to the
Battle of Antietam in September 1862. General "Stonewall" Jackson's
troops took the town and forced the surrender of 12,000 Federal
soldiers commanded by Colonel Dixon Miles. This was the largest
surrender of United States troops until World War II.

　　The carnage and desolation left by the Civil War saw the town
decline. Much of the population moved on. Those who might have
rejuvenated the town saw their hopes dashed by a series of floods that
destroyed much of the area in the late 1800's. Most of the area was
abandoned and slowly reclaimed by nature. There was a successful
experiment in education during the postwar years. Storer College,
one of the first normal schools for blacks, was established and continued operations in the area through the 1950's.

Wolcott

Maryland Heights
June 17, 1863

Friend Powers

　　Since I last wrote to you the 14th has been put through it.
Last Sunday night we were ordered to strike tents, and march
to Martinsburg, Virginia. We loaded our wagons and was all
ready to go when the Colonel received orders to stop where we
was until further orders. Then it was 5 o'clock Monday morning. About ten o'clock we received orders to go to the Relay
House. Gen. Briggs sent to Baltimore for 6 trains of cars to
take the Government stores. We arrived at the relay about 9
o'clock in the evening — went to bed on the ground — nothing
but the heavens to cover us — and without supper. Between 12
and 1 o'clock we were called up again and ordered to Harrisonburg. The cars did not come until morning — then another
dispatch said wait until further orders, at 3 o'clock we were
ordered to Maryland Heights where we arrived — 1 o'clock
yesterday morning.

　　I felt rather tired, we were put in the center of the line of
Battle and the stacks of guns are nearly mile and half from
right to left. All we have to do when the enemy makes their
appearance is to raise up and take our guns and pore a volley
into them. The Line is already formed and the guns loaded.
The Line has been formed since Tuesday morning — 3 o'clock. I
can see the rebel pickets on the Virginia side from where I am
sitting now. The force is small. I heard that General Hooker
was near Washington fighting Lee. We do not get any news
except what the scouts bring in and there is two that tell the

same story. Gen. Hooker sent a dispatch to the commanding Gen. if he could hold the Heights 2 days he (Hooker) would be up in their rear. The Gen. says he can hold it 6 days. This morning 50 men out of each company were called up and sent to risk digging rifle pits. Our detail is under the command of Lt. Col. Hall. I tell you this business has tamed our officers. They are not as independent. They have found out their lives are in great measure in the hands of the privates. They can take some notice of the men now and eat what the men eat. I had a hard time to cook my breakfast this morning — could not find anything to fry pork in, for a good while. I was going by a house and I saw a fry pan hanging up in a shed. I put my hand on it and somehow I got the cramp in my fingers and couldn't let go until I got to my quarters. I found it to be the thing Co. B wanted so I thought I would not send it back.

Powers, don't write until you hear from me again. We may be in another place before two more days. It is the intention of the commander of the rebels to go around us and not attack us. We will follow them in the rear and give them battle. The ground the chief engineer has picked out, that is if they should make the attempt on the Heights, could not be better for us, then 20,000 of the union soldiers on the Heights — they can hold 50,000 rebels in check 2 days and not work hard at that. We have some bulldog here that I can lay in very comfortable, fill them with grape and canister. It soon would make a hole in the rebels. Tell Nick and Allen not to write until they hear from me. Remember me to all my inquiring friends and I hope the 14th will give a good account of themselves. The pioneers are falling trees cross-ways over the bottom of the mountain so the cavalry can not go up to make charges on us. I do not expect you will get this as the mail communication is cut off between here and Frederick City. Lt. Wright said he would try and send it by some of the Quarter Masters to Washington.

The sun comes down warm. We are not allowed any tents. All the shelter we have is brush houses. The pioneers are cutting all the trees down.

Remember me to Mrs. Powers and the rest of the good folks of old Trenton. If we have a battle I will try and give you the first particulars of it — that is if I come out sound.

Good Bye
Yours Truly
J.R. Wolcott

Ross

Maryland Heights
June 19, 1863

Dear Father

As I have a few spare moments I will employ it by writing home. I wrote home from Relay House but don't know whether you received it, or not. We are now encamped in the Heights above Harpers Ferry having arrived here on Wednesday morning, after riding all night in the cars. Our men are throwing up entrenchments and rifle pits. All of Milroy's forces that were left after the battle at Winchester are here. Lieut. Randolph whose likeness I sent home was taken prisoner together with the whole of his battery. We don't hear any news here, none of us having seen a paper in a week. The cars don't run from the ferry now a night or two since the Rebs crossed over at Point of Rocks and destroyed a train of cars and tore up the railroad so it is very doubtful whether you receive this letter very soon or not. We all like it very much down here so far but we don't live quite as high as we did at Frederick. I don't know how long we will be likely to stay here. We left our Qr. Master at the Relay House and the Chaplain also. I suppose they will be on pretty soon and bring some news. We all feel confident that we can drive back any number of rebs that feel like coming to see us. If you could see the fortifications which were built on the Heights I think you would be of the same opinion.

General Tyler commands here with General Morris commanding our Brigade. I had a splendid time swimming in the Potomac River yesterday. Col. thinks of coming home to command a cavalry regiment. When the Governor was down he offered him the position, if he would take it, and if he goes I go with him, as Lieutenant, as he promised me the position if he went. There is no news of much importance to communicate so I will close. I am writing this while lying on the ground with the missing report book for a desk. Remember me to all my friends and my love to all our folks and when you write direct to Wm B. Ross, 14th N.J. Vols, Maryland Heights, Harpers Ferry, or on the march.

[no signature]

Harrison

Maryland Heights, Near Harpers Ferry
June 20, 1863

Dear Mother

I seat myself this first opportunity to pen you a few lines to assure you that I am enjoying excellent health. I suppose you have received the letter I wrote you while we were at the Relay House. It was written the same morning as we left in the afternoon. You will see by the heading of my letter that we are now at Maryland Heights. There has been no chance to write since we came here, and if we did write there was no mail. But I hear the mail boy is going to Frederick City this afternoon and I must say what I have to say, in as few words as possible. I wish merely to assure you that we are all well and in jubilant spirits.

The boys are all here without exception. I will write again

General R.H. Milroy USA

General William W. Morris USA

123

as soon as I know there are communications open. The trains are very irregular, and we can not tell when there is a mail.

We are at work digging earth works on the Heights, and I cannot inform you how long we will stay here. But you must not worry Mother, we are safe and sound. I thank God that we are all well. Give my love to all & tell them the 14th is going to do some good work for the Union, with the help of God. The boys are all anxious for a skirmish, but I don't think they will have it very soon, but rest assured the 14th will do its duty and also your son Albert.

I expect there has been all sort of reports concerning us, but now I must close as the mail boy will leave.

Your loving son Albert

Harrison

Maryland Heights, Near Harpers Ferry, Va.
Tuesday June 23, 1863

Dear Mother

I seat myself this evening to drop you a few lines to assure you that by the blessing of God I am in good health, and I earnestly hope this may find you enjoying the same blessing. I wrote to you last Saturday, but I don't think it has reached you, as there is no certainty of communication between here and Baltimore. The mail boy started for Frederick City last Saturday with the mail and he has not been heard from since to my knowledge. So I will write you a few lines again until I feel satisfied that you have heard from me, for I expect there is some anxiety in regard to the whereabouts of the 14th and all sorts of rumors concerning us. But I will assure you that we are at Md. Heights and all safe and sound. The boys are all well and in jovial spirits.

Charlie White and Chadwick are carrying on. They send their best wishes. I don't know how long they will keep us here but I think we will go on farther in Virginia. There isn't much danger of Rebs making an attack on us here unless they are driven into it.

We are about sixteen thousand strong. Our Brigade [the 14th New Jersey, 10th Vermont and 151st New York] is under the command of General Morris [General William Walter Morris]. We have been at work ever since we came here digging rifle pits, & we have plenty to eat, and the water is plenty, and as good as it was at Monocacy. Give my love to all the neighbors and enquiring friends, tell them all the 14th is safe and sound and ready to do their duty. I must bring my letter to a close as it is nearly time for roll call, so I must bid you good night.

Wednesday morning 24th

Well Mother as there is no signs of the mail going out this morning, I might as well write a few more lines. All is quiet on the Heights this morning. The weather is fair, we had somewhat of rain last week but it is getting dry and dusty under foot again. I went down to the Potomac yesterday to have a swim but the water was so muddy I gave out. I suppose you have heard often enough of John Brown's Cave. I watched for it yesterday, but I didn't see anything of John Brown (ha ha).

I don't think we will stay here more than four or five days. If you don't hear from me so often, you must not worry, for we may be so situated that there is no mail, and I am not certain that this will go through as there is no certainty in the trains for Harpers Ferry to Baltimore. Gil & Wes Van Dyke wish to be remembered. If you see their mother, tell her they are both well and will write soon. I tell you Mother the folks at the Junction didn't like to see us leave there, we had been there so long. It seemed like home, but I feel in hopes we will go over in Virginia. I have seen enough of the country in Md. but I am willing to go anywhere, where we can do the most good for the country. If you write there is no certainty of it reaching us.

Your Son Albert

John Brown

Vredenburgh

Harpers Ferry
June 24, 1863

Dear Mother

I have just time to scratch off a few words to you. We are here at Maryland Heights. Every night we have expected an attack, and been drawn up in line of battle every morning at 3 o'clock since we have been here. Twice we have been called out suddenly at midnight in a pelting rain awaiting an attack which the picket informed us would certainly take place. Stephen, one horse, and all my things are at the Relay House. Unable to get to me. I have nothing with me but a change of underclothes. When we left the Relay House last Tuesday night we expected an attack on the train at every curve and I dare not bring my horses.

The rebels here are thick around us. From the Heights we can see their camp and wagon trains in every direction. There are so many rumors that we can not tell what is true. I saw wagon trains of the enemy yesterday moving, with a glass, stretching from Charlestown Va. to Shepherdstown. The view from the Heights is splendid. You can see from Winchester to Hagerstown. Our men all bivouac. Col. and I are boarding at a small house — rather poor, but better than bivouacking. I sleep in my clothes boots and all on the floor. I was field (Brigade) officer-of-the-day when I first came, and as my duty was to post and visit all the pickets, am familiar with the ground. We have only about 7000 troops here and if the rebels come in 30,000 strong say, I am afraid we cannot defend it. I have just telegraphed to Steve to come up in the first train. We sent a boy to Frederick last Sunday after the mail but he has not been heard from since. Don't write at present, but if you do direct to Frederick.

Ever Your Affectionate Son
P. Vredenburg

[Obviously, in mentioning that they have but 7,000 troops on Maryland Heights, Vredenburgh is taking precautions against any mail being intercepted. The Union forces on the Heights totalled about 20,000 or more in the vicinity. Unfortunately, most of the men writing letters were also indicating their strength — and some honest estimates were among them.]

Ross

Maryland Heights Harpers Ferry
June 24, 1863

Dear Mother

As I understand the mail is going this afternoon I will send you a few lines with it. I wrote home from the Relay House, did you receive my letter? We left the next day for Harpers Ferry where we were encamped nearly as high up as the clouds. We can see the Rebs from the Heights encamped near the old battlefield of Antietam. The reports say about 40 thousand strong but we feel confident we will whip them when they come. The train which we came down on from Relay House was burnt by the Rebs on its return. We are completely shut in here no news, no papers, no mail, and no nothing, but I like it first rate. We left Qr. Master, Chaplain, Lt. Woodward at the Relay House. Our men have been kept busy building breastworks ever since we came here. I would tell the force here but it is against orders, suffice it to say, we have enough men here to knock the spots out of any force they can send against us. I suppose there is some excitement up North is there not? We hear something of the Rebs going to Pennsylvania but cannot tell much about the truth of it. Gen. Taylor is in command here and there are four Brigadier Generals beside him here so that will give you some idea of the force we have here.

There are three or four splendid brass bands here, one just opposite our camp — distant not more than a hundred yards and every evening we have a grand serenade from them. For my part I wish the Rebs would get up North, and stir some of those copperheads out of their nests. Perhaps if the war was carried to their own homes, they would then realize our situation and make some efforts to put this cussed rebellion down. I haven't time to write more at present. Only give my love to all my friends and my love to all our folk.

Burroughs

Vredenburgh

3rd Brigade 1st. Division 8th Army Corps
Md. Heights
June 28, 1863 3 P.M.

My Dear Father

I recd. your note from Jamesburg and one from Mother dated previous to our departure from Frederick. We are now incorporated in Hooker's Army, as the forces here and this station was yesterday turned over to him. I may as well give you chronologically a statement of our movements since we left Frederick.

On Monday morning the 15th inst. the Col. and I started under orders from our office at Frederick, on horseback for Frederick Junction, being the last officers to leave the town. We loaded the Regt. and luggage by two in the afternoon and with the 3rd Del. and Purnell Legion (they being all the troops there at that time) started for the Relay House, where we arrived about 6 P.M. We immediately selected our camping ground and on the following morning, erected tents etc. By noon we had completed our arrangements and repaired to the Relay House to dine. There we found a great many of the Union people and government employees, refugees from Frederick who had left that city. Just after we had finished our dinner, Genl. Briggs ordered our Regt. to go to Harpers Ferry forthwith in light marching order except that the men were allowed knapsacks. No trains had come from Harpers Ferry and we were informed that we would probably meet the enemy at Point of Rocks. We had nothing to do but to get ready and go; so leaving most all my things, as well as Steve, one horse and Dash, I started about 5 P.M. for the Ferry. A few of us officers had an open car on the rear of the train and amidst the cheers and "God bless you's" of the crowd we started. All along the road till it became dark the people cheered and waved flags, handkerchiefs, etc. until we almost believed that we had already won a victory. It was a beautiful evening, and sitting as we did on the rear of the train in an open car, we could not help but feel the elevating influence of the romantic and picturesque scenery. Mother can tell you what a beautiful ride it is from the Relay House to Ellicotts Mills and that evening it seemed more lovely than ever. The lovely, limpid, Patapsco, clear as crystal and still as slumber, reflecting the beautiful slopes, and villas from its opposite shore. The gay hilarity and good humor of the soldiers, the bright sunset, and the inspiring effect of sitting in the rear of a long train, loaded down with human beings, and going at lightning speed around curves, through defiles and over mountains, soon made us forget our serious mission. It seemed indeed more like a picnic.

We stopped at all the telegraph stations and could thus tell whether the track was clear as far as the next station each time. We halted at Monocacy Bridge till daylight as we felt pretty certain that we would meet a strong force at the Point of Rocks. We however, got safely through to Harpers Ferry by nine o'clock without seeing any rebels though we saw a signal flag at the Point of Rocks. On arriving here we were assigned (as above) to General Morris' Brigade and arriving on the ground found the rest of his brigade drawn up in line of battle expecting an attack every moment. We were placed on the left of the line of battle. We were allowed to fix ourselves as well as we could, till 6 P.M. when the men had to commence digging rifle pits which are simply a trench three feet wide and two feet and a half deep with the dirt thrown up in front which makes it as high as a man's chest. The next day the men worked again in the trenches till it rained so hard they had to stop. We field officers got a room in a small house to sleep in and therefore we got along pretty well but the rest had to sleep right out on the ground — no tents "no nothin" except a few boughs and branches to cover them.

About ten o'clock in the evening we heard a picket some two miles off fire off his piece, then another and another till the whole line of pickets were discharging their guns. The Col., Lt. Col., & I immediately flew to the door and as we opened it some soldiers came running towards us saying that we were attacked at the same time. Our Regt., which was only a hundred yards or so from us commenced firing off their pieces. I grasped my hat and pistols and started for the Regt. stooping low to the ground for fear some of our own boys would hit me and soon arrived there. It was so dark that it was impossible to see anything and it rained in torrents but I made them hear me and by the time the Col. got there had stopped their firing. I knew the enemy were not near us as soon as I got near the Regt. and the boys I suppose were firing off old loads for fear their guns would not go off. The Col. had us in line as quick as a flash and there we stood waiting to see what next would turn up. The pickets kept coming in one, two and three at a time exhausted and telling most exaggerated reports. The facts were the outer pickets had exchanged a few shots — thence all the alarm. We stood as I said three or four hours and then broke ranks again. All thoroughly drenched, at three o'clock we were ordered out again and there we stood in line of battle till morning.

We have been up every night since about three o'clock (as that is the most likely time of attack by the enemy) and stood in line till morning. The Genl. appointed me Field Officer-of-the-Day, the second day I was here so that I became pretty well acquainted with persons and things right off. General French commands here in the place of the old ass, Tyler, who commanded here at first. Yesterday Hooker came here from Poolesville. I was introduced to him and shook hands with him in Genl. French's tent. Both he and French look as if they drank too much. Hooker was cordial and affable in his manners, but he don't impress me as being a man of much ability. Hooker ordered our Brigade to go to Williamsport and therefore after our interview and after we had adjourned a Genl. Court Martial, of which I was a member, we all prepared to move by 6 P.M. But I think, from our not having received orders to start that Halleck telegraphed to Hooker to leave this place strongly fortified. I understand that Hooker recd. a telegram to that effect while we were in his tent. Hooker's intentions were to send all the troops from this place towards the enemy but Halleck frustrated them. I am glad we were not sent for it seemed as if sending us, without artillery or cavalry, to Williamsport to destroy the enemy's pontoon bridge there, was just sending us to be slaughtered. We have three days rations cooked ahead and expect every moment to receive orders to march. Hooker said in my presence that the enemy were numerically stronger than we were and that he should have forces enough to advance up on both sides of South Mountain.

What you see in the papers about the large forces and immense wagon trains of the enemy in Penn. and Maryland are true, for I have seen them going by for hours at a time from the Heights — with a field glass. I tell you Father, we should have McClellan in command. He is the only man yet that has shown the ability to manage the army and fight with a purpose. Nearly every man, woman, and child here likes McClellan. The officers and soldiers invariably like him and what is more, he is the only man the rebels care for. They never would have dared to have gone as far as Penn. if Mc had been in command. Hooker was called, in California, "blowing Joe" and that is all he is. One feint and a blow is as far as his strategy goes. Hooker went back to Frederick yesterday afternoon. He talked freely about the effects of certain movements in his tent in the presence of myself and a number of officers, which to say the least, was indiscreet. I am afraid he is too shallow potted for this crisis.

I should not advise you come and see me now and it is fortunate you did not start at the time you expected to. I believe Steve sent Dash and the gun home from the Relay House. Everything else is with me now. Give my love to Mother and all the rest. Direct any letters to me — Genl. Morris Brigade — 14th Regt etc.

Ever Your Affectionate and Devoted Son
Peter

Major General Henry W. Halleck USA

Ross

Hd Qrs. 14th N.J. Vols
French's Division on the march near Jefferson Ford
July 1, 1863

Dear Mother

We started from Maryland Heights yesterday to go I don't know where but I suppose to join the Army of the Potomac. I received a letter from Joe Nealy in answer to my letter which I wrote him. We haven't time to write more at present only that I am well and like soldiering as well as ever. We have halted for a few minutes and I thought I would write a few lines and put it in the next office. We came from Harpers Ferry — which was evacuated and the Division is commanded by Gen. French. We have about 20 thousand men with us. Wherever we stop I will write you, until then, Goodbye, my love to all.

Your Affectionate Son
Burroughs

Vredenburgh

Headquarters 3rd Brigade — Army Corps — Frederick
July 2, 1863 2 P.M.

My Dear Father

I recd. yesterday, the letter you sent me of the 17th inst. in reference to that check. You should not send it back till communication is safe and then if you direct to the cashier whose name I think is on the face of the check, he will send you a draft for the amount. But if you hold on to it for a few days all will be right. The bank is one of the best and will not be interfered with by the rebels.

We left Harpers Ferry last Tuesday and marched to Knoxville where we encamped on a clover field. I was soaking wet when I stopped and laid down on one blanket and put another one over me and slept quietly till morning with no bad result. It has rained incessantly since Sunday till yesterday noon. I think I can lie down in a mud puddle and sleep as well as in a bed. The people here were glad to see me when I returned. I got into Frederick yesterday noon in advance of the Division and assumed duties. I found the city in a terrible state of confusion. The streets were filled with drunken soldiers and desperate characters. The refuse of the "Grand Army" most of which has recently passed through here. Tell me if Dash and the gun arrived safely by Johnny Crithers. We march tomorrow morning at nine A.M. Where to I do not know.

Rebels are thick all around us as you see by the papers. I wrote a letter to you from Harpers Ferry last Sunday but I suppose you have not received it. When I decamped from the city I left a set of single harness, a new set of double harness, blankets, buffalo robe etc. My wagon is all right and I think I will trade it away this afternoon for a carryall which our mess (Col and Lt. Col) will go in for.

Your Affectionate Son
Peter

Harrison

Near Frederick City Md.
Thursday July 2, 1863

Dear Mother

Major General William H. French USA

You see by the heading of my letter that we are again in the vicinity of Frederick City. But we are not alone. The whole 3rd. Division is here. General French [Major General William H. French] is in command. He appears like a fine General and exhibits warm feelings for his men. We left or rather abandoned Maryland Heights, night before last after destroying all that was of any account. Since night before last we have marched 25 miles. We arrived here last night before sunset, and will stay here all day today until the remainder of the Division comes up. And then we will press on in the direction of Baltimore to join General Hooker. We number in the neighborhood of 20,000. Quite a decent little reinforcement for old Uncle Joe, ha.ha.

Company G are all well. I never felt better in my life than I have felt since we left Camp Hooker and God grant that I may continue in good health. We had a good night's rest last night and were all ready to shove on this morning, but as we are not going on this morning we will have the most time for rest.

I think within a very few months, perhaps weekly you will hear that the whole Rebel Army under General Lee, has been totally routed. I think they will wind up their existence in Maryland. The Lord will smile on the right.

Tell all that the 14th N.J. is going to do their duty. If we have a good chance the boys of the 14th will show the Rebs what our forefathers showed to the Redcoats at the Battle of Bunker Hill and Old Monmouth for instance. If you don't hear from me so soon you must not worry, for we may be on the march for two weeks or more. And perhaps there will be no chance of sending a letter or mail but I will write as often as I can.

The citizens of Frederick have been swarming out to greet us. I tell you they were glad to see us again. The weather is fine this morning, nice and cool. But I must now bring my letter to a close with love to you and John and may the Lord bless you and keep you from all harm and let me again tell you not to worry but trust in God who doeth all things well.

Your Son,
Albert

Photo: U.S. Army Military History Institute

Gettysburg
July 1,2,3 — 1863

In early July, 1863, two mighty armies converged upon the little Pennsylvania village of Gettysburg, situated about thirty-five miles southwest of Harrisburg. Some say it was soldiers looking for boots in the village that brought the antagonists together. In any event, it was here that the decisive three day battle was fought that would determine the outcome of the war. The South was determined to gain foreign intervention but it had to prove it could win. Having failed the year before at Antietam, Lee hoped to accomplish this goal in Pennsylvania. His army of Northern Virginia, perhaps seventy thousand strong, was opposed by about one hundred thousand Federals under

Devil's Den

the command of George Gordon Meade.

Fighting on the first and second day involved assaults, both to and from the nearby ridges. The Federal troops on Cemetery Ridge comprising Culp's Hill, Little Round Top, and Round Top to the south of Gettysburg. Lee placed his Confederates on Seminary Ridge about a mile west of Gettysburg. With little decisive results by the third day, Lee decided on a direct frontal attack. Many of his staff, including General Long-street, opposed assaulting such strongly defended works. Lee's will prevailed.

Base of Little Round Top

Lee ordered General George Pickett to advance, with this becoming one of the most famous military charges in history. Across the open fields came fifteen thousand proud veterans of the Army of Northern Virginia, the pride of the Confederacy. Musketry, grape, and canister produced the "hell of leaden hail" and tore huge holes in the long gray lines. "Rebel yells" plunged the Confederates forward. Some managed to breach the Union line but in insufficient numbers to hold it. Regrouping Federals drove back the Virginians and the battle ended. The field presented a ghastly sight of dead and dying

Gettysburg.....

humanity as both sides suffered in excess of fifty thousand casualties. This became the "high-water mark" of the Confederacy. Lee had been stopped. He broke off the engagement and started south leaving Confederate goals unfulfilled. Never again would the South be able to launch an offensive of this magnitude and it now became clear to some that it was just a matter of time before the North's superior resources would force the South's capitulation.

The Fourteenth New Jersey Volunteers were under the overall command of General French and held in reserve during the great battle at Gettysburg. Somewhat frustrated at not having taken part in the momentous conflict, they nevertheless fulfilled the important role of providing cover for the capital at Washington, D.C.

A congressional investigation of the conduct of the War examined General Meade's reasons for not using some ten thousand reserve troops, positioned within marching distance of Gettysburg. When asked to explain, his answer was reported as follows:

"A General planning to win a great battle must also plan to lose it. General Lee had the inner line of march to Washington, which I felt we could not afford to lose. With General French at the point I held him, if we were defeated, I could put him into the defenses of Washington before General Lee could get there. General French could hold it until I could re-enforce him."

Following the Confederate defeat, the Fourteenth New Jersey Volunteers were sent to Boonsboro Gap in anticipation of catching Lee's retreating army. The rebel army chose a southern route across the Potomac instead and successfully eluded the Federal "trap."

Gettysburg Photos: U.S. Army
Military History Institute

Harrison

South Mountain, Md., Frederick County
Monday morning July 5, 1863

Dear Mother

I seat myself this morning to drop you a few lines to assure you that I never felt better in all my life. When last I wrote you, our Division under General French were encamped within a mile of Frederick City and here we are at South Mountain, some 16 miles from Frederick. But our whole Division is not here only a portion of our Brigade. The 151st New York has taken their position within about half a mile from us while a part of the 10th Vermont is about 3 miles to our rear. I commenced writing you this morning but I had but two or three lines written before we, that is, our company were ordered to fall in to guard eleven hundred rebel prisoners to Frederick. They were brought in our camp last night by our cavalry. They were on their way back to Virginia but I reckon they didn't get there. Well Mother I suppose you have heard the good news long before you will receive this. The Rebel Army that came in to Maryland under Lee, will soon be played out. We have got the upper hand of them this time, thank the Lord. And if General Lee takes the half or the quarter of the Army over in Va., again that he brought here with him it will be almost a miracle. They cannot cross the river now, and they are in a trap. [This refers to a position that General Lee occupied on his way south after his defeat at Gettysburg. He was able to cross the river and escape.]

It is so reported that they have lost near forty thousand men in killed and prisoners. But I was saying the Company was ordered to fall in to guard the prisoners to Frederick 13 miles from here. But after marching about 3 miles we were relieved by the Vermont boys, who went on to Frederick with them and we came back to camp. Along with the 1100 prisoners our cavalry captured about 17 ambulances. The boys are well and in jubilant spirits. I hope this may find you and John, and all enjoying good health. May the Lord grant it. I don't know when this letter will go but I thought I would write and have it ready when there was a chance to sent it.

It is a splendid country through here. There is a valley each side of the mountain. It is impossible to see the sun up here it is so cloudy while we can see it shining in both valleys. I must close my letter for this time.

[no signature]

Ross

South Mountain Pass
July 7, 1863

Dear Mother

I received your letter today which was directed to me at Maryland Heights. We left there about a week ago marched to Frederick, stayed over night and the next afternoon started for this place having marched forty miles. We had a pretty rough time of it while we were at the Heights but now everything goes on seemingly. We are holding the pass through South Mountain expecting the Rebs to retreat somewhere through this part of the country. We are on the old battle ground which derives its name from this mountain. The tree in front of our tent has several balls in it and on Sunday I went to see where Gen. Reno was killed, it being about half way up the mountain under a large tree. The man who was showing me told me he was shot by a spy who was dressed in our clothes and was talking with him and when the Gen. turned around he shot him, but one of the Gen.'s aids killed the spy shorty after.

I believe Mr. Cowart is Brigade Qr. Master. Lt. Wright is acting in his place. There are lots of raspberries around here you can go out almost anywhere and pick your hat full. Major and all our officers are here except Mr. Cowart. We had nine hundred reb prisoners here yesterday which were taken on the battlefield of Gettysburg. The mail is going right off so will have to close. My love to all. My health keeps excellent. Direct to Frederick when you write. Save some of that homey for me until I come home. My love to all from

Your Affectionate Son
Burroughs

P.S. None of our men were captured

Vredenburgh

French's Division Morris Brigade
Boonsboro Gap Md.
July 8, 1863 9 A.M.

Dear Mother

I wrote to Father from Frederick on Saturday. On Saturday we recd. orders to march and started off as we were ordered to leave immediately. It rained in torrents and in a few moments we were underway. We took the road to Boonsboro. The City of Frederick was as still as death when we passed. All the stores are closed up tight. We started from camp at 3 P.M. and marched steadily through a drenching rain till 11 P.M. —

that is to Boonsboro Gap and most of the way up until Saturday was terrible but the men stood it remarkable well. We are now the advance infantry, that is our Brigade, consisting of the 151st New York, 10 Vermont and 14th New Jersey. On the 6th I went to a place called Monumental Hill situated about a mile N.W. of us. You can identify the spot on the map in the N.Y. Herald of the 6th inst. just where the "S" is of the words "South Mountain." I had a splendid view of the loveliest valley in the world from there. Hagerstown, Williamsport, Md. Heights, Sharpsburg, Antietam, and Shepherdstown. All appeared plainly in view. There was heavy skirmishing going on in the vicinity of Hagerstown and Williamsport, all the time we were up there. I could see every flash of the guns and every puff of smoke as it arose from the pieces, but not near enough to distinguish the men. I could see the cavalry at times and artillery moving through. It turned out to be the engagement between Gregg's Cavalry and the Rebs. All excitement here. The whole Rebel army is behind us.

I don't see how Lee is to get out without he cuts his way through us. The bridge at Williamsport, Falling Waters, Harpers Ferry are constantly destroyed. The Army of the Potomac came through here today and I expect we will then be pushed further on. We have been in the Army of the Potomac since the 1st inst., from the extreme left. We are located now on a slope running downwards towards the Southwest and are in a very strong position.

If Father has time he should come on and he may have a chance of seeing what he has never seen before — a battle. I can get him a place with the signal corps on Monumental Hill. He can see everything that takes place in the valley beneath us. The battle will certainly take place . . . this side of the Potomac. . . all the time and every moment makes Lee's chances of escape more desperate. I visited South Mountain this afternoon with a guide and saw all the particulars of the battle of South Mountain. There is a rude stone marking the spot where Reno fell. I had to draw on Faith for $200. I suppose he got the draft. I think Dash and my gun are at Thomas'.

Ever your Affectionate Son
Peter

Harrison

Antietam, Washington County, Md
Saturday July 11, 1863

Dear Mother

As I have a few moments to spare I will drop you a few lines to assure you I am enjoying excellent health. I have no time to give you a full detail of our last few days march as the mail is going out in 15 minutes. I simply wish to inform you that we are all well and the boys like active service first rate. I received a letter from you while we were at South Mountain. I was glad to hear you were all well.

I will write more the next opportunity. I hope this may find you all well. May the Lord be with you and bless and protect you all, direct as before. We are giving the enemy fits. And I think you will soon hear of the total demoralization of the Rebel army under Lee, pray for us. You wanted to know if I wasn't home sick. Not a once Mother. I have something to do besides getting home sick. I didn't come down here to play. I came to save the Union, and it shall be saved. May the Lord grant a glorious victory to our arms. I now close my love to John & enquiring friends.

Your Affectionate Son
Albert

Vredenburgh

3rd Corps 3rd Div. 14th Regt.
Fair Plains Md. Just East of the Williamsport Road
where it crosses Antietam Creek
July 12, 1863

Dear Doctor

I have just read your kind letter. The only one I will see before going into a desperate battle. We are now getting ready to go into battle and it has opened off towards Williamsport. The 6th Corps is engaged. We are about to inspect arms. I have had severe times lately. I am up in line of battle often but not yet having actually been under fire. Never mind that money till you hear from me. I don't think Will will want to use it. The rebels will give us a harder time here than at Gettysburg. Their army is nearly or quite as large as ours. We only have the terrain in our favor. The Corps are terribly cut up. Our Regt. is larger than most of the Brigades. We will have to go in first if the Corps attacks. I have been in fine spirits all along but I feel a little depressed this morning because the truth is found about the rebels waiting to retreat across the river. They would not cross if they could. Meade is the best gen'l we have had and an officer and soldier feels it. All is bustle and exciting around me. Love to Will and all.

Fondly
Peter

General Daniel E. Sickles USA

Harrison

Pleasant Valley, Near Maryland Heights
July 17, 1863

My Dear Mother

I guess you will believe now that I am in the midst of health, or I couldn't march with the Army of the Potomac, will you not Mother? When I can get over about 20 or 25 mile a day ha.ha. How are you marching with a big army? Our Corps came down here yesterday from Williamsport. It is now about 3 o'clock and raining quite hard. It rained the most of the time when we were at the Heights before, and I guess it is going to rain until we move from here, at least it looks now very much like it. Sergeants Foster, Chadwick & myself have quite a shanty rigged up so I think we can stand the storm. I haven't heard from you since we left Frederick City the last time, that was on the 4th of July. I wrote to you last week. I hope you have recd. it. I expect you worry about me as usual but I assure you I am getting along finely and like my bargain better than ever. It is true we see some hardship but what of that. That is nothing, I am willing to suffer anything to save and restore our old Union.

The war will not last a great while longer Mother, so keep a good heart. Trust in God & all will be well at last. The Rebellion has received a great blow. Look to Vicksburg, look to Port Hudson, Charleston I trust will be also in our hands. General Lee cannot long hold out. He will very soon see his folly. But it will be too late for him. The day is not far distant when our tattered banners will again wave in triumph over the South & North. Secession will be no more. God grant it. I don't expect you to make out half of that writing but perhaps you can study some of it out enough anyhow to assure you that I am well. The boys are well from the Bank with the exception of Sergt Diblin. We left him at Frederick but he wasn't very bad, we are drawing fresh meat for supper so I must stop and cook a steak, ha.ha. Porter House steak.

We are in the 3rd Brigade 3rd Division 3rd Army Corps. General French commands the Corps now as Genl Sickles [General Daniel E. Sickles] was wounded at Gettysburg. I don't know whether we will go over into Virginia now but I expect we will.

Your Son,
Albert

PS. I saw Capt. Sleeper & John H. Smith today, they look first rate. I have seen all my old chums in the 11th Regt. I heard there was quite a time in New York on account of the Draft. I wished to be there with Co. G

[Captain John T. Sleeper — 11th N.J. Vols. 1st. Lieut. Aug. 6, 1862;

Captain Vice Hill promoted. Killed in action at Spotsylvania Court House, Va., May 12, 1864. Private John H. Smith — 11th N.J. Vols. discharged at Convalescent Camp, Alexandria, Va. Feb. 25, 1864: Disability.]

New York City Draft Riots
July 1863

Although the War Between The States was fought primarily by volunteer soldiers, both sides resorted to conscription to fill manpower needs. It was in New York, perhaps more than anywhere else, that opposition to the draft took its most violent turn during the summer of 1863. There were many underlying forces that festered and caused resentment among the masses. A large number of these were recent impoverished Irish immigrants who were determined to make a living in the New World. Moreover, they resented both the propertied classes who employed them and the poor blacks that competed for their jobs. In addition, the spectre of religious bigotry reared its ugly head as the age old Protestant/Catholic animosity contributed to these combustible forces. It was also clear that the poor lacked the wherewithal to avoid military duty by hiring substitutes or buying exemptions. This, no doubt, fueled resentment and gave some the perspective that the struggle was a "rich man's war but a poor man's fight."

On July 12, 1863, the drawing took place and within twenty-four hours thousands of people took to the streets rioting, looting and attacking innocent people. Noteworthy among the latter were many blacks, who for whatever reason were held responsible for the war and its resulting privations. Fires spread destruction and hundreds of people were injured and killed before order was restored by veterans returning from the Gettysburg campaign.

Vredenburgh

Frederick City — Dill House
July 17, 1863   6 A.M.

Dear Mother

I have only time to let you know where I am as you see I am in Frederick. Yesterday morning we started from Sharpsburg and came to Brownsville about two miles west of Berlin on the Potomac. We started at daylight and I was in my saddle nearly all the time till 5 o'clock P.M. When I heard we intended to stay at Berlin a day I immediately got leave to come to Frederick. I started at 1/4 after 7, making over 22 miles in 2 hours. I wanted to settle up a little business I had there among other things and get my commutation.

I left both my trunks at Mrs. Hoskins. I suppose we will go into Va. now as that is the understanding. Our army is all around Berlin — for miles. The army is terribly affected by

Lee's escape. I never saw men so anxious to get into a battle. They had marched so many miles with patience in the hopes of victory.

The news on whole is favorable and I am in hopes we will finish up the war soon. Direct any letters to French till you hear to the contrary from me.

Love to all, Your Fond Son
Peter

Vredenburgh

Upperville, Virginia
July 22, 1863

Dear Mother

I moved in a few moments after finding my last letter to you of the 18th or 19th inst. and am now in Upperville, Va. just opposite Ashby's Gap. I expect we will move tomorrow to Manassas Gap. We don't know where Lee's army is but are trying to secure the passes through the Blue Ridge. The country around here is a perfect garden — rolling, fertile & luxurious. I wish some of our Monmouth County farmers could only see it. Our life here is similar to a perpetual gala day. Nothing moving till night but confusion, fighting, swearing & stealing all the time. Scenes which would harrow up your inner soul in ordinary times become so familiar that you scarcely give them a second thought. The whole road is sometimes jammed up, with men & teams for miles — men and animals dying along the roadside are common sights.

This morning I was riding through the village where crowds were going by all the time when a light colored negro called out to me and asked me "for God's sake get a doctor" to dress his wounds. He said he had been shot a short time since by a white soldier because he would not give him his pistol. There he had laid, none to inquire about him or arrest the man who shot him. I immediately did my best to get a surgeon but could find none. I came back and in a few moments the poor darkie died and ten minutes afterwards he was put in a bag and buried. Such a life here — you have to just fight and swear your way through to get anywhere or procure anything. I think I will always hereafter be able to meet the ordinary emergencies of civil life after I get through with the military.

Goodbye — I will write if possible from Manassas.

Peter

Harrison

Warrenton, Va.
July 26, 1863

Dear Mother

Warrenton, VA

Well Mother, you have not heard from me now in some time, and simply the reason is that I have not had time or opportunity to write until now. And another reason is that there has been no chance of sending a mail, but we have arrived once more where communication is open.

I am enjoying very good health as usual. Only feel a little tuckered out with the march we have had. Nearly the whole army of the Potomac lays in this vicinity. Our Corps went down to Manassas Gap last Thursday, and had a right smart skirmish with Lee's army or at least a small portion of it. Our Brigade was not called in action. But was ready on the Hill as the skirmish was going on in the valley below. We gave them a good whipping and then left the next morning to overhaul Lee before he could get down here and our purpose has been so far accomplished. And now if Lee comes this way we want to give him one more good whipping & then we will look for peace. Our Army is as large now as at any other time during the War. I have not time to write you much this time Mother, I only wish to assure you that we are well.

I must now close with love to you, may the good Lord over all, bless and preserve you.

Your Son
Albert C.

Ross

Camp of the 14th N.J. Vols.
Warrenton Va.
July 27, 1863

Dear Mother

As a party is going home tomorrow in recruiting service and as this is the first opportunity I have had since we left Boonsboro Md. I will take advantage of it. I can tell you Mother we have seen something of war since I wrote you last. Yes indeed war, with all its joys and sorrows. It is needless to narrate all we have been through since we joined the Army of the Potomac but I will give you some particulars. The longest march we have made in one day was 24 miles and we have marched some days with the rain coming down in bucketsful and then sleep all night with everything on as wet as it possible could be. We would wake up in the morning with the sun pouring down upon us and the mist rising from us like from a tea kettle.

The distance we have marched, since the 1st of July has been 178 miles. Day before yesterday we were at Manassas Gap, 28 miles from here supporting the 2nd Division which was fighting the Rebs. That was the first I saw of the gray back gentry. We were on a hill about 500 yards in the rear of the 2nd Division of our Corps and had a full view of them. I could see the Rebel's line of battle and a battery of theirs posted in their rear which was continually firing shells at the first line. I could hear their shells go wiz-wiz-wiz as they came on and then our skirmishers would blaze away at the rebs. I saw Gen. Spinola of the Excelsior Brigade N.Y. Vols brought in wounded. The next day we went all over the battlefield. I saw about a dozen rebs lying dead most of them shot through the head. Berdan's sharpshooters were the skirmishers and they never fire without hitting something. The Excelsior Brigade made a splendid charge and captured about 100 of the rebs. I have seen all the Freehold boys since we have been in the army several times. Charlie Hall who is in the 15th, Surgeon, Lt. Goney, Lt. Mitchel, Dave Oliphant, and Algernon Marcellous whom I went to school with at Billys. Goney Marcellous who went out in the 11th Regt. and who is a cousin of this one was wounded at Gettysburg but I have not seen him. He is the one who lives on the Branch road. I like this sort of life first rate. I think when this war is ended I will go soldiering again somewhere. I like excitement and the army is the place to find it. Of course there is a little bitter with the sweet but if a person always takes the bright side of this life, he will come out cat bird.

I have lived two days on our hard tack and coffee but when we did get enough I could eat all the more for it. Some of the officers, whom it must be remembered have to get their own provisions somehow, have to go around and beg crackers from the privates who are supplied by the government. We now have more than we can eat as there is a railroad running here and we can get our supplies through. Every day since we left Boonsboro Pass until we reached this place we could not send or receive any mail or supplies excepting a few which we got at Harpers Ferry. I haven't time to write more at present but will soon again. Give my love to all enquiring friends and write soon to

Your Affectionate Son
Burroughs

Wolcott

Camp in the field
August 8, 1863

Friend Powers

As I have not had a letter from you since I was at Trenton
I thought it advisable to write you up and make some inquir-
ies. I suppose you have heard before this that the 14th was in
the Potomac Army. Well it is so, bad luck to it. We were consolidated to the Potomac Army June 20th and I can tell you we
have had some hard marches and we are not done yet, but we
have managed to get along without fighting, but was very close
at two fights — close enough to support Gen. Buford at Boonsboro, and see the rebel shells explode sometimes not more than
100 yards distant. The reason we did not take part in the fight,
Gen. Meade did not want to bring on a general engagement
there as it would interfere with his plans. We were the only
Regt. of infantry there until that night and Gen. French our
corps commander thought the rebels were in strong force and
wanted to draw us in ambush. They kept themselves in the
woods — only a small party coming in sight. The fight commenced early in the morning and raged all day till after dark.
That night the balance of our (3rd) corps came up and the 12th
with it.

Then we were at the fight at Manassas Gap. We marched
that morning 14 miles out of our route to draw the rebels out of
the Gap. The 2nd corps got there ahead of us and the Excelsior
Brigade formed Line of Battle and kept 100 yards in their rear.
So if the (Excelsior) were pushed too hard, they would fall back
on us. Then we would have marched on the rebels with a
double time. I felt a little nervous at first — seeing our soldiers
fall and hearing their cries of pain. But every rebel that I saw
fall, done my heart good and they fell fast — soon as our boys
drove them from behind the stone wall. Our boys piled the
rebel bodies up for breastworks. We captured
1600 head of cattle and some sheep. I did not
learn the loss on our side but the rebel loss was
over 500, killed, wounded, and taken prisoner.

A rebel Lieutenant, wounded in the leg,
and was laying by a tree, told me he learnt his
trade in Newark, New Jersey and just before
the war broke out he went to Charleston and
enlisted in the rebel army. I forgot his name.
He said he was tired of the rebels and knew the
cause was hopeless. Our corps is camped near
Rappahannock Station and we came here last
Saturday. I expect we will remain here until
after this month and we get the conscripts and
drill them. I pity the poor devils. They will find
what it is to work for Uncle Samuel. I wrote a
letter to Nick while we laid at Upperville. I
think if I should ever get home again and a man

Union camp scene.

National Archives

should ask me to enlist I would knock him down. Traveling 20 miles a day with three hard tack and a small slice of pork does not agree with me, it is very seldom I cook my pork. I can eat it raw — when I cook it, it wastes so much. It rains every afternoon regularly and we have no tents and have not since we left Maryland Heights — Col. Truex swears he will not move again until we get them. I must close — write soon and tell Nick and Allen to do so.

I am yours Respectfully
J.R. Wolcott

Vredenburgh

3rd Corps 3rd Div. 1st. Brigade
2 1/2 miles Southeast of Sulphur Springs Va.
August 9, 1863 4 P.M.

My Dear Mother

It is Sunday afternoon and though the weather is warm, there is a pleasant breeze through our tent and everything is comparatively quiet and lovely. These quiet Sundays (when we have them) always makes me think of you all at home. We left Warrenton some days ago and till yesterday have been guarding an ammunition train. Yesterday morning we were relieved and are now with the rest of the Brigade.

I have just been appointed President of a General Court Martial which convened here on Friday, but adjourned till tomorrow morning. I have forgotten a good deal that I used to know about Ct. Martial and have no books, nor can I find any touching upon the subject, but I guess I can get along. I hope we will have no cases to try punishable with death.

I heard yesterday afternoon that Major Allison, our former Sec. of State, was over in the 2nd Division, paying off the troops. So Hall and I started immediately over to see him. He was very cordial and seemed glad to see us and without our asking him, paid us up to July 1st. George Taylor was with him and also Jack Smith, the treasurer's son. I sent $200 in money to Father by Col. Jonathan Cook. Tell Father about it. I have never heard from Father about that check nor of the draft I sent him. I wish he would let me know whether he saw the draft, so I would know whether Hoskins, who endorsed my draft is safe or not. Tell him to invest the $200 as he thinks best. Jack Smith is lying asleep on my cot here beside me. He seems exhausted with the ride we took to Sulphur Springs this morning, though he was well paid for his trouble. We drank immense quantities of the water and beguiled a few hours away very pleasantly, lolling on the green and listening to the last strains of the band which played incessantly near the Springs. We hear so much music here though, that I scarcely notice it now. Every night after tea, the bands strike up and you can hear from every quarter till late in the evening. We have no chance to read at night so that generally Col. and I light our pipes after tea and then getting snugly ensconced in our arm chairs and wile away the hours till bed time.

The mail is just closing.

From Your Affectionate Son
Peter

Ross

Camp of the 14th Near Bealton Station on the Rapidan River
August 9, 1863

Dear Mother

I received your welcome letter a few moments since and now I hasten to answer it. I wrote you from Warrenton but it seems you never received it and when Colonel went home I gave one to Lerr, one of his servants to give to you. So now I try it again. I forget all the particulars which have occurred since we left Boonsboro but will give you a few of them. We marched from Boonsboro Pass to Williamsport where we lay in front of Johnny Reb, for two days, letting him go across the river at his leisure, and one fine morning we were ordered forward only to find that the bird had flown. If men were ever in a bad humor they were then. I never want to hear again just to think of us lying in front of them for two days and letting them cross the river. We could have whipped them then just as easy as eating our breakfast but no it was not put down so on the partyramma. So after we found they were all safely across, we came to an about face and marched back through Sharpsburg and over Antietam to Harpers Ferry, where we crossed the river at night on a pontoon bridge.

I wouldn't have given two cents for our army after we came to Williamsport. You could hear the men all around saying they never would go into Virginia again. Now that they

Union camp at Bealton Station.

had let the Rebs go. When they might have bagged the whole, but someway or other we all got across and are now on the sacred side. We marched from the Ferry, a place called Upperville, near Ashby's Gap and the scene of a great cavalry fight sometime since. Our Regiment went out on pickett the same day we got there, and Colonel made his Hd. Qtrs. near a house about two miles from town. I went up to the house to get some water and the lady asked me if I could not

get someone to stay in the house all night for there was none there but her and her niece and two daughters. After hearing her story, I very accommodatingly offered her my services (for I had faint visions of coffee with milk in it and some good bread floating before my mind). She was very kind and when I told her I would stay she asked me if I had been to supper. I told her I had not and she then got me a supper and the way I piled in the eatables was a caution. I stayed there all night and until supper time the next day when we got marching orders. Before I left they filled my Haversack with good things and one of the little girls gave me a needle book and pin cushion filled with pins. I offered them greenbacks but they would not take a cent for my staying with them so I bade them an affectionate fare-well promising if I ever came that way again to come and see them. We then took up our beds and walked to Warrenton Va. and from there, here.

Altogether we have travelled since July 1st, over two hundred miles through all kinds of weather and sometimes with nothing to eat, when we stopped for the night. I saw officers in the regiment offer 10 cents for a hard tack which he would not pretend to eat at home. But here I am after all our adventures sitting in our tent, feeling just as well as I ever did in my life, never having been sick for a moment since I started preferring this sort of life from any I have yet experienced.

Quarter Master Cowart hasn't made his appearance yet. Col. Hall wrote to him yesterday that if he did not return immediately, application would be made for his discharge from the service. You need not tell this to anyone for it might make a fuss. I received a letter from Let, a short time since. I would like to be home to attend the levee at the Seminary Hill. You get Mimmie to write me a good long letter, telling me all the news and how the levee passed off. Ask Pop to find out what the Colonel is going to do. Some say he will take that cavalry regt. If so, you may expect to see me home again soon. What has become of Aunt Jane? I never hear from her any more. Give my love to all From

Your Affectionate Son
Burroughs

Ross

Camp of the 14th New Jersey Vols
August 11, 1863

Dear Sister

I had the extreme pleasure last evening of receiving a letter from you and as it closed with the injunction "write soon" I feel only bound to write a letter this afternoon while I have an opportunity, for we are under marching orders and it is no telling where we may be tomorrow. Some say we are going back to the 8th Corps at Baltimore and some that we are going

to New York and then again that we are going to Fredericksburg or along the Rappahannock somewhere which I think is
the most sensible conclusion to form at present. I guess we
have been to the Springs as well as some of your northern
folks. The White Sulpher Springs are only two miles from here
and I have been to them several times and had both the pleasure of drinking and bathing in the notorious waters. It tastes
exactly like the region below, or to give you a better idea, like
matches. The grounds surrounding them are perfectly enchant-
ing. The splendid hotel which graced the place in former years
is now burned to the ground, nothing standing but its huge
walls and pillars to remind one of days gone by when it flour-
ished in all its glory. They say it was a splendid affair but it
belonged to an Eastern man and therefore the Rebels said it
must come down but the grounds surrounding it still flourish
in all their magnificence. The springs still bubble the same as
when surrounded by the sparkling beauties of old Virginia
instead of by Uncle Samuel's soldiers with their sunburnt faces
and ragged apparel.

The park surrounding the springs are the most beautiful I
ever saw and in their days of prosperity could have been little
short of a paradise. Such a number of statues are still here,
some with an arm knocked off and some with a head off and
then there would be one lying prostrate and the fountains all
demolished and their fine sculptured work lying around loose.
But enough of this, it is impossible for me to describe the
devastation which one sees daily in marching through Virginia.
I guess they are all heartily tired of this secession business and
wish this cruel war was over.

How did the levee pass off at the seminary? I should like
to have been home to participate in the grand affair. How is
fruit going to turn out in New Jersey? They don't raise any
down here but we live highly upon blackberries of which there
are a profusion. We have some gay times down here once in a
while and I like this life very much. I believe I have nothing
more of importance to communicate so will close hoping soon to
hear from my Dear Sister. Remember me to Garrett and Mr. &
Mrs. Schenck and give my love to all the folks at home.

Your Brother
Will

Vredenburgh

3rd Corps 3rd Div. 1st Brigade
Near White Sulphur Springs Va.
August 13th 1863

Dear Mother

I received your letters of Aug. 6th and 10th the last including stamps. I also recd. one from Will dated July 25, '63. I have
nothing new to write. My being on Court Martial relieves me

from duty with the Regt. and as we often adjourn a few moments after convening I have plenty of time to ride around and amuse myself generally. I had a very pleasant time last night. We sleep under a canvass sheet raised in the middle and fastened at the side with ropes, very pleasant in pleasant weather and vice versa. Last night about 12 o'clock one of the severest thunder showers burst forth that I ever witnessed. My cot was near one end of the tent and I was awakened by the corner of the tent coming down over my head. I got up about as soon as if someone had hollered "fire" etc. As I did so down went my cot in the water, blankets and all were nearly submerged. Col. Hall had a bath about the same time and by the most assiduous efforts with a little swearing succeeded in getting a light. Our clothes, boots, and everything was drenched and as I endeavored to get my cot further toward the middle of the tent, away I went down in the slush, bed and all, which, considering I was dressed very much after the style of the costume of paradise, was disagreeable. The next move by Col. Hall upset the table and contents and the corner of the tent that was down gave a pleasant wave over our heads as if it would fan our poured brows. By that time our beds were wet through so we just took a drink of whiskey, lit our pipes and smoked it out till morning. It was fun to look around the camp at daylight and see the officers and men sitting around in heaps on rails, stoves, and anything to keep them off the ground.

Steve is with me and suits very well. He is a smart ingenious fellow and acts as valet de chambre, groom & general adviser. Bill is in Baltimore at a livery stable and wants to come back.

Long Branch, NJ was an exclusive seaside resort in the 1800s. The West End Hotel is pictured below.

Affectionately Your Son
Peter

Ross

Camp of the 14th N.J. Vols
August 13, 1863

Dear Mother

As I am at leisure today I will write you a few lines so as to keep you from thinking that I have forgotten home and its associations. Everything is unusually quiet about here with nothing to do but sleep and eat. I would like you to see us cooking. We all have to cook all we eat. The only cooking utensils we use is a tin cup and frying pan of small dimensions. We generally take turns. The Adjt. and I sometimes he cooks the coffee and I fry the pork and sometimes when we are fortunate we get ham by way

of variation. I should like to
be home to take a trip down
to Long Branch and get a
good wash. The only place we
have to bath in is the Rapidan River, quite a mud gutter
in its way. If I could get some
influential man to speak to
Col. Truex about me for a
commission I think I would
stand a good chance as there
will be some vacancies in this
regiment before long. Mr.
Chandler for instance would
have some influence with
him. I will send you 50 cents
to get me some stamps. We
cannot get any here and I
dislike to send a letter
franked. I am still in good
health and believe I am now 20 years old. We haven't been paid
since I was home but am looking for the paymaster every day.
No man at present. My love to all. Tell Min to write and tell me
all the news. Direct as before

The Rapidan River.

Your Affectionate Son
Burroughs

Vredenburgh

1st. Brigade 3rd Div. 3rd Army Corps
Near Bealton Va. August 23, 1863

Dear Mother

I recd the letter from you that mentioned Aunt Dora's
return home last. I think I have sent none since. Changes are
of frequent occurrence here. Col. Hall has been in command of
the Brigade and I of the Regt. at times. Yesterday I was appointed president of another Court Martial. Rose is to be Court
Martialed; his trial comes on tomorrow morning. He has some
apprehensions for his safety. I should not wonder if he was
dismissed the service. Our Regt. every few days acts as picket
guard on the Rappahannock from near Rappahannock Station
to where we are encamped. This picket duty is rather ticklish
business and particularly perilous here. The river is only about
25 yards wide though quite deep. The other night I took the
Regt. out on picket and after establishing the posts, went up to
a fine house to establish Hd. Quarters. I found a very pleasant
family in the house consisting of a middle aged woman and five
daughters. Her husband and two sons are in the rebel army,
but she cordially invited me in to dinner. Of course I responded
that I didn't care if I did and partook. In the evening I sent for

Capt. Alstrom and we had a delightful time. They were all bitter Secesh but seemed mightily pleased with our company. I slept on their stoop at night as I had to be up frequently and left after breakfast in the morning. There was picket firing a half dozen times during the night but one gets so used to that that it is scarcely noticed. I had to laugh when I arrived at camp the following morning to find your letter warning me against visiting Seceshers etc.

I think I will ride over to the 1st. Corps tomorrow to see Ed Taylor. I saw him a few times while we were at Warrenton but I left him there when I came away and have not seen him since. Don't let Will come in the service. I would rather pay the exemption money than have him in the army. We don't even pretend to guess or think of where we may go next. It looks as if we might stay here some time. I sent Father $100 by Col. Cook. Let me know when he gets it.

With love to all I am your

Affectionate Son
Peter

Stults

Camp Near Bealton, Virginia
Sunday August 23, l863

Dear Pa & Ma

Dinner just over, had beefsteak, fried potatoes and tea — that is what a soldier considers a good dinner. You need not fear of my starving. If there is anything in the country eatable, I have a first rate scout in the person of my cook. He finds lots of things, of course we buy our ham and bread, that can't be borrowed. Green corn and potatoes we borrow. Our regiment came off picket duty this morning. We picket the north fork of the Rappahannock. No rebs have troubled us. Still the boys fancy an enemy at times and fire a shot or two. There is nothing new with us of importance since my last to you excepting the visit of the paymaster. He was on here the first of last week. By the first of September we will have two months pay due us again, but we don't expect to receive it under a month or more.

Officers call was sounded this morning for the purpose of the assembling of the officers to vote for a sutler (our old sutler having given up the business) A Mr. Merino is likely to be our sutler, John Hunt of Bergus Mills was nominated and would have been elected if all of our officers had been present. Sutlers charge enough to get rich but I doubt if many of them make much. A sutler in this vicinity charges $1.00 per lb. for cheese, 20 cts for a lead pencil, 15 cts. bottle ink, other things in proportion, still there is such a rush on the arrival of a wagon that they have to be protected by guards.

The guerilla Mosby often picks up a train of sutler wagons

on the route from Washington here — that takes off profits fast. The news from Charleston is encouraging. I think it must fall and that will be a hard blow for the Rebellion. If newspaper reports are to be credited, the rebel army of Virginia is greatly demoralized. I think if an advance were ordered we would find them in fighting trim as it always has been found. I also think the rebel army of Va. must suffer defeat before the rebellion is crushed.

In my last to you I spoke of being under marching orders. We have as yet received orders to march at that time it was reported that the rebels were trying to flank us by way of Manassas Gap, to Washington, D.C. It is Sunday today but it appears nothing like it will take place. The program of duties is the same nearly as on other days. Tell Mary Ann she must write me, she should practice besides. I want to hear from her very much. Tell her I saw some of the fashionable ladies of this part of the country taking a pleasure ride not long since. They were pleasantly seated in a cart. The driver, a young dark riding one of the oxen, our boys allowed it. Would not do in Jersey. The people of this country are having hard times — suffer greatly. It is very warm again today — had a shower Friday night. Write soon — give me all particulars of farming and so forth. My respects to all.

Marcus

John Singleton Mosby CSA

Ross

Near Bealton Station Va.
August 24, 1863

Dear Pop

Your welcome letter was duly received and I now will write a few lines in return as I have the time. We still remain in the same position in which we were a month ago with no signs of our moving very soon, but of course we cannot tell what a day may bring forth. You wished to know about how far we are from Fredericksburg etc. They call it 35 miles from here, and 60 miles from here to Washington. We are very comfortably situated now, having drawn tents yesterday. The first we have had since we left Md. Heights almost two months since. They are those small shelter tents. Two men carry one between them and when they are up make quite a good shelter. We draw rations every day having more than we can eat. Today we have potatoes, molasses, soft bread, fresh beef, and onions. So you see we live in regular hotel style — quite different from a short time since when one or two hard crackers were all that we had for one days rations. It doesn't seem very healthy here although I still keep in good health. This morning's reports show 147 "present sick" and 90 "absent sick." Most of those present with diarrhea.

It is a splendid country around here for farming purposes

U.S. Army Military History Institute

but in a whole day's march, you won't see an acre under cultivation except in little patches around the negro houses. We get Baltimore papers the same day they are issued, arriving about four o'clock in the afternoon. From reading the papers I guess there will have to be some drafting in Jersey after all. There will be considerable fun when the conscripts come in for this regiment I think. When you write tell me about how many men have volunteered for our regiment. Tell Colonel we are all wishing for him back again with those two hundred men he promised us. I believe I have nothing more of importance to write at this time. Hoping soon to hear from you again and sending love to all I remain

Your Affectionate Son
Burroughs

Harrison

Green Wood Farm, Near Bealton, Virginia
Thursday afternoon, August 27, 1863

Dear Mother

Before the drum beats for Brigade drill I will scratch you a few lines to inform you that I am "forked end down," have a good appetite, and feel first rate in general.

The weather has assumed a great change since night before last. We were about two miles from Camp in the afternoon on Brigade Drill and it commenced raining. The General dismissed us but too late. We were soaked well before we reached camp, the General included. General Morris is well thought of by the whole Brigade. And he is as smart as steel. It has been quite cool since the rain. It is good healthy weather and as good as medicine to the boys in the hospital. I hear Corporal Byran has been united in the arms of ceremony or rather matrimony, ha.ha. He must have thought somebody would run off with her, I guess if he waited until the war was ended, which will not be a great while. The Johnnies are almost played out, but I must bring my letter to a close. Good night, may God protect you all

Albert

Ross

Head Qrs. 3rd Div. 3rd A.C.
August 28, 1863

As I have a few spare moments I will write you a few lines. I am now in a new position at Division Headquarters, Gen'l Elliott. I like it very well but am kept pretty busy writing. It is to be a permanent position I believe, and on the march I will ride. I miss my old associates in the Regiment some, but the Brigade that they belong to is in this Division so I will see them once in a while. There is some talk of sending our Division to Texas but I hardly think it will be done. How are you getting along with the drafting business in Jersey? I guess you won't get all your quota by volunteers. Do you hear whether Colonel is getting any volunteers or not. There are any quantity of conscripts coming here almost every day. Five of them are to be shot on Saturday, for deserting. I had a letter from Mimmie some short time since. I don't know whether I told you of it or not. I believe I had nothing more of importance to say. Remember me to all my friends and write soon to your

Affectionate Son
Burroughs

Harrison

Green Wood Farm, Near Bealton Station, Virginia
August 31, 1863

Dear Mother

It is Monday morning and nothing to do as usual but lay off and think of the future. We have had general inspection and muster this morning lasting about an hour and if you notice the date of my letter you will see it is the last day of summer, being the end of two summers I have been in my country's service.

I feel fine since the weather has grown cooler. It is uncommonly cool for the season. There is no news Mother, of any importance. All is quiet along the Rappahannock. I reckon Capt A [Alstrom] will not get me in the invalid corps and as to getting a furlough that is out of the question.

If our chances were as slim as the Johnnies, I would make up my mind that our cause was caved in, and would want to be crawling out of the back door, before I was kicked out, ha.ha.

Beauregard [General P.G.T. Beauregard C.S.A.] must feel rather white to see our little monitors [Union Ironclads] crawling up on Charleston. And the next thing we hear will be that the city is either in our hands or in ashes. It don't make much difference which.

May God bless you all and protect you from all harm.

Your loving Son Albert

General P.G.T. Beauregard CSA

Vredenburgh

1st Brigade 3rd Div. 3rd A. Corps
Near Bealton Va. September 2, 1863

Dear Mother

I believe the last letter I recd. from you was dated Aug 22nd and included one from Will. I have written once since, I think. The other day while I was down to Bealton Station to see Elias Conover off, a young man with his coat off came up to me and spoke. I recognized him in a moment as young Lindslay, Uncle Lindslay's brother, you know, who used to be in Tomerville. He looked well and said he was employed in the telegraph office (in the government employ). I was very glad to see him and invited him up to my quarters about 6 miles from Bealton. Four or five days ago, Dr. Vanderveer from Tomerville called on me. He said he used to keep his horse in Grandma's stable and I think I recollect having heard some of my Aunts speak of him. At least I told him so. He is now Surgeon of the 5th N.J.

I witnessed the execution of the 5 deserters in the 5th Corps last Saturday. It was a solemn scene, I can assure you. Alexander Ward, the "special artist" of Frank Leslie's Illustrated was about 60 yards off from me fronting the spectacle and I wish you would send me the copy with it in and I will return it, marking where I was. I was on horseback on your left as you look at the picture from where Ward stood.

Last Sunday Elias Conover's son and I took a ride over to Warrenton to see Ed Taylor. I found him quite low with the dysentery but he said he was getting better. Elias Conover was here Thursday and Friday of last week. I took him over to Sulphur Springs and he seemed very much pleased with the ride and place. We are living very pleasantly now. I have about $200 and with money we can get decent living from the sutlers.

It is extremely cold at night but though I am very uncomfortable sometimes I experience no injurious results. The night before last we were ordered to get ready to move at a moments notice, but have not moved yet. I rather like the glorious uncertainty of our life as it keeps up continual expectations of a change, which is always courted by a soldier. We have Brigade drill nearly every day now and I am very fond of it. I have been in command of the Regt. for the last two weeks, but am still on the Court Martial that I spoke of in my last letter. Genl. French detached me a few days ago as assistant Inspector General, that is, Inspector Genl. of the Division but General Morris commanding our Brigade replied that he wanted me with the Regt. as I was the only field officer with it on duty.

Write soon, with love to Father and all
I am your Affectionate Son
Peter

Ross

Headquarters 3rd Div. 3rd A.C.
Washington, D.C.
September 2, 1863

Dear Sister

　　Your welcome letter reached me a day or two since and I will now try and accommodate you as you said I had not written you in so long. But if you did not receive a letter from me it was not my fault for I wrote one sometime since, the receipt of which was never acknowledged. I suppose you have heard I have got a new position but if not I will tell you that I have the honor to be at Division Head Quarters of 3rd Division 3rd Army Corps. General Wm. L Elliott. I find my duties a little more arduous but you know I was never afraid of work ha.ha. Will Gulick was over to see me a few moments before your letter came. I was sorry I had not a chance to tell him about what you wrote of his folks in your letter. I don't know when I will see him again as his camp is about five miles from here. He looks very well indeed, not quite as fleshy as formerly but the same old Bill. It made me think of old times to hear him laugh once more. We are having delightful weather here just now but I don't suppose it will continue long. We are now under marching orders but it is impossible for us to tell where is to be our destination. Some say New York, others Texas and some say across the Rappahannock but it makes little difference where I go now. I should like to be home and get some apples and peaches. We don't see anything of that kind around here. I often see some old acquaintances down here that I had forgotten all about almost. There is no news at all here and nothing to write about. I only write to let you know I am still alive and to get you to write in return.

　　My love to all and write soon to your
Affectionate Brother

Will

Vredenburgh

Inspectors General Dept.
Hd. Quarters 3rd Div. 3rd Corps
Near Bealton Va.
September 5, 1863 9 P.M.

Dear Mother

　　If you have received my letter dated a few days ago you will not be much sur-

Pontoon bridge across the Rappahannock River.

prised to see by the date of this that I have been favored with one of the most pleasant offices in the service. My duties consist in seeing that all army regulations and orders are enforced in this Division. Such as related to the condition of the troops, ordnance, commissary and Quarter Master stores, and to see that every Regt. has all it is entitled to and if not, why; and what would improve the condition of the troops in any particular. To see that the troops are drilled, that the camps are properly located, tents properly pitched and raised. That all men and officers are present or properly absent. That public property is not used for private purposes or improperly, which enables me to prevent the terrible cruelty heretofore so prevalent in this Division as well as the rest of the army. In fact there is no end of my duties or labors if I choose to go to the full extent of my authority. My course is wherever I see any wrong inflicted or right withheld to prevent the one and enforce the other by my own orders, or if that fails by reporting the fact to Corps Headquarters. I am in a position antagonistic in fact, to a certain extent, to the Brig. Genls and all other officers and men in the Division. My predecessor reported that Gen'l Elliott did not drill the men sufficiently and he was immediately notified to attend to it etc. I have to make out weekly, semi-monthly, and monthly reports of the condition of affairs in the Division so that I can employ my time you see. But as an offset, I am free to go, do, and act as I please, anywhere within the limits of the army and am not under the control of anyone short of Corps Hd. Qrs. I can travel without asking leave from anyone as my duties call upon me to visit picket outposts and fly around generally. I also have orderlies and clerks sufficient to meet the necessities, though I will never have a mounted orderly tagging after me as I don't like the looks of it. I rode over to Warrenton this afternoon to see Ed Taylor but found that he had gone home on a leave of 20 days.

I wish you would send by Col. Truex a box of shaving soap and my gold cord that I took off my pants you know, when I left home. If you cannot find it don't buy a new one as I can get it here I expect. I think of writing to Frederick to have my things sent on here as I will soon want my winter clothing and have none here. Don't you or Father think I am bragging in my above enumeration of "duties" because I merely mentioned them to give you a clear idea of how I am situated. Tell Will to tell Judge Barclay that our Hd. Quarters are where he married his first wife and I often talk to the ladies about him. I wish you would also send me a lot of good stockings (not yarn) if you can.

With love to all

I am your Affectionate Son
Peter

Harrison

Green Wood Farm, Fanquir Co., Virginia
Sabbath Morning September 7, 1863

Dear Mother

I must now take up my pen, and scribble you a few lines to assure you I am enjoying good health. Inspection is over and I have mounted my Guard so I will have nothing to do until Dress Parade this afternoon.

David Twiford is on Provost Guard, and has been on guard at a house some two miles from camp ever since we have been here — and where do you think it is. You are no doubt aware that Judge Barclay took his first wife from Virginia. Well it is at his wife's daughters, Mrs. Robert Ashton and when they found that David knew something about Judge, you can imagine they were highly tickled so Dave told them there was a Sergt in his company that knew more about him than he did, so when Dave came to camp again he brought an invitation from Mr. & Mrs. Ashton for me to call the very first opportunity. So as they have three or four daughters you can imagine that I did go ha.ha.

So a night about a week since I started off and reached the house and had a long talk with the family, concerning old Judge and his young wife of which they knew nothing about. They had heard nothing from him since the Rebellion broke out. I was very much pleased with my visit, and with many thanks for my visit I returned to camp again. They told me to come often but I haven't been since, as one of his daughters is sick they would talk me to death if I went very often, ha.ha. They would come mighty slim for provisions if it wasn't for our army. They have one son in the Union Army and one in the Rebel Ranks.

The old lady painted him out to me, in case I ever fell in contact with him but I don't think I would talk with him. I would much rather talk with the daughters. They are pretty good looking girls.

Their slaves have all run away and they are in the midst of misery, for they have no crops whatever. Only a few vegetables in the garden. The night I was there, the old man said he had just flour enough for breakfast so you see they just live from hand to mouth. I tell you Mother, the people North don't know what suffering is. When the farmers come to lose all their cattle, tear down their fences & burn them, then have their houses searched and everything in the shape of eatables taken from then, they can begin to realize what suffering there is in Virginia. But such is war's desolation. There are better days coming let us look ahead and look not behind us — remember Lot's Wife.

General Joseph B. Carr USA

Major General David B. Birney USA

I believe I have turned out all the news I can think of, so I will close for this time.

I remain your Son
Albert

Vredenburgh

Hd. Quarters 3rd Div.3rd Corps
September 7, 1863 — 9 P.M.

Dear Mother

I have just finished business in my office and feel like writing a few lines to you. I wish you would send me a watch good for something, that one say, that you bought me last spring. The one I have does not run well now, in fact, not at all and, if that little one you bought will suit you had better send it by Col. Truex or some of his party.

We had a grand review of the 3rd Corps today. General Meade was the reviewing officer and I had a good look at him. Stoneman, Birney, Mott, Carr, French and others of less celebrity attended. It was a grand pageant I wished you all could have been there. Henry, particularly, would have liked it. I see by the papers that court is in session and Father is presiding. I should like to be there. I told you I think about my having seen Linslay and Dr. Vanderveer. I have not been to Bealton since and therefore have not seen Linslay.

Give my love to Aunts Dora and Mary, and Mary Taylor if you see her. How is Sally getting along? I hear Jim is a Secessionist, in his own way.

Ever Your Affectionate Son
Peter

Ross

Hd. Qrs. 3rd Div 3rd Corps
September 10, 1863

Dear Mother

I received your letter a few days since and I will now try and answer it with all your questions. In the first place, I will tell you how I came to be in my present position. Gen'l Elliott wanted a clerk at the Hd. Qrs. and had tried quite a number out of our Brigade but none seemed to suit him and somehow he found out my name and had me detailed. I have been here nearly three weeks now. I did not want to come at first and the Major came over twice to see about getting me back, but twas no go so I was compelled to stay. I begin to like it better now

though. Major has been appointed Acting Inspector General of
the Division and he is here as also Lieutenant Walker of our
Regiment who is Commissary of Musters. I don't have as much
spare time as I used to with the Regiment but perhaps it is all
the better for it keeps me out of mischief. The pay is the same
but there is one advantage, on the march I ride, and that is
what used to trouble me the most. I wrote to Mimmie sometime since but haven't heard from her in reply yet. We had a
grand review the other day. Our whole Third Corps was out
and General Meade inspected them. It was a grand sight I can
assure you. Everything goes on about as usual here. We are
looking for Colonel back every day. I believe he didn't succeed
very well in getting volunteers. I had my likeness taken which
I will send you with this, there is a travelling artist a short
distance from here and I thought perhaps you would like to see
how I look. Don't you think the mustache looks fierce? No more
at present-write soon. My love to all.

Your Affectionate Son
Burroughs

*General George G.
Meade USA and staff.*

Vredenburgh

Inspector General's Department
Headquarters 3rd Div. 3rd Corps
September 11, 1863

My Dear Mother

I have just received two letters, one from you, and one from Father both dated the 9th inst. I can never tell which of my letters you have received without you describing them by date.

I tell you what I wish you would do, and that is to express me a box of something to eat. We are very scant of vegetables here and there is no fruit at all. Can't you express me a box, say about two feet long and wide and one foot deep, partly filled with apples and a few bottles of apple whiskey. I would rather you should not send me anything but apples, and apple-whiskey as with those two associated articles I think I can regulate my bowels and "register" so as to keep in fighting trim all the time.

My pay will not be increased by virtue of my appointment. I only rise in importance and responsibility. In case of battle I would join the regiment though I can keep out if I choose, but I would rather be shot through the hat or even coat, than to be thought shirking. Don't send me anything else but what I have written for and not them if inconvenient. If you send the apples or whiskey, get the best you can and I will send the money to you. I don't care for expense in such a small way.

If this letter is disconnected recollect that I am now at Headquarters and might have been tempted before writing to "take a drop of something strong" to tell the truth Mother, I took a small drink with the Medical Director of Hospital whiskey and feel it a little — just a little. Tell Father I will write to him tomorrow or next day.

Ever Your Affectionate Son
Peter

Vredenburgh

Hd.Qrs. 3rd Div 3rd A. Corps
September 12, 1863

Dear Mother

I wrote to you last night under rather unfavorable circumstances and asked you to send me a box of apples and I now write to say that I don't want them. They would be more trouble to you and expense than they were worth and I don't want you to bother with them at all.

Tell Father in reply to his questions, that I am on General

Elliott's staff and am as permanently appointed as any other officer, as long as our regiment remains in this division. I can get myself relieved if I request it. I am studying hard to perfect myself in the duties as possible, and I think I understand them very well now. Don't send me any flannel blankets or anything else except what I have stated. I mean to write to Nocross to send me some gin cocktail as the Doctors recommend it to repel dysentery and none can be gotten in the army. I am in excellent health now though and have not been sick a day that I recollect of since entering the service. Be as courteous to Col. Truex as you can Mother, for he has been very kind to me always, and is keenly appreciative of the slightest rebuff. I will write to Father tomorrow or the next day. Tomorrow is my hardest day. I have to write a weekly report, long and tedious in its details, in the morning; and inspect all the horses, wagon's harness, mules, in the Hd.Qrs., supply, and ammunition trains, ambulance corps, and hospital wagons in the afternoon. I like the business though and feel a great deal of satisfaction at being able to stop abuses, which heretofore I have seen and been unable to remedy.

With much love to Father and all the rest

I am you affectionate Son
Peter

Vredenburgh

Hd. Qrs. 3rd Div. 3rd Corps
September 14, 1863

Dear Mother

That sketch of the execution of those five deserters is in "Harpers Weekly" and not in "Leslie". I wish you would please send it to me. There is to be an execution of two more in this Corps, this week.

There was very heavy and incessant firing yesterday towards Culpeper, and we thought the guns were not more than four or five miles off. You spoke of Father coming here. He could not get a pass without a great deal of difficulty. With much love to him and all.

I am your affectionate Son
Peter

Vredenburgh

Hd. Qrs. 3rd Div. 3rd Corps
September 17, 1863

My Dear Mother

We have moved from our old encampment and as I suppose you have undoubtedly heard of it before this time will write a few lines to relieve any anxiety for my safely. We took up the line of march Tuesday evening at 7 P.M. and marched to the banks of the Rappahannock and encamped on the Northern shore at midnight. I slept in the crotch of a worm fence and slept tranquilly till morning. In the morning we started early and arrived at a point parallel and two miles westward from Culpeper; that night slept on a hillside after partaking of a luxurious supper of green corn, roasted, that being the only meal I had that day since early in the morning. This morning we started again and came here a distance of a couple of miles or so and say 2 miles southeast from Culpeper.

Here we arrived about ten o'clock this morning and were arranged to receive an attack. We are still arranged in line of battle, but how long we are to remain, the Lord and General Meade only know. After this I am going to mess by myself and I won't have to wait starving for any wagon to come up. You understand, the wagons are sometimes miles to the rear of the column, and we frequently arrive at midnight or long after dark at our place of encampment and then can get nothing till the wagons come up. Now I mean to have a small coffee pot, tin cup, frying pan and haversack and travel on my own hook. Let Steve cook you know — wait on me till I finish and then I wait on him, till he expresses himself satisfied. Steve behaves excellently and is perfectly honest. I never think of touching my valise, clothes, papers, or anything except what I carry about me. He does it all. You would laugh to see how Col. Hall and I as well as other officers, generally, affiliate with the niggers. Ever since I and Col. have been in the army the darkies and we have eaten off the same dishes, with the same knives and forks and dipped our own spoons in the sugar and knives in the butter when we had it. Steve carries my canteen and "Josh" (Col.'s Nigger) carries his and when we or they want a drink up goes the canteen to the mouth of the suffering individual. I believe I have got so that I rather like the niggery savor and think of letting Stephen wear my dress coat awhile to impart a pleasant fragrance to it. I now travel with the General and have it much more pleasant than when following the regiment. I can get better fodder for the horses and better quarters for myself as Generals always select the best places for themselves and staffs.

We hear cannonading frequently towards the Rapidan, say 10 miles off, and I am pretty reliably informed that the rebels are this side of the river.

I wish Henry could be here to see us march sometime. I should think it would be about as exciting all the time, as a runaway is at home. We go right across the country here and do not pretend to follow roads as a general thing and to see the artillery and baggage and supply trains work their way over some of the places, is wonderful and exciting. We forded two rivers yesterday; the Rappahannock and the Hazel. The water was not deep, only about up to the middle but the ascent on the opposite side of both the rivers was very steep and dangerous. I saw a battery wagon going along the bank with ten horses to it and one of the hind wheels on the near side went over the edge and away went the wagon down the bank. The wheel horses were thrown up in the air the same as a man could throw up a kitten. The off horse was lifted entirely over the near horse and came down on his back, on the top of the driver who rode the near horse, and stranger than all, he was not killed but I expect terribly injured. I was watering my horse in the Rappahannock at the time and was close to the place. We passed in our march close by the homestead of John Minor Botts. The whole country is fast going to decay. Fields are overgrown with weeds, fences down, plantations deserted, roads that were once great thoroughfares now looking like blind roads, the farms and even the gardens utterly void of cultivation or care. There will be terrible suffering here next winter for those who are left to suffer, and if you could only see it, connected with the abuse, cruelty, extravagance, and demoralization of the army you would pray harder than ever for this "Cruel War" to end.

Peter

Vredenburgh

Hd. Qrs. 3rd Div 3 Corps
September 22, 1863
Before breakfast

Dear Father

I received both of your kind letters and hope to profit by their good advice. The last one I should say was written under rather unfavorable circumstances. We left our position last Tuesday, and marched to this place, about 2 miles west of Culpeper. I have a chance to enjoy a little cure liberty now and very frequently ride up to the town. I can go without asking anyone. We had 8 days rations issued last night to the men and rumor is current that we are going on a reconnaissance in force. Culpeper is on table land [plateau] and you can easily see the Rapidan and 20 miles beyond it.

The rebels are supposed to be on the south bank in force. We will probably move today, the wagons are still running with the rations from the depot to the Brigade commissaries and as soon as the rations are issued I suppose we will start. I expressed $260 to you yesterday. You will have to pay the express as they would not take pay here. I have still about $250 left. Col. Truex is expected on every day. I get letters from him occasionally.

This is very pretty country but sadly depleted by the war and slovenly farming of the inhabitants.

Ever Your Affectionate Son
Peter

Ross

Headquarters 3rd Division, 3rd A.C.
September 24, 1863

Dear Mother

I now am permitted again to write you a few lines but from necessity they will be very few for we are under marching orders and there is no telling where the next half hour may find us. I am still at my old place at these Headquarters enjoying myself as much as can be expected. Charlie Bartruff returned a few days since and said he wished me to express his regrets for not being able to wait and see you. How do you like my likeness? I can never look pleasant in a picture as you can see by that. We are looking anxiously for Colonel and Quartermaster to come back. I suppose if a fight comes off I will be deprived of the pleasure of being in, while I am in my present position. I don't know anything to write about so you must excuse me. Write soon and direct to Hd. Qrs. etc. Love to all from

Your Affectionate Son
Burroughs

Vredenburgh

Hd.Qrs. 3rd Div. 3 Corps
September 30, 1863

Dear Mother

Col. Truex arrived here last night and brought good news from home and that bundle you sent. Steve left yesterday and through my advice, got home. I was afraid he might get used when he comes back. I wish you would please send me some Canton flannel drawers. I don't want the tight ones you know, but the Canton flannel with strings to tie them around the ankles. Have plenty of room to tighten or loosen them around the waist. I wish you would please tell Father to let Steve have what money he wants inside of a $100, and deduct it from what I have sent. I sent my watch home by Steve. Tell Father also that I wish he would deposit $100 of the money in the Freehold Bank as I want to send to New York sometimes, for things and can then pay by sending a check. I sent $14 in a letter the other day to New York to pay for a pair of pants I had gotten and have not heard from it yet.

Ever Your Affectionate Son
Peter

THE BATTLE CRY OF FREEDOM

The insignia with the slogan "The Union Forever" was taken from a common letterhead of the time.
The slogan also begins the chorus to "Battle Cry of Freedom."

The Battle Cry of Freedom by George F. Root, Published by Root & Cady, 1863. Source: The Free
Library of Philadelphia, Music Department.

4 The First Encounter

October 1863 — February 1864

October, 1863, begins with the regiment resting near Culpeper, Virginia, and fully expecting to remain inactive through the winter of '63-'64. However, unbeknownst to the men of the 14th, General Meade had other plans, and their first major engagement of the war rapidly approached.

The front on the Rapidan in Virginia became active in late November, 1863. General George Meade, at the head of the Army of the Potomac, crossed the Rapidan River and took offensive action against Robert E. Lee's Army of Northern Virginia. There was fighting at Raccoon Ford and Morton's Ford. Meade had tried to get Lee to fall back toward Richmond as both armies maneuvered for advantage. On November 27, 1863, there was fighting at Robertson's Tavern or Locust Grove, Catlett's Station, and other nearby locations. The 14th New Jersey Volunteers, part of the 3rd Division 3rd Army Corps, Army of the Potomac, led the advance at Locust Grove. They suffered sixteen killed and fifty eight wounded in their first major engagement. General Morris rode to the front congratulating the men for their bravery and as new troops they could not have fought better, accomplishing everything that was expected of them that day.

The Rixey House — Culpeper, VA (General Birney's Headquarters).

The campaign was not a Union success, however. As General Meade pushed toward the Valley of Mine Run near Locust Grove, General French's Corps, of which the 14th N.J. Volunteers were a part, mistakenly took a wrong road and became engaged with Confederate Jubal Early. With the loss of the initiative, the Federal offensive bogged down. There was additional skirmishing but Lee's position was so strong that assaults were cancelled. For example, Corps Commander Warren called off an assault by his

National Archives

troops on a rebel position. The Army of the Potomac broke off
operations and crossed the Rapidan River to winter quarters.

Harrison

Near Culpeper, Virginia
Thursday Eve. October 1, 1863

Dear Mother

Yours of the 27th Sept came duly to hand this afternoon
and as I have a very small piece of candle I will pen you a few
lines in answer. Although there is no news of any importance
perhaps I can make out a few lines. I was very glad to hear you
recd the check. Well Mother, our Colonel has returned to the
Regiment. The boys were all glad to see the old Gentleman
back again. He came in camp night before last amid cheers &
shouts throughout the Regiment. He appeared highly gratified
with the reception.

Corp Byram isn't likely to be here in a month yet, he has
been down to Culpeper I hear with conscripts since we have
been laying here. I believe I don't want his job bad. I think we
will have rain before morning, it sprinkles a little already. I
feel in hopes we shall have some rain for it is much needed in
these parts, it being very dry and dusty. I haven't heard from
Corp. Charlie White since he went to the hospital, and don't
know what hospital he is at. I thought I would hear from him
before this, but he hasn't written. We expect our Orderly back
in a week or two. Eseck is well, he is on guard at the ammunition train.

All is quiet along the lines there being no signs of an
attack. It is the general belief that this will be our winter
quarters, if nothing serious turns up in the meantime. Give my
best respects to all the neighbors and enquiring friends.

Does Adlum & Cole [Harrison's employer before the war]
do a rushing business? They'll make a fortune I think in the
grocery business in Red Bank if business is as good as when I
was concerned in it.

Well Mother, I have scratched you a sheet full and still my
candle stays with me but it will soon be gone. Sergt Prickett
has just come in my tent, he sends his best respects. Sergt
Foster, Corpl George White, Joseph Hartshorn & myself tent
together. Just step in and take a sly glance at us, you would
see four just as happy "sogers" as there are in these diggings, &
just as good looking! George & I make an agreement about a
week since not to shave our chins until we get home. I present
a fine appearance on Dress Parade already, ha.ha. Please send
me some stamps Mother for I cannot get any here. There is no
danger of the letter getting strayed away as long as we are
laying here still. Capt Goudy of Company F sent in his resignation and it has been accepted. I suppose he will be at home
with his pretty wife in a few days, and Capt Patterson of Co A

has received the commission of Major in the 33rd Jersey so there will be vacancies for some lucky fellows to fill. I believe I am now about written out & my candle will also be out. So I must now bid you good night, and may God bless you all, my love to you & John.

Write soon & I remain Your Affectionate Son
Albert C

Vredenburgh

Hd. Qrs. 3 Div. 3 Corps
October 2, 1863

Dear Mother

The watch you sent me does not run well and I will return it as soon as I can. Please send me a good silver one with a double case to prevent the crystal's breaking. See that it is new. I wish you would go to New York and see Barney Hagerman and tell him to make me a genteel sack coat, very heavy dark blue beaver — deep pockets on both insides as well as out — to button up to the neck, well lined and warm with a single row of buttons in from — for a Major of Infantry. Then get from him, 3 very heavy undershirts and 3 pair of canton flannel drawers, with a buckle behind. He will know what will suit me. Then purchase a toothbrush, a little hair oil, fine tooth comb, some Castile and fancy soap, a good stiff whisk and clothes brush and a largest sized strong valise to put them in. Also a pair of common strong horse blankets — on Courtland Street I believe is a good place.

Never mind the blankets though now. Also tell Barney to let me have a heavy, good sized cape — something dark and appropriate for me. Also please get 2 bunches of tooth picks, one box of Brown's trachces and then let Steve bring the valise to me. I am sorry to trouble you so much. Can't you take Steve to New York with you to carry the valise? If you cannot go to New York yourself just send this letter to Barney Hagerman (with "Smith & Rice" 122 Fulton Street N.Y.) and I guess he will attend to it. I refer you to him because he is pretty sharp and can tell where to get the best things. I want the coat to be handsome — without outside pockets in the breast. Also buy me a couple of pounds of good Killicarrick tobacco. Tell Steve to get me a good horsebrush, mane comb, card and course sponge for the horses. If you cannot go to N. York immediately you had better write to Barney telling him to have the coat and cape ready. Get the thick ribbed flannel shirts if you can find them, also a small black cravat. The drawers I think you had better make than buy as you will likely get them to fit better. I will write to Barney myself today and tell him to make the coat and cape and hold on to them till be hears from you or me. If Steve gets well and is able to be out I wish you would let me know, so that I won't be without a man longer than is necessary. Let him wait though for the valise.

Ever Your Aff. Son (in haste)
Peter

Vredenburgh

Hd. Qrs. 3 Div. 3 Corps
October 4, 1863

Dear Mother

I wish you would send me a good big sponge for myself and none for the horses as I will take my old one for that purpose.
Gen'l Elliott has been ordered to join Rosecrans and Gen'l Carr now commands this Division. The change does not effect me as I am appointed by Gen'l French. Ed Taylor came over to see me today, but I was absent. I will ride over and see him in the morning. Cowart has not arrived here yet.

Affly Your Son
Peter

P.S. I would like to have a large or good-sized flask to carry ardent spirits in, with a cup attached — a glass one surrounded with cullon or leather.

Vredenburgh

Hd. Qrs. 3rd Div. 3 A.C.
October 9, 1863   6 A.M.

Dear Mother

I received your letter of the 3rd inst. late last night. Jim Bedell told me that Steve expected to start on Thursday (yesterday I suppose) I am obliged to you for your suggestion in reference to leaving so much in the Bank. I think $25 will be sufficient, tell Father. We have recd. so many orders to be "ready to move" lately that we do not attach any importance to the orders any more. Last night word was brought that the enemy's cavalry were in our rear, threatening the railroad and we have been on quiver ever since. Today our Div. has a review. Ed Taylor called to see me yesterday but I was absent.

Affectionately,
Peter

Harrison

Camp at Union Mills, Va.
Friday October 16, 1863

Dearest Mother

I expect you are near about worried to death in regard to your absent son in not hearing from him. But of course you must be aware that our army has been on the march and I am safe and sound feeling first rate. Only foot sore as I have marched somewhere in the neighborhood of 75 mile since last Saturday. I wrote you a letter last Saturday night but had no chance of sending it so I made up my mind I would write you a few lines this morning, and have them ready to send the first mail that goes out. Well Mother, I will endeavor firstly to give you a few details of our late march in as few words as possible.

We formed in Line of Battle near our camp at Culpeper last Saturday morning then came orders to march as quick as we could get packed up. So off we went marching about three mile on Sat. halted at the old camp of the 5th Jersey Regt., and were there the remainder of the day, ordered to fit for the night and make ourselves as comfortable as possible, so we put up our tents laid ourselves down to sleep and about ten minutes after we were fixed, orders came to pack up, and be ready to move on. So passing a sleepless night, we started on the march at sunrise, crossed the two branches of the Rappahannock, having to ford one, water up to the middle, and dark as blazes. I tell you it was wild enough but we didn't care for that as we thought after crossing the stream we would park for the night, but nary so, our Regt. had to go on picket, (Sunday night). We were posted about 11 o'clock and then for a fire the first thing. Well we were on picket until Monday night, routed out at 12 o'clock, expected to have a brush with the Johnnies. Our com-

Centreville, VA

pany went out as skirmishers, were called in, in half an hour, started again on the retreat, as you are aware that we have been retreating all the while. And a hard day's march on Tuesday — 25 miles. Parked at night at Green Ridge up by daylight on Wednesday, halted at Bristoe Station & received a mail. (I received your letter) Parked for the night at Bull Run, up again before daylight yesterday & marched through Centreville & halted at Union Mills. This is the position the enemy held when General McClellan was checked here and a strong place it is, it seems almost impregnable, its no wonder he didn't make an attack.

National Archives

Union camp scene.

We shelled a woods last night but the Rebs have not showed themselves.

I don't know how long we will hold this position but I rather think we will stay here the remainder of today, one of the men in our company was shot last night through the leg, (Emily) sent away to hospital [probably Private Theodore E. Imlay, wounded, discharged, January, 1864 at Newark, NJ].

It has been raining all the morning and still continues, but I think it will clear away soon. I don't know whether you can read this or not as I am in a hurry & just simply wish to give you a letter in hand of matters & things in general & I feel as like old Lee will get too much Meade [General George Gordon Meade].

We had fighting in our rear on the whole march but with no serious loss. The Rebs fought hard for our Train & captured part of it, but we recaptured it, also 6 pieces of artillery with it & 700 prisoners. I will send you one of my locks. My hair is getting long. But I don't think I shall have it cut this winter. It curls all around my neck. I comb it back of my ears.

Give my love to John & yourself and remember me to all friends write soon. I close, God bless you.

Your Son,
Sergt Albert C. Harrison

Vredenburgh

Hd. Qrs. 3rd Div. 3rd A.C.

My Dear Mother

I wrote to you last night at ten P.M. This morning at 4 A.M. we started for Bristoe Station a few miles southwest of this station but brought up here and have encamped. We may stay here a month — we may move in five minutes. I have been all the afternoon, busily engaged posting the pickets: that duty the general always imposes on me as I have had considerable experience in that way, and it is a ticklish, dangerous and important trust. While we were at Bull Run a few nights ago, I had the posting of the pickets for the whole corps and at the time we expected to be attacked before or early in the morning. The rebels have deserted this vicinity as far as we can learn, where to turn up next the Lord only knows. I have now seen considerable of the historic grounds of Bull Run, Manassas, Fairfax etc. It is a fine level country and splendidly located for fighting purposes. I passed this morning, the old fortifications and entrenchments constructed by the rebels in 61 and where their "Quaker Guns" held us in check previous to McClellan's advance in the winter of '61. I have not yet seen the spot where the first Bull Run battle occurred.

I am remarkably well and never enjoy more than when on

the march as there is always some excitement then. These moonlight nights are perfectly charming in "the field." We have a very large, cheerful fire built in front of our tents and after supper we, that is the General and staff, bring our chairs out, light our cigars or pipes and while away the hours till long after tattoo, in harmonious conversation, jokes and songs. The soothing effect of the general blaze and lambent moonlight made still more agreeable by the sweet cadence which floats on the night air.

[no signature]

Vredenburgh

Hd. Qrs. 3rd Div. 3A.C. Catlett's Station, Va.
October 21, 1863

My Dear Mother

Sure enough a short time after I wrote to you on the 19th inst. we were ordered to move. We went to Greenwich, thence to this historic spot. The railroad has been completely destroyed by the rebels since we arrived, and we are now to wait here till it is rebuilt — probably a week or so. The rebels heat up the ties, put the rails across the heap and then set it on fire. As the iron rails get heated in the middle they bend with their own weight, thus the ties are burnt and the rails spoiled at the same time. I wish you would write every day, till Steve starts or makes up his mind to stay, as I will keep a look out for him after he once gets on the road.

Ever Your Aff Son
Peter
Give my love to Father

Vredenburgh

Catlett's Station, Va.
October 22, 1863 7 A.M.

Dear Mother

The mail is just starting. Steve arrived 5 minutes ago. He stayed at Col. Truex Hd. Qrs. all night. Everything is right.

Ever Your Affectionate Son
Peter

Vredenburgh

Inspectors Genl's Office
Hd. Qrs. 3rd Div 3rd A.C. Corps
Catlett's Station Va. October 23, 1863

My Dear Father

I received two letters from you and one from Mother yesterday, all dated on the 19th inst. Steve arrived safely yesterday morning with all the things. I was mighty pleased to see him and freely forgave all the inconvenience he had caused me by his absence. The articles suit exactly and I feel a good deal better among my peers when well dressed. It never pays an officer enough to enable him to dress well and it looks mean to see him neglect it.

We are likely to remain here for two or three weeks at least, as the railroad has been completely destroyed from Bristoe Station to the Rapidan. Our Corps will have to quickly rebuild it. I think this last move of the "Grand Army of the Potomac" throws all its other maneuvers in the shade. Meade is now in Washington. My duties on the march and in camp, among other things is to post and visit the pickets. The reason I offer this is I have become acquainted with a number of Jersey families who live in the vicinity. They are loyal people and I have been very kind to them in furnishing safeguards to their property. I mess now with General and dine exquisitely. The people here are very destitute and God only knows how they will survive the coming winter and I can't help but feel sorry for them but I suppose its one of the results of the war. I expected you and Mother to pay for the things I got out of the money I sent. I have paid "Smith & Rice" for everything else I ever got off them except this last bill...

Affectionately Your Son
Peter

Catlett's Station — Orange & Alexandria Railroad.

Wolcott

Catlett's Station
October 24, 1863

My dear old friend Powers

This being the first leisure day I have had since October 10th and I think I cannot pass away the time to a better advantage than writing to you. I will give you some idea of my travels since Oct 10th. The 3rd Corps left Culpeper on the night of Oct 10th between the hours of 8 & 9 o'clock — marched all that night

and until the next morning. 8 o'clock we crossed the Rappahannock and encamped until that night 12 o'clock. We took up our
line of march for Bealton Station where we arrived at 4 o'clock
the next morning. We took aboard a new supply of rations,
then went to bed and slept until 3 o'clock next morning. We
was called up and ordered to be ready to march at daylight. We
got underway at 6 and arrived at Warrenton Junction about 11,
where we laid until the next morning. At 6 o'clock we started
again, at daylight we found that the rebels were closer up on
our heels than we cared for. At the train station we had to
come to a halt, the rebels appearing on our right flank at 12
o'clock our boys opened fire upon them and the fight bid fair at
one time to become a general engagement. The train made off
in single column. The trains reached 35 miles and it took
several hours but our turn came to go. I had a fair chance to
look at the battle. I had a good view of both parties. Our boys
broke at the first charge the rebels made but the officers soon
rallied them again. Our boys made a charge on them and the
rebels ran in turn. Our boys captured some 200 prisoners and 5
pieces of artillery. The rebs were well dressed, better clothed
than I ever saw. Their clothing all being new of a blue-gray
cloth and they had good calf-skin boots instead of shoes which
we are furnished. I asked one of them where they got so good a
boot, they said they came through the blockade. I suppose they
were English made.

Well, about 6 o'clock we got our train moving again. The
rebels were fast retreating toward the woods. Started on a
double quick and went along all night until within 2 miles of
Bull Run. One of our supply wagons broke down. I stayed back
to help fix it up again — in running order. Then it was past
midnight the train was a mile ahead of us but Buford was
behind us with a strong guard. We started off with the wagon
to catch the train. We knew the train would be detained at the
ford — at Wolf Shoal. We was coming into a dense woods when
we heard three guns fired but we paid but little attention to it
— thought it was one of the guards firing off his piece. I was
ahead walking carrying a lantern to light the road up. I going
along with my head down when I saw but a few feet ahead a
cavalry lying in the road. I called out to one of the men in the
wagon (4 of us in all) they came out and took a hold of his wrist
and could just feel his pulse. It was just fluttering and we
unbuttoned his coat and shirt. He was shot through the heart.
We knew that the bushwhackers were around and not far off
and I can tell you I felt a little nervous. I did not know how
soon I would get a ball through me, then I wished I was out of
the army. We put the body in the wagon and started again to
catch the train. I had to pilot the wagon through. I bet the
mules had to run with their load. Good fortune would have it
the train had stopped a few hundred yards ahead. I reported to
Col Truex. Cowart and he sent back a Rgt. of cavalry to picket
the road until Buford should come up. The next morning we
arrived at Fairfax Station. A cavalry belonging to the 4th New
York, he said that 4 of them were going along behind the train
when they were fired upon. One of them fell and he was taken
prisoner and the other 2 got lost by death.

Catlett's Station, VA

It is very cold and stormy today. I wish I could be somewhere where I could have a warm house & fire to go to. I think I could appreciate it, but I must not complain others have to bear with so much too. My house is comprised of a wagon with the storm beating in at both ends. Well Powers, my fingers are so cold I shall have to bring my letter to a halt — front right dress, without doubly, right face, arms a port, break rank.

As Ever Your Friend
Jacob R Wolcott

P.S. Remember me to all inquiring friends, I suppose you have named that boy of yours by this time. When you write you must inform me the name. I have no doubt but that you feel proud. You must give my regards to Mrs. P & the little ones.

Good Bye
JRW

Harrison

Near Catlett's Station Virginia
Tuesday October 27, 1863

Dearest Mother

With pleasure I take up my pen this afternoon to answer yours of the 23rd received by me yesterday and very happy I was to hear from you once again, to hear that you were quite well as this leaves me well & in jovial spirits. Well Mother, when last I wrote we were at Catlett's Station & now we are about two miles from there expecting to move at any moment. When I wrote last I spoke I think of our Brigade being encamped in a splendid place. Well yesterday about sunrise we were leaving those good quarters, marching about half a mile or three quarters of a mile from there our Brigade halted expected to move on, until about two o'clock in the afternoon. I made up my mind we were going to lay there all night so Foster, G. White, Hartshorn & myself went at work & stuck up our shelter tent, & had things comfortable once more. We had just turned in when the order came to pack up and move off immediately, so our anticipated good night's sleep was played & in less than 10 minutes our shelters were down & everything packed & off we went. Then our whole Division was on the move. We came along by the camp of the 1st Division & they were ready to move so I made up my mind that there was an all nights march at hand. But after tripping along for about two miles I was agreeably disappointed by seeing the old Colonel ride down the line and order the men to close up in four ranks. Then came the welcome command to halt, (fix bayonets), stack arms & rest. So we laid ourselves down & slept, were routed out this morning at daylight, got our break-

fast & expected to move right off but it is now nearly sunset &
no move yet. The boys have all got their tents up again but how
long we will stay it is hard to tell. We may lay here two or
three days & we may be off in fifteen minutes. The sky is
overcast & I shouldn't wonder the least if we had a few flakes
of snow before tomorrow morning, for it is very cold. I froze last
night. I am sitting before my tent by the fire, writing, the boys
are running with wood & in fine spirits. I would much rather
see this kind of weather than to have it so warm. It makes us
lively as crickets.

The lock of hair looks natural Mother, you must not worry
Mother when I tell you of our hard marches, for it is nothing
more than can be expected of a soldier's life & if it don't worry
me, you need not for if I was out of my time today I should
enlist again. Remember our ForeFathers, how they suffered for
the cause of Freedom. Must we not fight manfully with the
help of the most High God to maintain it. (Yes) In God is my
strength. Let us ever look, He will supply our wants & bind up
the wounded spirit. You want to know what we do with our
things when we are on the march. Well Mother, they are not
carried in wagons I'll assure you. As our shoulders are broad
enough to carry all we have to carry. We take our houses &
grub on our backs, in our knapsacks & haversacks. I think if I
don't hurry up with my letter I will be covered with ashes.
There comes Eseck. He sends his love, he is still on guard at
the Ammunition Train. I must answer some more of your
questions. You want to know what we do with the Rebs after
we capture them. Why treat them as prisoners of war. Send
them off to the nearest prison. Fort Delaware for instance,
until they can be exchanged or paroled, and now I must close
or I will be too late for the mail so I close with love to you &
John & remember me to any who may enquire.

Good Night
Albert C.

Vredenburgh

Office of the Acting Ass. Insp. Genl
Hd. Qrs 3rd Div. 3rd A.Corps
In the field near Bealton Station, Va.
October 30, 1863 10:00 P.M.

Dear Father

I received your letters, speaking of the $5.20 purchase,
and also one from Mother, two or three days ago. We moved
here today, and seem likely to remain for a few days. We have
changed the location of Hd. Qrs. three times since I last wrote.
The enemy are reported a mile and a half in front of us about
10,000 strong, but from our late movements I don't think we
will come in collision with them soon. We made many narrow
escapes though on our retrograde movement from Culpeper.

Lee, in person, arrived at Greenwich an hour and ten minutes after we left, where he arrested a deserter who told him that our army was concentrating at Bristoe Station. Lee then held on for Ewell's Corps to come up and that occasioned a delay that enabled us to elude him. On our march from the Warrenton Branch Railroad to Greenwich we could see the dust and wagons of the Confederates off about 6 miles to our left.

The rebels completely destroyed the Orange and Alexandria railroad from Bristoe Station to the Rappahannock and have even removed all the iron from Bealton to the said river for the purpose of making horseshoes. It is now however, reconstructed as far as Warrenton Junction. I shouldn't be much surprised if we turned up soon at Falmouth. I bought a field-glass the other day for $10, so don't buy any for me. My things all suit me exactly and I am now existing very comfortably. The General is very friendly and seems to have a good deal of confidence in me.

Ever Your Aff. Son
Peter

A scout has just galloped by towards Corps Hd. Qrs. from the front and from his speed he must have important communication. We may move in twenty minutes.

Peter

Vredenburgh

Hd. Qrs. 3rd Div. 3 A.C.
November 2, 1863 9 P.M.

Dear Mother

I received yours of the 30th inst tonight. If you have not yet purchased the towels don't do it as I have sent to Washington for them, but if you have gotten them, then send about 1/2 a doz. by mail. Leave one end of the package open and the postage will only amount to a few cents. All the sick from the army have been sent to Washington and 8 days rations have been issued to the troops so that we will move tomorrow or next day. Gen'l Carr told me tonight that we would advance and throw down the gauntlet and the enemy could picket up if he chose to, which literally interpreted means that we will cross the Rappahannock and take position, if possible and let the enemy attack if advisable. The pontoons came up tonight, so that we may move any moment. Our pickets are frequently attacked, and from the force the rebels must have had to have so utterly demolished this railroad, I think they are strong enough to offer open battle. If they do not then we will probably move towards Falmouth. Sunday is always my busy day, from morning till night. I am inspecting trains, camps etc and making reports upon my investigations. Otherwise, Sunday passes off as every other day. The same work, the same details, the same levity and the same music. And I candidly assure you it is more bother to remember the day of the week, than of the month.

I will write at every opportunity if we move. With love to all, I remain your affectionate Son

Peter

Don't show my scraps to anyone out of the family.

Harrison

Near Bealton Station, Va.
November 3, 1863

Dearest Mother

I will take up my pen this evening to drop you a few lines in answer to yours of the 30th which came duly to hand also the Standard & their contents.

Well Mother, since last I wrote nothing has transpired worth my mentioning. Oh yes, I am sorry to say I was too hasty. A load of boxes came in camp this afternoon & there happened to be one for one of my tent mates, J.W. Hartshorn. It was from home and the most of the articles were eatables, comprising jelly cake, sponge cake, pound cake, sausage, preserves, pickles, apples & cider. Well there is no use in talking I am full up to the neck. Oh yes, there was some first rate butter. I forgot that, well we just had a first class Jersey supper. I am now smoking some of Conny Osonoce, it is very good. Please thank Conny for his kindness & I also thank my Mother for sending it, as there are four of us that tent together. You see the four cigars just fit, ha.ha. It is warmer tonight than it has been in some time heretofore. I think in all prob- ability we will have rain before many hours. It is likely we will move from here before long. I rather thought last night that we would move on today. But we didn't as it happened. I was over to the 2nd Division yesterday afternoon & saw Lieut. John Sowder, Capt. Sleeper & Jeff Thompson. I took supper with Jeff, they are all well. I also saw John H. Smith. He was around as usual, also John Mount from Long Branch. I guess John knows him. [These men were members of the 11th N.J. Volunteers]

Well Mother, I can tell you in double quick time where I would rather be, that is just where I am most likely to get a shot at the Johnnies (that's where I live). What kind of a soldier would I be if I was afraid of danger & hardship. I wouldn't give a pinch of snuff for any such soldier as that. They are no good to our country. I have not seen to tell the truth as much hardship as I expected when I left home. And I thank God that it has been no worse. I feel that I have been richly blessed. Not myself only but my dear Mother also. I feel to thank God most fervently that you have been spared to me. I believe there is nothing that I need at this present time. But if we ever get in winter quarters I think I shall call for a box, so if you should happen to go to New York any time between now & freezing weather you can get something from Aunt Clemming perhaps or Uncle Henry seems to be well up in the Market. But I must now bring my letter to a close by bidding you good night & may God bless you all & keep you firm in the Faith.

Your loving Son
Albert

Vredenburgh

Headquarters 3rd Div. 3rd A.C.
November 6, 1863

Dear Mother

I received your letter of November 3rd last night and the towels at the same time. I had already sent to Washington for some but I can easily let some one else take them from the sutler who is to bring them. George Patterson arrived tonight with Col. Hall's servant. I wrote to Capt. Conover who is now at home to bring me a bottle or two of apple whiskey and if Henry has any of the same that he had before I left, I wish he would let Capt. have some if he calls for it. I am not very particular, that is not enough to put anyone to any inconvenience. How I should like to be home now to enjoy the shooting but I am afraid that my shooting this fall will be entirely confined to larger game. There are quantities of rabbits, quails, and grey squirrels here but it is contrary to orders to discharge fire arms in this vicinity. The enemy was supposed to be in force in front of us and this side of the Rappahannock yesterday and we have been under marching orders for the last two days, but we may stay now a few days longer.

Your Affectionate Son
Peter

Vredenburgh

Hd. Qrs. 3rd Div. 3rd A. Corps
November 6, 1863 12 o'clock midnight

Dear Mother

I wrote to you early in the evening but since then we have received orders to move at 6 o'clock tomorrow morning, and attack the enemy at Kellys Ford, if necessary to effect a crossing there. One Brigade is to be thrown across the ford immediately upon our arrival to hold the place while the pontoons are being laid. Kellys Ford is distant eight or ten miles from here and the rebels have been in some force between here and that point since our short and happy sojourn. Gen'l French commands the left wing of the army now, and consequently Maj. Gen'l Birney now commanding the 1st Div. in this Corps will take command of the Corps.

I have never since I left Maryland Heights felt any apprehension of injury though having been frequently in position where an engagement seemed certain to occur. Nor do I now have any more anxiety or thought of being killed or wounded than if going with Henry, over to Bob Crawfords, to shoot quails. I believe the same state of feelings is prevalent throughout the army, as the men and officers always seem pleased when an action is contemplated. I will write you the first opportunity after the march.

With love to all
I am your Affectionate Son
Peter

Vredenburgh

Hd. Qrs. 3rd Div. 3rd A.C.
Brandy Station Va.
November 10, 1863

Dear Father

I received yours of the 4th inst. this morning. I have written frequently during the last week and I suppose you have heard from me by this time. We are likely to remain here a few days. I was under fire the other day and several were killed and wounded around me, four I think, and there may have been more. The skirmishers in battle have a very dangerous duty to perform. They are the men, thrown out in advance (say a half or 3/4 of a mile) and having taken intervals of 4 or 5 yards, advance to "feel" the enemy. The enemy do likewise of course and then the skirmishers have a succession of quasi-duels, no man knows what bush, tuft of grass, or hillock may conceal his deadly foe, but onward they must go till routed by a charge of superior numbers, cavalry or checked by artillery.

I am ex-officer on Gen'l Carrs' staff so that you can keep track of me in this collateral light, without I may make tracks so fast that the devil himself couldn't follow. I was among the foremost in our late, gallant advance upon Washington. You ask about the pickets. They are the guards thrown furthest out towards the enemy to prevent an attack or surprise. They are usually put about a mile from the camp or main body, three men on a post, with a sergeant or corporal, and the posts are from 50 to 150 yards apart. They are the only safeguard to the main body of troops and have to be placed and instructed in their duties with a great deal of care. The enemy are sometimes a mile or two and others not a hundred yards from our own pickets.

Of course, all depends upon the proximity of the troops and the nature of the ground. Any arrangement you make with what little funds I send home will suit. I will send a hundred or so more in a few days. I received Maria Brinckerhoff's letter this morning too, with yours and will answer it very soon.

Your Affectionate Son
Peter

Ross

Hd. Qrs. 3rd Div. 3rd Corps
Brandy Station, Va.
November 11, 1863

Dear Father

As the past week has been a very exciting one to the Army of the Potomac, and especially to our division, I will give you a few particulars in regard to our movements. On Saturday, the 7th inst. we struck tents and moved toward the Rappahannock. The 1st Division, in advance. We arrived at Kelly's Ford about 11 o'clock where we found the enemy posted on the opposite side, in rifle pits and behind a brick wall opposite the ford. The 1st Division rushed across the ford and captured 400 prisoners, together with their breastworks. Our batteries belonging to the 3rd Division firing over their heads into the woods to prevent a strong force from advancing, which they had there. About dark, our Division crossed on a pontoon bridge and took up position about half a mile from the river, on the left of the 1st Division. Nothing occurred during the night, and in the morning our Division was put in front. So about daylight we started after the rebs in the direction of Brandy Station. We had not advanced more than 5 miles when we came upon their pickets, so we halted, threw out a line of skirmishers, and drove them about a mile over a very high hill.

Brandy Station, VA

When our main line reached the hill, we found the enemy posted with artillery and infantry, on another hill about half a mile in advance, so we threw out skirmishers, and advanced in line of battle, our skirmishers commenced firing, and our battery threw the shell into them in profusion, and they returned the compliment in good style, knocking three men out of the 138th Pa. the first shot.

General Carr, who

commands our Division, at present, was standing on the hill watching the proceedings and as he had the Division flag with him they of course supposed it must be some general and they turned their battery on him and his staff, when their shells came over our heads thick and fast, as I was riding along with the rest of them and wanted to see the fun. The General told us to separate, so we got out of range pretty soon. One shell struck about 11 feet from me but did not explode.

All the houses along the road are deserted except by perhaps an old negro woman or man. One house I went up, when we came up, the rebs had been using it for a hospital. The floor was covered with blood, and on a table in the front room lay a man's arm, which had just been amputated.

We advanced to this place, where we halted firing and skirmishing all the way here. We are now 5 miles from Culpeper and 30 miles from where we started on Saturday. Since writing this letter I received one from Capt. Conover, from Mother. In answer to her questions, I will say that I am still as well as ever, sleep very well at night, as I have as many blankets as I want, and get enough to eat. Although when we were on the advance, our wagons were left.

[no signature]

Harrison

At Brandy Station, Virginia
November 12, 1863

Dear Mother

Yours of the 4th came duly to hand and I was very happy to hear from you. To hear that you were well. I am on duty today but I guess I can have time to write you a few words. I am on the Brigade Headquarter Guard. I have my guards housed in an old dilapidated building which is a little the worse for wear. I wrote to you three or four days ago stating that we were again on the march and we still remain in the same vicinity we were when I wrote, at Brandy Station. At some former time this has been quite a nice little place, there has been about 20 houses but some of them are no more.

Dear me, the wind blows through my shanty and fills

Brandy Station, VA

U.S. Army Military History Institute

my eyes full of ashes, for I have a fireplace in one corner. One of the men has been over to camp & says the paymaster has made his appearance & also that Colonel Cook is there. So I shall send you $20.00 & then you can get your spectacles Mother. You had better not send any of that to the Bank for you may want to use some. And I may want to send for some things if we ever stop for winter. It is quite a pleasant day but yesterday & the day before I can tell they felt like winter. It froze very thick ice night before last.

I must now close, write soon. I cannot tell how long we will lay here. But I think we will move on in a day or two if it isn't too cold & don't storm.

I remain Your Loving Son
Albert

Stults

Camp Near Culpeper Court House, Va.
November 23, 1864

Dear Ma

It is rumored in camp that a general movement is afoot and that we will likely move this afternoon, or tomorrow quite certain. We are provided once more with new eight day's rations, which is enough to show that something is going on. Which way we will go I know not. It has been supposed that we should attempt a crossing at some of the fords of the Rapidan River. Now it is rumored that we will go down to Falmouth and cross there. We will know when we get there. It is reported here that Butler has a large force near the White House but on the Peninsula Route. If I were to prophesize that Butler's and Meade's forces were intended to unite at some point with the intention of capturing Richmond, I might not miss, then perhaps I might.

I have in store a stock of provisions for the march. Ham, bread, and you can judge that eight days rations are not a trifle in weight, or bulk, besides I must necessarily carry rubber and woolen blankets, besides accoutrements. The men are well supplied with winter clothing.

I haven't received a letter from you in a long time. I received gloves last night, very good pair of cotton gloves lined, a good article. Send also a package of envelopes, the best in the market. Buff

*General Meade's Headquarters —
Culpeper, VA.*

and I want very bad some baking soda or something of the kind, if it can be sent. No troops have moved up near us. We drill at 2.30 P.M. My respects to all — my health is good

Marcus

Vredenburgh

Hd. Qrs. 3rd Div. 3 A.C.
November 25, 1863 9 P.M.

Dear Mother

Owing to the unfavorable weather we did not move this morning as expected, but every sign indicates that we will be off early in the morning. The artillery is moving by and the yelping, hallowing and swearing of the teamsters make a lively noise outside. Since I have been at Hd. Qrs. I have occupied a tent with the Medical Director of the Division and have become very intimate and friendly with him. We pass the evenings alone together and prove to be very congenial. You perhaps would like to hear how we both live in one small tent. I used to think two tents hardly large enough — we have our beds in this shape — heads together, the stove towards the door and table as you see at the foot of my cot with three pipes, two whiskey bottles, two tin cups, a box of cigars and writing material on it. The floor is constructed of damp ground and if anything drops it drops in the dirt. Steve makes an excellent valet de chambre and helps me always to don though never to doff my good clothes. You would hardly believe how scrupulously clean and neat I always keep it here — much more so that I ever did at home. And I suppose it is hardly necessary for me to state that your predictions about my becoming lousy have proved false. Nary a "pinch back" or "broad white belly" has had the audacity to attack me yet — though the soldiers have had lively times with them. Nothing is more common than to see a soldier in a semi-nude condition sitting on a hassock scrutinizing and you can generally congratulate him for his successful efforts.

They say we will have a fight this time with the rebels before we cross the Rapidan and many will cross the Jordan first. If any accident should occur to me, my first and last thoughts will be of you and Father. But I have no apprehensions, though I suppose is as dangerous, perhaps more so than in the ranks — as my duties as aid are incessant and ubiquitous on the field. The General frequently compliments me by asking my advice about the position of the troops and adaptability of the ground. I most always select their camping ground and move their camps as I think proper, within the proper distance. I have authority to order the Brig. Genls in this Division to change their ground, if I wish, but I always of course, say "by command of Gen'l Carr."

Your Affectionate Son
Peter

Ross

Headquarters 1st Brig. 3rd. Div. 3rd A.C.
In the Field near Mine Run, Virginia
December 1, 1863

General Order

The Brigade Commander deems it his gratifying duty to express to the officers and men of the 14th N.J. Vols. commanded by Colonel Wm S. Truex, his appreciation of their bravery and endurance throughout the engagement on the 27th of November. The occasion was one which presented the perils of the battlefield in the most discouraging form. It was necessary to form the line of battle in a dense woods and at the base of a hill, with the enemy in position on its crest, protected by breastworks.

The Regiment was under fire for three hours and for a portion of that time the crossfire of the enemy rifles made rapid and terrible havoc in the ranks. Its duty being to hold the line without advancing beyond a limited distance. The Regiment performed its entire mission, and drove the enemy from the crest, and held it until their ammunition exhausted and the veterans of the 1st Division arrived to relieve them. Our distinguished Division and Corps commanders have spoken of the Regiment in terms of high commendation. The Brigade Commander is proud to lead such gallant and patriotic hearts.

By Command of Brig. Gen'l Morris
M. Leonard Acty. Adjt. Genl.

The above order is one published to the Brigade by Brig. Genl. Morris showing his appreciation of the manner in which our Regiment fought on the 27th of November at the Battle of Locust Grove Va.

Wm. B. Ross
Sergt Major

Vredenburgh

Hd. Qrs 3rd Div 3 A.C.
December 4, 1863

My Dear Father

I suppose you all feel considerable anxiety after my safety
and therefore hasten to inform you of the same. You cannot
depend at all upon the accounts you see in the papers of our
engagement. On the 23rd inst. an order was issued from Army
Hd Qrs. that on the 24th at 7 A.M. the 2nd Corps would proceed to Germania Ford on the Rapidan — the 3rd and 6th to
Jacob Mills (3 miles above) the 5th to Germania too and the 1st
to Culpeper Ford a few miles further above. It rained so on the
24th, that the troops did not start till light on the 26th inst.
and we (the 3rd) arrived at the Ford about 2 P.M. We found a
few of the enemy's skirmishers at the Ford but they retired and
allowed us to build our pontoon bridge, though one Brigade
could have detained us for hours if they had wanted to and a
few thousand could have kept us at bay till the crack of doom. I
thought, it looked suspicious at the time. We all crossed safely
by dusk and moved on a couple of miles though a dense wilderness when we discovered ourselves on the wrong road and
returned to the Ford and bivouacked. On the following morning, we took up the march and steered toward "Robertson's
Tavern" (the point where all the army was destined to meet),
but had proceeded but a short distance when we found the 2nd
Div. of our corps halted in front of us and we therefore halted
too.

We waited here about 2 hours when we heard artillery
firing off to the left about 3 miles which showed that Warren
(of the 2nd Corps) had crossed and was feeling the enemy. A
few minutes afterwards, we heard the booming of cannon to
our right which told us that the 1st corps had crossed and met
the enemy's skirmishers. Now or but a very few minutes afterwards, before our own skirmishers commenced firing, and we
were all immediately ordered forward. We went about a half a
mile, still in the woods, when the column was halted and the
2nd Division deployed (i.e.) put in line of battle in two ranks
and advanced a half a mile to our front. Gen'l Carr ordered me
to go and see how the line was formed and learn the direction
of the line. I found the 2nd Div. in line in a dense wood fronting
towards Orange C.H. I could not see the cleared land which I
was told was some distance in front of them. The firing at that
time was very brisk among the skirmishers and though an
occasional bullet would whistle by the reserves, none of the
soldiers firing could be seen from where I was. I reported to
Gen'l Carr and he immediately ordered me to take the Division
and put them in line of battle on the left of the 2nd division
joining them with our right and extend our left over far enough
to join with Warren's right, if possible. I conducted Gen'l
Morris command of our right Brigade towards the left of the
2nd Div. but before I reached the left, the firing had ceased to a

certain extent, and I received orders by an aid from Carr to halt the column. While standing, talking to Gen'l Morris, the firing opened again with vigor among the skirmishers and Gen'l sent me another order to go on and form the line as quickly as possible. I immediately told Morris where to go and saw him get his 1st Battalion in line and order the 14th N.J. (his 2nd Battalion) in position. I then went back to meet the 2nd Brigade which had been ordered on, for the purpose of conducting that to its position.

As I came with the 2nd Brigade, near where I had left the 1st Brigade, I saw it had moved further through the woods and was firing very sharply. The bullets began to whistle past or rather thick. Col. Kieffer, commanding the 2nd Brigade, wanted to put his men in line of battle but I would not allow him to do so and rode forward to find exactly where the left of Morris' Brigade was, so that the right of the 2nd could be established, (recollect the woods was as thick as could be and you could not see a 100 yards in any direction). I found the 14th N.J. just coming into line on the left of Morris' first regt. Col. Truex was at this time, at the head (on foot) of his regiment and led them right up to their position in the line, as bravely as a man could do. Col. Hall had his proper place, smoking his pipe, the firing at that time was increasing in intensity in geometrical proportion and the Col. and all his men fell down on the ground till they might get the order to fire. I had left my horse about twenty yards to the rear, in a ravine, and now as I had discovered the position of the 1st. Brigade, hurried back to Kieffer to bring him up. But if I attempt to enter into details, I will never get through with this letter, and will therefore say, that the 2nd Brigade and finally the 3rd. came along and took their proper positions.

The firing all the time increasing rapidly and extending gradually from right to left, so that by the time the 3rd Brigade was in position the firing had extended along the line. I should add that by this time the (our) line had reached the edge of the woods and formed about 10 yards behind a worm fence on the right while the left had taken a course around the edge of a hill in a horseshoe form or rather forming an "L" with the other two brigades.

The rebels were across a field, partially cleared, but their actual line was at this time hidden almost entirely by the scrub oaks. The firing now became terrific and the artillery beginning to open, it seemed as if hurricanes, thunder and earthquakes were striving with each other to make the most uproar. Gen'l Carr was back in the woods about 250 yards and kept his aids riding backwards and forwards to find how his line was kept up and report progress. I remained on the line all the time sometimes near one brigade and sometimes near another. I was not at as much risk if the ground had been cleared but thousands of balls passed near me mostly over my head and many a poor devil was hit far in the background.

The 14th acted most heroically and stood two distinct charges of the rebels. Their high state of discipline made them stick to the Col. and he and Col. Hall and many of the line officers behaved as well as men could have done. I recollect once the right regiment of the 2nd Brigade turned from a charge of the rebels and would have run right through the 14th, when Col. Truex ordered, "Charge Bayonets" and the 14th did so and turned the fleeing regiment and the rebels too. Col. Truex was the one officer who showed any skill in the whole field. For instance, Gen'l French ordered Gen'l Carr to put his troops in position etc. Gen'l Carr did not look at the ground nor know about it but sent me and I did all that part of the duty with advice or command, while Gen'l Morris never gave a single command to his troops. Now Father, how can you expect our army to accomplish anything if managed in this way? What I write about my part of the duties I do not mean in a braggadocio sense, and I would not want to tell you an untruth. But I write confidentially the facts to you knowing full well that none else will hear of it.

Now we failed to gain a decisive victory that day because there was no officer present where the battle was, in seeing distance, who had authority to command, "Forward." Three or four times the rebels were checked and routed in disorder, yet our men had to let such golden opportunities for a rush slip because none would say, "Forward Boys." Our Gen'l instead of giving me directions to take the Divisions and put them on the left of the 2nd Division in the same line, should have gone down himself and seen the country in person, and not have trusted to the reports of his staff officers.

At dark the firing ceased very suddenly. The 6th Corps had formed a 2nd line of battle in rear of our line and at dark the woods was alive with stragglers, skulkers, the wounded etc. I was roaming through the woods, till 10 o'clock looking for the 3rd Brigade which retreated early in the action and did not behave well. It is commanded by Col. Smith, son of Horace Smith, from Trenton who used to shoot with me — you know. It was terrible to see the wounded, and many a poor fellow would cry out to me for help but I could not leave to assist him. All old officers say they never heard musketry more fierce, not even in the battles of Antietam and Gettysburg. You can imagine 16,000 men on our side alone, all firing as fast as they could.

We started the next morning at light, southeasterly evading the battleground (though the enemy had evacuated) struck off to Robertson's Tavern again, we having been at the time we commenced the engagement, on the wrong road. We arrived at Robertson's Tavern at 4 P.M. and thence proceeded a couple of miles or so and took position in front of the enemy's entrenchments — facing towards Orange Court House, at nine o'clock at night. Gen'l told us we would see a severe fight in the morning and as it was Sunday we fully believed his predictions. In the morning, I went up to the crest to view the rebels, and sure enough a mile in front of us was their long line of rifle pits and artillery in position. Now I readily derived why they had let us cross the Rapidan so easily, and why they had contested so severely our passing their flank on the wrong road. They wanted us to come on the plank road and had accomplished it. Our position at this time was; the 2nd Corps on the left of the 3rd Regt. The 1st Corps next on the right of us, the 6th next

General Gouverneur K. Warren USA (left) and General George G. Meade USA (right).

and on the extreme right, while the 3rd Corps held in reserve in rear, the whole time. The skirmishers on both sides could be seen apparently just beneath us and I watched them with the glass, for hours the firing between them was kept up all the time and I could distinguish every motion with the glass. And to see the men on opposite sides sneaking up, invisible to each other, till the deadly missile was sent, yet plain to me I could hardly refrain from riding down, on my horse and telling our men where their foe was concealed. This was kept up for three days you see, and I would watch this skirmishing by the hour.

We remained thus all day Sunday when Gen'l Warren told Meade that he could take the right flank of the enemy (he was on our left you recollect, I mentioned) and it was all arranged, that on the next morning at 8 A.M. artillery was to open on our right by Sedjwick (6th Corps) then by the 1st, 3rd, and 2nd successively. At the same time Warren was to charge the enemy's right the 3rd corps the right center, the 1st and 6th Corps the points (simultaneously) opposite to them and thus there was to be a grand artillery opening followed by a terrific charge along the whole line — but Alas! At 12 midnight, Warren sent word that he must have more troops etc. the 2nd and 3rd Divisions of our Corps started at 2 in the morning (and most bitter cold it was) to join Warren. At 8 o'clock as true as gospel, the artillery opened on the right, then it approached gradually our position, till all along the line there was a continuous fire of artillery, though the rebels did not reply at all (with a few exceptions). We, that is the 2nd and 3rd Division of the 3rd Corps and the whole of the 2nd Corps were waiting behind a small piece of woods (all closed in mass) for the little word, "Forward." but it did not come. Finally Meade came down and he and Warren talked earnestly sometime. Warren told him that he found the enemy with 18 guns in position and the rebels all wide awake in line of battle behind their entrenchments at daylight. And that he did not attack because he thought he could not carry their works. Meade looked excessively chagrined and in a little while the two divisions of the 3rd Corps were marched back again to their encampment.

All day Tuesday, we kept in the same position and on Tuesday evening we started at 6 o'clock and marched all night, crossed the Rapidan at 4 and bivouacked for a couple of hours on the north bank. We started the next day at 6 o'clock, went a mile, stopped two hours, went another mile, stopped an hour or two, and thus fooled along the road, delayed at one time by a train — their artillery, then other troops, and finally ended with starting fairly on our course for Brandy Station at midnight. And marching all night along another road and reaching Brandy Station at daylight the next morning making just a week since we started.

I have not tried to write more or read this over. I have a half a dozen reports to make out between this and tomorrow night and have scribbled this off — "Said Source". I never supposed mortals could stand what our soldiers have. The wagons were not allowed to cross the Rapidan — so we slept in the open airs every night without covering, save our overcoats, and right on the ground with only an india rubber blanket under us and the weather has been actually piercing all the time. I bore a good deal but the rank and file bore five times as much. Poor Joe Lake has had his left arm taken off. Our Regt lost say 64 killed and wounded. I have just recd. a letter from you dated Nov. 29th, one from Jim and one from Mother.

Affectionately Your Son
Peter

PS. 2 of my inspectors out of three were killed

Wolcott

Camp At Brandy Station Va
December 4, 1863

My Dear Old Friend Powers

I received your letter of the 21st on the 25th. I was glad to hear from you. This is the first opportunity I have had to write since I received it. We left Brandy Station on the 26th. The troops crossed the river and encamped for the night. The next morning they took up their line of march on the Richmond Turnpike where near King's Farm the skirmish line met the enemy and commenced to skirmish with them. The rebs falling back slowly until about 11 o'clock. The 3rd Division came up and relieved the 1st Division. The rebs making a stand and the fire became hotter and the artillery opened on both sides. The 14th laid behind a rail fence and the 122nd Ohio had the front line until one o'clock. The enemy fire became so hot that the Ohio Rgt broke and turned to run. When Colonel Truex ordered the 14th to fix bayonets and charge — the 122nd Ohio turned back to their work but the rebels came on at a bayonet charge. Colonel Truex with sword in one hand and a pistol in the other, in front of the Regt. drove the rebels back over the fence, killing & wounding a great many of the rebs. The 14th held their position until their ammunition had run out when they were relieved by the 10th Vermont of our Brigade. Our Division fought all day until late in the evening when the rebels fell back and left their dead & wounded in our hands. Our Regt. lost 15 killed and 47 wounded & 5 missing — 4 or 5 have died since. Co. B had 4 wounded and none killed. The 14th stood better than Gen Carr thought they would. He came up to Col

Truex and congratulated him on the bravery of the 14th and told him he had saved the 3rd Division from a disgraceful stampede by his coolness and quietness in rallying the 122nd Ohio when they broke. If they had been permitted to run back on the 2nd Division the whole Corps would have been forced back upon the 2nd Corps. The rebs took the advantage at once and threw their Regts. against the 14th but the 14th proved themselves made of good stuff.

On Saturday morning the rebels could not be found. We buried our dead then took up line of march for Orange Court House looking for the enemy — gone about 5 miles when the pickets found them behind strong earthworks. Gen French ordered the Corps to halt and drew them in line of battle and awaited orders from Gen Meade but for some reason they did not make an attack that day.

On Sunday Gen French was to take the batteries in front of his line and French detailed the 3rd Division for that purpose. The 1st Brigade was to charge the front, the 2nd Brigade was to go on the left and the 3rd Brigade on the right and each Brigade had orders to fire upon each other if they faltered. It was certain death for the Brigade charging the front. The rebels had a battery of 6 guns in front and right behind that another and on the front battery they had stakes pointed and set so that our boys could not get to the guns before the rebs could fire — and mow them all down. 8 o'clock came and with it a death like stillness as everyone in our Brigade did not expect to get to the battery or back again and it made them feel rather sober. 8 o'clock has passed and 9 o'clock is at hand and the 2nd Corps has not commenced to open yet. Gen French had deployed his skirmishers and can see the rebel pickets in two groups of a dozen some are stamping their feet to get them warm and right in front is 24 cannons looking you in the face. 10 o'clock has come and down came Gen Meade and he seemed very much excited because the battle has not commenced. Gen Warren and French said they could not take more than 200 men in the works alive. So both armies stood facing one another all day and soon as it became dark the troops started back to the river, crossed at 3 o'clock on Tuesday morning and we got back to Brandy Station Thursday morning about 9 o'clock tired out. I thought I would have a good sleep. I've had only one night's sleep since last Thursday — week, but I was ordered up out of my bed at 9 o'clock. The rebels were reported to be crossing in three different places and we must get our trains to the rear. We worked until morning — the news came that our boys had driven them again. But I should try and take a good sleep tonight I am almost

Union burial detail.

U.S. Army Military History Institute

asleep now. Lt. Col. Hall saw one of our boys fall and he ran to him and took his gun and accoutrements and took his place in the ranks — fought like a brave boy — when the boys saw that I tell you that they jumped into it and returned the enemy fire in good earnest. I must close and go to bed I am so sleepy I can hardly keep awake — love to all inquiring friends.

Yours Truly
J R Wolcott

P.S. I saw in yesterday's Baltimore American a quotation from the Richmond Enquirer that the rebels drove the Yankees back from five miles. All I have got to say is that they lie. We drove them and they left the battlefield and their dead & wounded in our hands — that looks as if they had drove us? Good Night. Once more I wish you would send me one of the Trenton papers that has the account of the battle in it. I have little faith in the newspaper reporters. They generally keep in a safe distance — all the news they get is what someone tells them.

J R W

Winter Quarters 1863-1864

Shortly after the Battle of Locust Grove, the Fourteenth New Jersey Volunteers retired to winter quarters at Brandy Station, Virginia on the site of an old rebel encampment. Of the nearly nine hundred men who had set out from Freehold in September, 1862, nearly one hundred had died of sickness, sixteen had been killed in battle, some were on detached service, others hospitalized and a few deserted, leaving a total of approximately six hundred men fit for duty.

Unfortunately, the above letter from Jacob R. Wolcott, dated December 4, 1863, was the last of the collection. Private Wolcott continued to serve with the 14th Regiment throughout 1864, before taking ill in the winter of '64-'65. Private Wolcott died in January 1865, with official records indicating "heart disease" as the cause of death, and was buried at Poplar National Cemetery at Petersburg, VA.

During the winter of '63-'64, a deep religious revival swept through the Regiment. It included all faiths and was under the direction of Chaplain Frank B. Rose. Several churches and places of worship were erected. Sergeant Albert C. Harrison's correspondence reflects these deeply held religious convictions, citing prayer meetings, Testament readings, etc.

The men were well supplied by organizations such as the Sanitary Commission and settled into the routine of camp life.

Wounded at Culpeper, VA.

Vredenburgh

Hd. Qrs. 3rd Div. 3rd A.C.
December 6, 1863   9 P.M.

My Dear Mother

I received yours of the 2nd inst. and was surprised to hear about poor Peter Strong. I wish you would tell me what the cause of the separation is, between him and his consort. Nothing could have surprised me more. Tell Jim, not to join the 34th, he will always regret it. It will just interfere with his studies and it may probably change his whole future career. Col. Truex (as I wrote to Father tonight) is making application for Brig. Gen'l and says if he gets it, will take Jim on his staff.

I wish Mother, you would send me a box, with some apples, and apple whiskey in. Buy the whiskey off Henry, or at some other store and have it put up in a common box and labeled plainly. We are now encamped within 2 miles of Culpeper and our Hd. Qrs. are in a fine large house in the rear of the troops. The Medical Director and I have a large room upstairs, with a fireplace and everything is lovely. I wish you would send me a few lemons too in the box. Everybody is getting boxes but I always thought it more bother than they were worth. But if you are willing, to take to trouble, I am willing to bear the expense and risk of loss. I would like some tobacco too, in the box.

Your Affectionate Son
Peter

Vredenburgh

Hd. Qrs 3rd Div. 3rd A.C.
December 7, 1863

Dear Father

I wrote to you yesterday. Col. Truex intends to try and get commissioned Brig. Gen'l and he ought to succeed. I think he is the best officer in the Division. If you can do anything with Parker I wish you would though. I don't know that he (Truex) has asked him to yet. Col. says if he gets appointed he will take Jim on his staff while I will be made Lt. Col. of course. However, I hope Col. will succeed not from any selfish motives but because I think he deserves it. Tell Jim not to join any regiment, he will get under some inferior officer who will do him more harm than good.

I bought a very handsome horse today for $120. Rather old but good, worth more than the grey I sold for $175. We are on the alert here all the time and I guess in a few days will shorten our line of communications. I think we will be compelled to.

The account in the Herald is nearer the truth than any other that I have seen. I wish you would ask mother to keep it for me. It is a little too "Frenchy" but on the whole, tolerably correct. We are here now within a half a mile of John Minor Botts, and I intend to call on him tomorrow. I am headover ears in business now and only scribble these few lines while waiting for a paper to arrive so good night.

Your Affectionate Son
Peter

Ross

Headquarters 3rd Div. 3rd Corps
Nash Mansion, Brandy Station
December 8, 1863

Dear Sister

I will occupy the few leisure moments that I have in writing to my highly esteemed and dearly beloved sister. I suppose you have heard by this time the particulars of the recent fight, in which the old 14th so nobly sustained the glory and honor of her state and country, by dealing death and destruction to her enemy. So it is needless for me to write about that. I was fortunate to come out safe, but am sorry to say many of the Regiment never lived to tell of the trials they passed through.

We are now quartered in a fine mansion, owned by a family named Nash, on the line of the railroad about one mile from the Station. All that is left of the once happy family, is the old lady and one daughter. One son was killed about a year since, while in the rebel army, and her husband is now in the old capital prison at Washington, having fired on some of our men when we first came to Brandy. The house is very much like Mr. Cowart's, a splendid place. They have a very fine piano in it, and as Captain Alstrom is Provost Martial now, and stationed with us, it comes very opportune and we make the country around hideous with our howls. I believe I have nothing more to say on this, only I think it quite likely we will stay here all winter. Remember me to Garrett and write soon to your

Affectionate Brother
Will

Residence of John Minor Botts near Culpeper, VA.

"...from the portico of my house, I and my family have seen nine battles fought on my own fields, and just before my own door, between hostile troops, who but yesterday as it were, boasted of a common history, a common nationality, and a common destiny."

John Minor Botts
May 26, 1864
Monmouth Democrat

Vredenburgh

Hd. Qrs. 3rd Div 3 A. Corps
Brandy Station Va.
December 10, 1863 9 P.M.

Dear Mother

I think I will see you all about the 1st week in January. That is to say I have determined to make application for leave, after I get through with my "monthly reports" which are due from me on the 23rd and as I have not been off duty a day since I entered the service I ought to obtain it. We are within a half mile of John Minor Botts' place and last evening, Col. Hall, Woodward, Ross and Alstrom and I went over to his house to indulge in a little music. I have been there several times. He has two daughters, but they are not very interesting. I herewith enclose you his signature, perhaps Father would like to see it.

Cols. Truex and Hall had a box put up for them in Washington by a grocer they knew there and I was present when they opened it this morning. First Col. Hall opened a basket filled with sausage (which Col Hall detests), then a large (tremendous) piece of head cheese, then another basket of sausage. Col. Hall was now fully exasperated and began to swear most emphatically that next time he would write exactly what he wanted and not trust a greasy grocer to pack his boxes for him and with that he seized another covered basket remarking in jest, "I'll bet, the d____n fool has put sausage in this too", and lo when opened it was filled to the rim with sausage. Col. couldn't do justice to the case by swearing, so he quietly walked off.

I went to Culpeper this morning. We have only cavalry there now. Rose and two of the surgeons lost their horses the day before yesterday. They turned them out to eat grass and the horses strayed beyond the camp lines and were of course stolen and they will never get them again. You have to watch your property very close in the army. A horse is taken if you leave him tied five minutes out of sight.

Your Affectionate Son
Peter

Vredenburgh

Hd Qrs. 3rd Div. 3rd A.C.
December 11, 1863 11 P.M.

Dear Mother

I received the appointment this evening of Inspector
General of this Corps. The Ins. Gen. formerly was an old officer
of the regular service and very efficient, but resigned a few
weeks ago and was succeeded by another officer of the regular
service who has been relieved tonight. I understand that the
first mentioned officer means to return soon, but I don't know
certainly. Gen'l French raised me over other officers who
outrank me, and yesterday sustained me in a matter wherein I
appointed a Brigade Inspector and two Brigade Commanders
protested against my interference. The Inspector Gen'l en-
dorsed on the document, that "the Inspector Gen'l of the 3rd
Div" had a high reputation for zeal and ability and should be
sustained." Don't mention this out of the family, as I only tell
you because it will please you and Father. I hope I will be able
to perform the duties, but they are so onerous and difficult that
I feel doubtful about it. All the property in the Corps must be
confiscated if condemned at all by me and I should think from
what I have seen that that alone will keep me busy all the
time. But aside from that I have the same kind of duties as
now, only increased and aggravated tenfold and I have thought
all along that I had too much already. But I mean to try it as it
is the most honorable and conspicuous position in the Corps
next to the General commanding. My duties will take me all
over. Every man in the Corps will know me, and I am clothed
with a coextensive power with the Gen'l and am especially
enjoined to exercise all authority on the spot to further the best
interests of the service, that is I can order and say "by command of Gen'l French, do so and so," without seeing the Gen'l
first and getting his permission. Of course if I abused the
power I would soon be fetched up for it. I recollect Lt. Col.
Hayden, who was the former Ins. used to select the positions
for the Corps whether going into battle or camp. He seemed to
be always flying about, fixing the picket lines, moving the
divisions and Brigades and was apparently one of the most
ubiquitous officers in the Corps. I mean to follow in his illustri-
ous footsteps and snoot into everybody's business except my
own, and make myself as feared as possible. I am not certain
that I can get home as soon now as anticipated.

Your Affectionate Son
Peter

[In early December, 1863, Sergeant Harrison was transferred to the
Ambulance Train of the 3rd Division, of which the 14th Regiment was
a part. He will later be transferred to the Ambulance Train of the 6th
Army Corps, headquartered at City Point, VA, and despite the fact
that the 14th Regiment, N.J. Vols. will be attached to the 6th Army
Corps, Harrison will lose contact with his comrades. There is a seven-
month gap in the Harrison collection, beginning after his
correspondence of January 21, 1864. We will not hear from Sergeant
Harrison again until near the end of September, 1864.]

Harrison

Ambulance Train
3d Division Park
Near Brandy Station, Virginia
Friday December 11, 1863

Dear Mother

I seat myself this evening in new quarters to pen you a few lines to assure you that I am by the kind mercies of God enjoying good health earnestly hoping this finds you all in the self same enjoyment.

Well Mother, now you have read the heading of my letter, I suppose you want to know the very first thing what I am doing in the Ambulance Train, I will tell you I am now Sergt. in the Train, and hereafter instead of carrying gun and equip-

Union ambulance train.

ment, I throw them aside, and have my horse to ride, so long as I behave myself. So Mother you see that your son Albert has got up in the military world about one inch or more. And I reckon he learned when he was quite a small chap how to behave himself, especially when there was anything at stake. I have you to thank for all that. I left my company yesterday, have been with the Train two days, and like it first rate. But I cannot help liking it, as there is no hard duty to perform and you can imagine yourself that it is worth something to get rid of picket duty, especially in winter, and no guard duty, no gun & rigging to be cleaned etc. Oh, I tell you its a large thing for this child, now I will tell you my duty, I have three wagons & three teams and nine men to look after. It is my duty to see that the wagons are kept in repair & that the men take good care of the horses. When my teams are sent out, of course I saddle my nag and go with them. That's the whole sum and substance.

Lt. Patterson secured the position for me. Therefore he's to blame for my good luck.

Well Mother, now I will want something else in my box, that is a vest. I am not particular what kind you get, so that is good and warm. You can fit it by John. I think there will be no danger of our moving from here this winter. So when you get the box ready mother, you can send it. My boots will be doubly good to me now. I believe I have nothing more to say. Our train is about a mile from camp. I intend to go over in the morning if I live, to get my mail.

Direct hereafter thus,

Sergt. Albert C. Harrison
Ambulance Train
1st Brig, 3d Division 3d Army Corps

Vredenburgh

Hd Qrs. 3rd A. Corps
December 12, 1863   10 P.M.

Dear Mother

I received your letter of the 10th inst. tonight. I wrote to you yesterday, telling you of my elevation to Corps Hd. Qrs. I have been very busy today investigating the papers of the office and getting the hang of things. Gen'l French was very cordial today when I reported to him for duty and earnestly is prepossessed in my favor. I think now that my appointment may be of longer duration than I at first anticipated and soon as feasible I mean to try and get appointed by the President Corps Inspector with the Rank of Lt. Col. I stand the best chance now. Hitherto I have not done anything towards helping myself upwards, but now I think I will try and get this appointment. If French is pleased with me he can recommend me and then the President will certainly select me permanently for this

Corps. I will wait though a while to see how the office and I affiliate. I have any quantity of influence now and can get a leave as soon as I can spare the time from the office. I may not be able to get home by New Years.

Your Affectionate Son
Peter

Vredenburgh

Hd. Qrs. 3 A.C.
December 13, l863

Dear Father

I recd. a few moments ago, your letters of the 10th and 11th inst. I don't know whether you have exactly hit it, writing to Newell, TenEyck etc. as Col. has already secured their influence and they may think he hasn't confidence in their sincerity and therefore gets you to influence them too. I won't say anything to Col. yet about your writing to them, and if things go wrong he will not have us to blame. I only meant to secure Parker's [N.J. Governor Joel Parker] influence as Col. said he had not heard from him yet. If Col. is successful I will then exhibit your letter. Perhaps if you have a chance you had better let TenEyck and Newell know that Col. did not ask you to address them particularly without you did so in the first instance.

I am now Inspector General for the Corps and am "obeyed and respected accordingly." I will move my quarters tomorrow to Corps Hd. Qrs. so that you should direct your letters hereafter "A.I. Gen'l Hd Qrs. 3rd A.C.."

I am fixed so pleasantly here now, that I hate to leave, but have no alternative. I have a fine, large room with an elegant open fire place, plenty of hickory wood, and a good stable for the horses. However, I can make myself tolerably comfortable anywhere. I have sold both the horses I brought out with me for more than I gave for them and have now a slashing pair of handsome bays, sound, kind, thoroughly broken and worth $75 apiece more than they cost me. I only gave $125 for one and $120 for the other. I think I will wear a silver leaf before the 1st of April.

Your Affectionate Son
Peter

Harrison

Camp of the 3d Division
Ambulance Corps
Near Brandy Station, Va.
December 15, 1863

Dear Mother

As I am now at leisure this evening I will take my pen and scratch you a few lines. I have just finished eating a hearty supper. I wish you could have been with me to dine. You wouldn't think then that there was any likelihood of my starving.

I paid a visit to camp last night and to my delight I found there was a letter from you. But to my sadness on reading I found you were low spirited, and when there was no necessity for it.

I have told you often Mother, that if you believed what every one said, you would always worry. And now I would like to know what Van Dyke knew concerning me or the late battle. Why he didn't know anything about it and he has been away at the hospital for a long time. But he is like a great many others, if they cannot find truth enough to tell why they will hatch up a few lies, and that's no hard matter for him to do, I know him too well. I am sorry that you don't and I cannot imagine why you listen to anything of the kind when you hear from me so often. But I know your weakness and I know too well that you worry at all such rumors. But you worry I see Mother thinking that I will be killed. Now Mother you say you prayed for me. Has not your prayers been answered? Most assuredly; thank God; then you know that God will hear and answer all those that pray in faith believing that their prayers will be answered. Faith, Mother is what we want.

As to the last battle Mother, it will be worth more to me than gold, and may prove to me far more than you are aware of. You must not say anything and I will tell you that my good conduct in the engagement was highly complemented by our Col. and Lt. Colonel and I will not be forgotten. It was partly through that I gained my present position, which I would rather have than a lieutenant's pay. When I last wrote I told you the particulars. Well Mother, I believe there is nothing of importance for me to write you farther. The boys were all well in camp and in first rate quarters. I finished my house today. There are only two of us in the shanty. A man from my own company and a fine fellow. He is a married man, a Key Porter [Keyport, N.J.]. He does all my cooking and he understands his business. I have just as nice a little cabin as any one would wish to rest in. You said you would have to pay $8.00 for my boots. That don't make any difference to me. It is likely we will be paid in the course of a month so you will not be out of money this winter if I can help it rest assured, and I told you in my last letter that I wanted a vest. If you haven't bought it yet you had better get me a regulation vest to button up close in the neck. Give my love to Grandmother, I was happy to hear the old lady keeps so well, also to John and bear me in remembrance to your neighbors and any who may enquire of your Union loving Son.

Albert

Ross

Hd. Qrs. 14th N.J. Vols
Near Brandy Station
December 16, 1863

Dear Mother

Your welcome letter by Lt. Kerner reached me today. He has my gloves in his valise which I will get this afternoon. I am back with the regiment now, having been appointed Sergt. Major, in Fisher's old place, who has been promoted to a lieutenancy. Charlie Bartruff was Sergt. Major before him. We are going to move again tomorrow I hear, where to, I cannot say. I saw the Quarter Master a few moments since. He looks well and hearty as ever. Major Vredenburgh has been appointed Inspector General of our Corps, a very huge thing by the way. I wish him all success for the Major was very kind and used me very gentlemanly while I was with him. I am glad to hear you are to have someone to live with you, and enliven your time a little, for I suppose you miss Mimmie and Burroughs a little, now and then. You wish to know about Brandy Station. Well, it is composed of a station house about the size of Jamesburg but not near as Homely. And three small frame houses are in the immediate vicinity, very much after the style of the little house at the bottom of the hill past Skenck Bennett's house. John Minor Bott's house situated about half a mile from the station. A few evenings since, we paid him a visit. Capt. Alstrom performed some operatic pieces on the piano. Lt. Woodward and myself doing our part in a vocal way. He and his three accomplished daughters did all in their power to make our visit agreeable, and the evening passed away very pleasantly, leaving with many invitations to call again. How is Aunt Jane? I hope she is well by this time. I don't think I can get home this winter as my duties will be such now as to prevent me coming just now. I have nothing more to say at present.

Burroughs

Vredenburgh

Hd. Qrs 3rd Army Corps
December 18, 1863

My Dear Father

 I received a few moments ago, letters from you dated the
15th & 16th inst. I fully appreciate your fatherly advice and
think I have been often influenced by it. I sometimes tell the
General portions of it, and he laughs and tells me to "be sure
and follow it." Do not think I make an expose of any letters. I
have only two or three letters at the present time in my possession for I invariably burn them. I have not yet moved my
quarters but intend to do so in the morning. For the last week I
have ridden over to Corps Hd Qrs. every morning, and remained till night. My mess here is so agreeable that I hate to
leave, but I will have to come to it.
 The Inspector General Department is a separate one
consisting of an Inspector General, located at Washington, an
Inspector General of the Army of the Potomac say, at army Hd
Qrs., an Asst. Inspector General of each army corps, and an
Acting Asst. Inspector Gen'l for each Division and Brigade in
each Corps. It is a department established to see that every
other department does its duty. To see that all orders,
circulars, and regulations are observed and that everything
goes on as contemplated. For instance, to see that Commissaries issue proper subsistence, at proper times in proper quantities, that they make proper return vouchers, and abstracts for
the same, that none is misappropriated. To see that Quarter
Masters make their proper returns, vouchers, and abstracts,
that they have sufficient on hand of what may be required, in
their particular department. That public property is properly
purchased, cared for, and issued or disposed of — to see that
the Medical Department plays up and locates their hospitals
properly, and save and account for the hospital funds. To see
that Corps, Division, Brigades and Regimental Commanders
do their duty, drill their troops, promulgate and have orders
from the different departments observed and obeyed. These
and a thousand other things I might mention and would not be
near the end. In panca verba, the Department is the eye of the
Commanding General. The commander in chief cannot personally see that "all goes well", and therefore the Inspectors,
branching off as far as Brigades, are his special agents to carry
out what he would have done. You can get an insight from
what I have said of what an Inspector should do, but you really
see nothing but the outside. Each department is vast and
complicated, requiring close and arduous study to understand
it. There are but very, very, few persons who understand the
departmental business thoroughly that they are in, let alone
posting up on any other.
 The reason is, that there are so many orders, circulars,
and changes made since regulations were published, being
capable of different constructions, as our acts of legislature,

that it requires extensive study and application to learn and understand them. I send you herewith a blank of the Monthly Inspection Report, which I have to make out every month. You see it is not only a check upon the Adjutant General's Department but shows the discipline etc. of the troops. This blank looks easy but it takes me two days to make it out, though when completed it is much more voluminous than it now is.

All property to be inspected for condemnation in this Corps has to be done by me whether the same be medical, ordnance, or quarter master's stores. And I order the disposition to be made of it. Thus the government trusts thousands of dollars worth of property to my discretion. I suppose I decide upon over $500 worth a day now on average. There is no reviewing power. My action is final. The commanding General has the power to make any disposition of such property he pleases, but nine hundred and ninty nine times out of a thousand he leaves the papers to the Inspector. I have thus given you some idea Father of my true position and have to say in conclusion, that it is a burning shame that persons, for positions that might affect the country peculiarly as much as mine, should be selected with so little care and previous examination, for fitness. It is so though, with every department.

Peter

Harrison

Camp of the 3d Division 3d A.C.
Ambulance Corps
Near Brandy Station, Va.
Friday December 18, 1863

Dear Mother

Yours of the 12th came to hand last evening, and much pleased was I to see such a long letter from you. I also received a standard at the same time. The weather must be altogether different with you than it is with us. We have had no such storms. Although it has looked very much like storming. It rained quite hard yesterday and when it commenced it froze as soon as it touched the ground. It rained some last night, but it is quite pleasant this morning.

You want to know if I don't think the war will end, this winter. Well I haven't bothered my brain much with the prospect lately. But I can tell you one thing certain, that it is nearer to a close than when it broke out ha.ha. I am not very anxious myself, I would like to get another dig at the Johnnies. I tell you just how I think. That is this. That between now and next August this rebellion will be crushed out, and another thing I have become so habituated to this kind of a life, that I feel perfectly at home. Where ever I throw down my old rubber blanket and I am better acquainted with old Virginia soil than with my own Native State.

You say you always felt that you would like for me to go in a battle if I could come out all right, same here. And anxious to get in another one, but you can cease to tremble hereafter so long as I hold position in the Ambulance Corps. For there will be no danger of my getting into battle so let your mind be at rest and don't meet trouble half way. It is time enough when it comes.

It seems that you have a great many sudden deaths in Red Bank. So Mother if you can look at the matter in the right light you will see that God is able to preserve life in Virginia as well as in Jersey. And I am just as safe here as at your side. For what is to be, will be. That is certain; nothing is impossible with God. No doubt Theodore Fields, feels very badly on account of the death of his brother [Private Elliot Fields, killed in the action at Locust Grove]. But he died a noble death. He fought with all the vigor and zeal of a lover of his Glorious Country. God grant to reward him in Heaven.

You want to know if we have any Church. I haven't heard a sermon preached since we were at Culpeper before the retreat. Anyhow we haven't been situated to give the Chaplain any chance. But he does his duty and I believe him to be a good man. I have talked with him a great many times since we have been in Virginia. But now I am away from the Regt. I don't see him so often. I think after we get fixed up finally that he will have Church Sundays. Then I shall saddle my horse and ride over. It was plagued lonesome for me here the first day or two. But I soon became acquainted with the boys from the different Regts. and now I am home.

[no signature]

Vredenburgh

Hd Qrs. 3rd Army Corps
December 21, 1863

Dear Mother

I received the letters in which you sent the lip salve, and the one speaking of the diary. I also received the diary for which I thank you very much as it is just what I need.

I left General Carr's Hd Qrs. yesterday with professions of regret on his part, and am now pleasantly ensconced in a room with a fireplace in it at Corps Hd Qrs. Captain McBlair, brother to Miss McBlair who visited Liddie Conover is my roommate. I haven't quite as much writing to do now as I had before as I have clerks to do it all except a few reports I have to make; But there is no end to outdoor work. I wish you would please send that box and two pair of india rubber straps if you can buy them in Freehold. Pay Charley Voorhees that $10 and I will charge the same to Steve.

Affectionately
Peter

Vredenburgh

Hd Qrs. 3rd A.C.
December 27, 1863

Dear Father

General French informed me a few days ago that he intended purposing my name to the President for Ins. Gen'l of the Corps. I immediately wrote to Senator TenEyck asking his aid in getting the nomination confirmed in the Senate. Had I better write to Newell too? I think if TenEyck thought I had written to anyone else he would let me take care of myself. If I succeed I will have the rank of Lt. Col. Don't write to anyone for me, but I would like to have your opinion.

Your Affectionate Son
Peter

Ross

Brandy Station Virginia
December 27, 1863

Dear Mother

Your kind letter reached its destination this morning and I will now take this opportunity to answer it. I should like to come home, in accordance with your request very much, and I want to see you fully as bad as you do your Burroughs, but I think it will be to my interest to remain here this winter. Next spring or summer perhaps, you will see me around your part of the country. In regard to Lieut. Bartruff's coming on to get married, I think, that if the lady reports that they are to be married about Christmas, she will be mistaken as he cannot get away until about March.

On our march across the Rapidan the last time, I had a horse, which saved me considerable marching. On the march anyone can pick up a horse along the road. I got a first rate one on the last march, which stood me through. The night we recrossed the river, our Division was delayed considerable, by several batteries getting stuck in the mud, so that it was about 11 o'clock before we got barely started, and just then the 2nd Corps came along and away we went down the plank road, on the double quick, as we had to close up to the 2nd Division of our Corps. It was a splendid moonlight night and cold as Greenland, and such fun as we had hollering at each other, and making fun. Ed Danberry who enlisted from New Brunswick, with John Manning, had to fall out, as he could not keep up and was taken prisoner by the rebels. We had a letter from him the other day and he is now on Belle Island, Richmond. Mimmie is acquainted with him, I am glad to hear Aunt Jane is convalescing and regaining her usual good health. My pay is now $20. a month, and duties not very heavy. I will have all the detailing to do, such as picket, guard duty etc. I like my gloves very much indeed, just the thing I wanted.

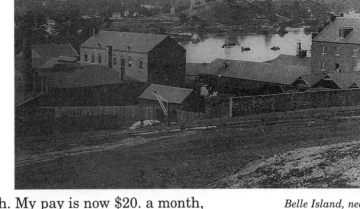

Belle Island, near Richmond, VA.

Your Affectionate Son
Burroughs

Harrison

Camp of the 3d Division 3d A.C.
Ambulance Train, Brandy Station Virginia
January 3, 1864

Dear Mother

It is Sabbath afternoon I will take my pencil and scratch you a few lines as my ink is played out. I forgot to tell you to put a bottle of ink in the box. But I can get some at the sutler's when I go over to camp. This leaves me in excellent health & I hope finds you all in the same enjoyment.

Now Mother, I suppose you want to know if the box has arrived, well it has not yet made its appearance, although I have been looking for it the last three or four days. I went down to the Station yesterday and searched around but saw nothing of it. But I guess it will be along in a day or two. I did not intend to write until I had received it, but I thought you would be rather anxious to hear from me. The weather is so cold I don't believe anything in the box would spoil if I didn't get it in three weeks. I was at camp last Saturday & found the boys all right side up.

I expected some of the boys would be over to see me today but they didn't come. It's so cold they don't like to go out any better than I do. I wish you could look into my cabin. You would say if I froze to death this winter it would be my own fault. I have been putting on two extra logs on my building, mudded it good both outside & in. Then lined on the inside with old feed bags. I drew two new pieces of shelter tent the other day, and now I have my roof double, the two of us have two blankets each (wool blankets) one under us & three over. Well now I can tell you, we live, and when that box comes we will live still better. I am all anxiety to see it, for I want some buckwheat cakes, the first thing.

Well Mother there are not so many going home on furlough as there was. It is played out for about thirty days. It seems they are giving thirty days furlough to men that reenlist for three years longer, the three years commencing at the expiration of their two years. But I believe they can't give me any furlough under those circumstances. I would like to come home very well, but I believe I will not be sold, for a furlough. I will do so, without compulsion. I can just stay with Uncle Sam as long as he has got a hard tack. That's what's the matter. I wish every one felt as well contented as I do, all I want is enough to eat & wear, & that I have always had, but when they go to pinching my belly then they get my dander up instantly, but I must now close, and get some wood.

Your loving and Affectionate Son,
Albert

Union Sutler

Ross

January 16, 1864

Dear Mother

Your letter reached me in due season, and now I will try and answer it. It still keeps very muddy down here, with no signs of improving. I got my guitar from Frederick last week, but haven't been able to get any strings for it yet. I should like to be home and get a sleigh ride once more, it being nearly two years now since I had that pleasure. I had a letter from Mimmie since I wrote you last but haven't answered it yet. I should like to see Pop down here. They say it is pretty hard to get through Washington, as everyone has to have a special pass to come down to the army. The father of one of our men got as far as there last week, and couldn't get any further. If he does conclude to come, he had better go to Mr. Sprague who used to live in Freehold and perhaps he could get him a pass. He keeps the Kirkwood house in Washington. Everyone is as well as usual down here. I would like to get home and see you all if I could but Mr. Lincoln says no, so here we have to stick. I will send you those pictures shortly on.

Your Affectionate Son
Burroughs

Harrison

Camp of the Ambulance Corps
3rd. Division, 3rd. A.C. Brandy Station, Va.
January 21, 1864

Dear Mother

It is true the winter is fast passing away and it cannot pass any too quickly to the soldier, even if he is in good quarters. He soon tires of that and longs for a dig with the Johnnies. And is never happier, than when he can after a long day's march stretch out his weary limbs on Mother Earth, with naught but the bright blue sky for a covering. Excitement is the life of a soldier. Here we lay this winter nothing to do, we cannot but await with anxiety the coming of spring.

I was out this morning at Headquarters, and I thought I would ride over to the Company, and who should I find but my old crony Charley White, who came from Camp Convalescent, last Sunday. He looks first rate and sends his love to all.

I saw Capt. Alstrom this morning for the first time since he was home. He said he enjoyed his visit, and had a good time in general. All is quiet in the Train this morning.

I heard this morning that a Regiment of the Rebs came across our lines and gave themselves up together with their families.

The weather is quite pleasant today. The travelling is miserable. Tell Susie I have written to her. I must now close — write again soon. My love to you & John, and bear me in memory to any enquiring friends.

Your ever loving son,
Albert

Vredenburgh

Hd Qrs. 3rd A. Corps
January 22, 1864

My Dear Father

    Jim says he has written to you about my intercourse with Mr. TenEyck. He said fairly that he would assist me. I called on Gen'l French tonight and asked him whether he had forwarded my name etc. He replied that he had not for the reason that he did not know how long he would stay here himself, that he had understood that the army was to be reorganized and so he had not recommended me. I told him that I could get enough influence to secure me the appointment if he recommended me. He said if anyone was I.G of the Corps, with his approval, I should be, and that he meant to forward my name as soon as he stood on sure footing himself. I thereupon thanked him and withdrew. There are some other officers from the regular army applying for the position, but I suppose with no success yet.
    Gen'l recommended that I should not get my friends at Washington to work for me yet as I "would exhaust my strength, before it would pay." If he is candid his advice is good — if not, I don't want the position anyhow. The General seems favorably disposed toward me, and he says the appointment will have to be confirmed by the Senate. I did not of course, dispute the question with him, but I am certain that it does not have to go into the Senate. I will just wait calmly till the matter is settled.

Yours Affectionate Son
Peter

Stults

January 23, 1864

Dear Ma

    Tonight's mail brought me letters from home — glad to hear of continued health. My health is excellent as usual. The box has started you say but have not reached me yet. It will be along by the first of the week.

Military news is scarce. Nothing stirring everything quiet along the lines. The picket line has been moved two miles farther from our camp.

I am afraid that Grandpa will never get well. He must suffer greatly. You speak of flannel for shirting. I prefer the plaid to blue or gray. Black and white is my choice if it is in market. I guess I shall have to have another pair of pants before I come home. You have a pair on hand have you not? A pair of blue pants? The kind I want after this. Black requires too much brushing, and corduroys are out of date. If you can get me up a shirt, send along in about a couple of weeks. Shirt & pants. You can mail or express, perhaps the latter is quite as cheap, and then you can send other things.

A small detail goes out tomorrow morning. Four or five officers go. I am not detailed. My turn is next I suppose. The last time I was out it rained the third day out. And rather a severe time of it we had, I can tell you. The weather has been quite warm of late and mud is knee deep or less. We are making great exertions to improve camp appearance, in the way of corduroying the avenues and paths. The boys are going to build me a nice comfortable tent next week. Captain had his finished today. The tent I now occupy is comfortable but small and rough in appearance. I would not wish for a more comfortable tent than we can build of pine logs. A tent 10 feet long, 7 feet wide gives plenty room for one family. The bunks in one end and good brick fireplace in the other. You speak of our wheatcakes and how we baked them. Bill Sodon gets them up in proper shape, are baked in the tent we live in. I get our wheat flour at the commissary 4 1/2 cts per pound. The sutler has buckwheat for 10 cts. per pound.

The Governor of Vermont is expected on soon. The Brigade will be reviewed and have parade. The 10th Vermont is in our Brigade. It is reported the Brigade will be strengthened by a new Vermont regiment. The 10th has been recruited full, Vermont's quota being filled already. Application has been made to have the Lt. Col. and Capt. Conover of D, and all the orderly sergeants to go home on recruiting service. General Morris being very desirous that the regiment be full. It is reported for a certainty that we will be paid off next week. We will be agreeably disappointed if not.

My Respects to all
Marcus

Stults

January 29, 1864

Dear Ma

Very pleasant weather we are enjoying now, rather warm for comfort and decidedly too warm for health. The doctors are worrying dreadfully and prophisize an abundance of chills and fever if it should continue as warm. We are hard at work corduroying and draining our avenues. We can make it comfortable in time no doubt, but the situation is miserable in the extreme. The weather is very favorable for our work. I don't think I remember as great a length of period of warm weather during any winter. I suppose there is very little difference in the climate of eastern Virginia and Jersey. I had a great disappointment today. I walked two miles to witness the execution of two deserters and on reaching the place appointed, learned they were respited or pardoned, don't know which. The former most likely. The condemned were members of Jersey regiments. One a William Smith of New Brunswick. As many as seven deserters were sentenced to be shot today. Don't know if the others were respited or not. They were connected with different corps. You will think I was favorably disappointed. Perhaps I was but it is too bad that a crowd of thousands should assemble and then no performance. Don't you think so?

Our pickets often pitch in some deserters from the rebel army. The papers say numbers are coming in every day from different parts of the picket line. That looks favorable.

You can send pants and shirt and a large bottle of Arnolds Writing Fluid. Anything else you please, at your convenience. I am not certain that I shall come home. I may. I would like to see Grandpa very much. Lt. Col. Hall, Captain Conover, and all the 1st sergeants of the regiment left here a few days back for Jersey on recruiting service. Very nice health and my respects to all.

Marcus

Vredenburgh

Hd. Qrs. 3rd Army Corps
February 1, 1864 2 1/2 A.M.

Dear Mother

I have been sitting up till this late hour reading "David Copperfield." I wrote to you early in the evening, saying that Steve intends to "enlist" and asking you to see about Prince etc. I now write to say that I have hired a nice looking darkey, recently a slave for a rebel officer from Georgia. He seems very bright and intelligent and I give him $16 per month — the same I paid Steve. Steve will likely be home in a few days. I feel sorry to lose him, as he has been most faithful.

Your Affectionate Son
Peter

Vredenburgh

Hd Qrs 3rd Army Corps
February 7, 1864

Dear Mother

We have just returned from an expedition to the Rapidan and I find letters from you, Will and Jim. I had just returned from Washington (where I had been ordered on business) last night when our Corps was ordered to move in haste (not giving me time even to eat) in rear of the 1st Corps to the Rapidan at Raccoon's Ford. The 2nd Corps likewise went to the River somewhere near Germania's Ford. I left Steve to take care of one horse and the cabin and started with Charley, my orderly, alone and sometime after the other officers.

I found the Hd Qrs. last night after considerable difficulty and laid down wet and cold and hungry on the floor, without any blanket over me (mine having been mislaid) at ten o'clock at night and awoke at one o'clock, chilly and sneezing and nose stopped up. In fact, all the symptoms of having taken a heavy cold. But I there procured a buffalo robe and woke up this morning all right.

We started at daybreak, this morning and advanced to within a couple of miles of the Rapidan, waited there till dusk and have now returned. What the design was you will know before I will. I understand to make a demonstration in aid of Butler.

While we were waiting about 2 miles this side of the river, I asked the General to be allowed to go on and take observations. I went to the picket line (with Charley) and there dismounted to take a look at the rebels with my glass, who were in large numbers on the opposite bank of the river. They were not more than 700 yards off from me and I could almost see their features with the glass. I rode to the advance picket or vedette who stood on a crest in the middle of a field while the main line of pickets were in rifle pits (Jim, he knows all about them) a hundred yards or so in the rear. The pickets advised me to move the horses as the "Johnnys" had been firing briskly at them a few moments before I came and the bullets had struck all around them. I then sent Charley back with the horses behind a hillock and took a seat on a stump and commenced observations. The rebels had rifle pits along the bank and eight out of ten of them were dressed in our uniform and had it not been for their red battle flag, which flaunted defiantly in the breeze, I would have supposed they were our own men. I gazed at them for a long time, quite interested to see them walking about, talking and laughing apparently unconcerned about us as if we were not in sight. How I wished for a gun then! After I had started back for the General, I met a colonel who had command of the pickets about 400 yards in rear of our line and he called out to me, "you were pretty lucky"

Why so, said I? "because" said he, "the rebels have been firing like the devil at those pickets where you have just been with your horse and their balls whistled all around them." I dare say if I hadn't sent Charley off out of sight with the horses, they would have been fired at. The morning was a little hazy so that it was almost impossible to draw a bead on a man at the distance I was, but a horse might have been hit — one time out of five. At dusk we all moved back again. The road was terrible and I think, gave me a pretty clear idea of Burnside's "mud

Hired servant of an officer of the 6th Army Corps, stationed at corps headquarters.

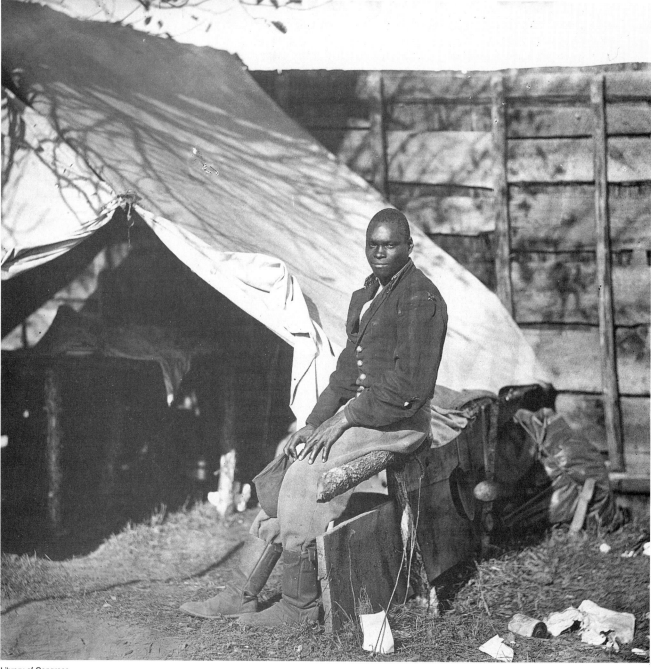

march" last year.

As I stated in the commencement, I have been to Washington this last week. I went to Alexandria after papers connected with the Office and thence to Washington. I carried that demijohn you gave me, to get whiskey in it. I "toted it" as I would say, all around Alexandria and Washington, filled it with $6 worth of "Old Rye", put the demijohn on a box and as the box was being placed on the cars, it fell, smashed the demijohn and presto, quick! — away went my $6.00 and trouble, "quicker" as Col. Truex would say, "that hell can scorch a feather." I wish you would see whether Prince is well enough to come here and first whether the Formans wish to five him up. I wrote two letters, same date about him. Consider the 2nd one unwritten and act on the 1st. Don't engage him but let me know whether I can get him if I want and whether he will be able to stand the life. I mean to give him $200 a year and I will send word by Steve in a day or two in reference to him. I engaged another darkey at $16. per mo. but he was afterwards offered $22 and I think, means to leave me.

Your Affectionate Son
Peter

General Butler USA and staff. General Butler is seated, second from the right.

Vredenburgh

Hd Qrs. 3rd Army Corps
February 13, 1864

My Dear Father

It has been a long time since I have written to you, but I believe I have told Mother all the news. I am living very pleasantly now and I think I have risen very perceptibly in the estimation of my brother officers since I bought that whiskey. I actually have to keep my door locked most of the time to keep out those whom I don't want to bother with. From appearances I think French will command this Corps and then I shall undoubtedly be permanently assigned here. I am bound to rise high in the opinion of everyone here or else be displaced as a nuisance. I am taking a different position here than any other Inspector has taken. I go on the ground of perfect independence in everything. I yesterday reported every officer at the headquarters employing soldiers or servants and though it affects the officers very much peculiarly and makes hard talk, yet it will all work well in the end. I even had the audacity to tell the Adjutant General of the Corps that I meant to report the two men he had and I did so.

I stick my nose into everything and strike mercilessly in every direction. The Inspector General told his clerk (who told me) that I sent him the best report he received from the army and I know by his demeanor towards me that he thinks a great deal of me and will back me in what I do. I know of two officers of the regular army who are trying to get the position here as Inspector, but the time has not arrived yet for me to try.

I received a letter from Mother yesterday mentioning that she had received two letters from me, but I wrote one subsequent to those two which she had not yet received. I expect Steve has arrived by this time, and he can tell what I want and so I will not recapitulate now. I have not been paid yet, but expect to be soon. I will keep you advised of my success or defeat and which I will know about this month I think.

Your Aff. Son
Peter

Ross

February 13, 1864

Dear Mother

It is some little time now since I wrote you but as someone
is going to Freehold almost every week, I thought you could
hear the news from them. We still remain in the same place
and expect to stay here for two months yet. My guitar is great
company for me. I can pass many a pleasant moment with it.
Lieutenant Bedell is discharged and went home yesterday. He
was discharged on account of disability. I was pretty sick for
one or two days last week. I think I got cold and brought on a
fever, but the doctor put the quinine into me and stopped it, so
now I feel almost as good as new. What is going on in Freehold? Is anybody getting married that I know? I hear Hon.
David Patterson has bought the hotel next to the court house. I
suppose he will carry on there in grand style. When have you
heard from Let? When you write to her next, please tell her she
has forgotten to answer my last letter.
Nothing more to write about so I must close hoping soon to
hear from you.

Your Affectionate Son
Burroughs

Vredenburgh

Hd Qrs. 3rd Army Corps
February 16, 1864

Dear Mother

The darkie I have keeps improving so fast that you need
not bother with sending out a man without you hear of a first-
rate fellow like Steve or John Higgins. I have a contraband just
from slavery, and he is good enough now, but you can't depend
on these runaway darkies, as they may take a notion any
moment to go further North. So if you hear of a man whom
Henry knows to be steady and trusty — let me know. Hasn't
Steve arrived at home yet? He left me last Tuesday. I couldn't
settle with him as my diary is at home and I told him to ask
you to send me a copy of the leaf on which his account has been
kept.

Your Affectionate Son
Peter

Vredenburgh

Hd. Qrs. 3rd Army Corps
February 26, 1864

Dear Mother

I have just received yours of the 22nd inst. I am very glad to hear that Will is out of danger. Why didn't you send me an exact copy of my diary of Steve's account? I can't tell anything about it from what you send me. There is one credit of $9.00 cash which I have marked X that I forget about. If I saw how it looked on the leaf I could recollect. You had better tear out the leaves and send them to me.

Don't bother anymore about a man without you hear of one that is par excellence. I have one I am breaking. I break a nigger or a soldier just as I used to a dog or horse. And I have this nigger half broken now. Wouldn't Will or Henry like to come out and see us here? I should be very glad to see them. Tell Henry or Will (not both together) that I will send them a pass to the army if they say yes.

Your Affectionate Son
Peter

Germania Ford on the Rappahannock River.

National Archives

Vredenburgh

Hd Qrs. 3rd Army Corps
February 29, 1864

My Dear Father

We are again under marching orders, that is, ordered to be ready to move on short notice. We recd. the order Saturday night. The 6th Corps have gone in the direction of Madison Court House or James City while the cavalry are demonstrating in the direction of Germania Ford. Our division, the 1st. of our Corps, has gone too, with the 6th Corps. I saw Kerner tonight who says Will is out of all danger. I don't think I will remain here long as I am in bad order with nearly every officer at Hd. Qrs. including the General. We had a set-too the other day. I reported truly all officers having soldiers in their employ as I am ordered to do and because General Birney who was commanding the Corps at that time, issued the order, Genl. French viewed my faithful report with disfavor. I also reported the Medical Director and Commissary of Subsistence in regard to the expenditure of the Hospital Funds and General gave me particular fits. I got mad on the start and talked back as I never thought I could. We made to do, argued the matter and played the Devil with myself generally. I told him that before I would sacrifice my manhood by not having the moral courage to make a true report, I would go back to my regiment. I was with him three hours and since that time I have marked a change in several of the officers. I don't care a snap for the whole lot of them though, and I look as up at any time and start the fire. I weigh a hundred and forty six pounds and am perfectly well. My eyes never hurt me any more.

I expressed $150 home to Father today by Adams Express Co. and I herein enclose the receipt.

Your Affectionate Son
Peter

Kerner has arrived. Tell Will as I was trotting by this morning I passed a very intellectual looking gentleman who turned out to be Reybold from Eatontown. A Methodist minister there, he is trying to get the Chaplaincy of the 8th N. Jersey.

Ross

February 29, 1864

Dear Mother

Your short note sent by Lieutenant Kerner, he just handed me. I am happy to say I am now about as well as ever, but sorry to inform you that my application to come home was not granted. So shall have to wait until George the Meade gets in a more pleasant humor. I was pretty sick for about a week but when I found I couldn't get home, I concluded to get well without that pleasant remedy, so today finds me in my usual good health. I expected Pop down with Lt. but he said he expected me home every day. I am sorry to disappoint you, but when you want to go anywhere down here you have to ask someone else beside your own self. We are under marching orders. The 6th Corps went on a reconnaissance yesterday, and the report is that the Johnnys had all left our front. Adjt.

Buckelew is at home now, he is coming back on Thursday. I believe I have nothing more of importance to write. My love to Aunt Jane, Mimmie and everybody else who wants it.

Write Soon Your Affectionate Son
Burroughs

Just Before The Battle Mother

THE VACANT CHAIR.

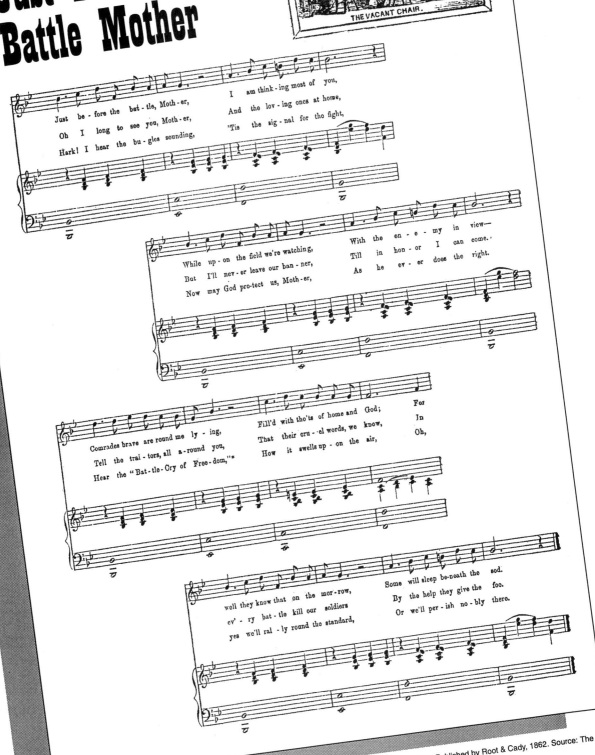

Just Before the Battle Mother by George F. Root; Published by Root & Cady, 1862. Source: The Free Library of Philadelphia, Music Department.

5 Confronting the Hailstorm

March 1864 — October 1864

In March, 1864, the 3rd Corps was broken up, and the 14th Regiment N.J. Vols. became part of the 3rd Division attached to the 6th Army Corps, Army of the Potomac. As spring approached, all attention seemed focused on the billigerents in the East. The Army of the Potomac was poised for its spring offensive in Virginia which would flank Lee's Army of Northern Virginia, push on to Petersburg and finally end a year later at Appomattox. Despite heavy losses and poor supplies, the Army of Northern Virginia was still a formidable force. It believed in its cause, maintained high morale, and trusted the invincibility of Robert E. Lee.

In early May, 1864, the Army of the Potomac moved against the Confederates at the Wilderness. Grant ordered Hancock's 2nd Corps, Warren's 5th Corps, and Sedgwick's 6th Corps across the Rapidan River at Culpeper Mine and Germania Fords. They were opposed by Confederate generals Ewell, A.P. Hill, and Longstreet. Warren's Federal Corps led the assault supported by Sedgwick's forces but were driven back by Confederate fire. Both sides became locked in mortal combat. Northern generals Sedgwick and Warren moved west along the Orange Turnpike but were successfully blocked by

Union engineers cutting road on the south side of the North Anna River in May of 1864.

General Ewell. In the meantime, the rebels inflicted heavy losses on Hancock's Corps. Cavalry forces were also engaged in deadly combat at the Wilderness. Sheridan fought Stuart at Todd's Tavern and General Gorden attacked the Federal flank when the battle finally ended. Losses were heavy on both sides, 18,000 Federals as compared to 12,000 Confederates. In addition, both sides lost valuable commanders. Confederate General James Longstreet was severely wounded and Union General

John Sedgwick was killed. Sedgwick was supervising the placement of cannons when he was shot in the face by a sharp-shooter.

The Fourteenth New Jersey Volunteers were engaged at the Battle of the Wilderness. On May 5, 1864, the regiment suffered heavy casualties; again on the 8th of May, in support of Warren's Corps, which was battling Confederates under General Longstreet, the 14th drove the rebels back inflicting heavy losses. Colonel William Truex was placed temporarily in command when General Morris was wounded. Heavy skirmishing continued on the 10th and 11th as General Grant ordered the Army of the Potomac southeasterly in an attempt to flank General Lee. There was severe fighting at Spotsylvania Court House. On May 12, 1864, Hancock's Corps opened a general engagement along the entire line which inflicted heavy casualties on Southern forces. Again, there followed several days of maneuvers and skirmishes bringing the 14th N.J. Volunteers to North Anna and Jericho Ford by May 24 and then to Nole's Station where it destroyed some eight miles of track of the Virginia Central Railroad.

Meanwhile, General Grant decided against a frontal assault on Lee's works, opting instead on another flanking movement which sent the Sixth Corps southward toward the Hanover Court House and Cold Harbor Road. By the 31st of May, the 14th had captured a number of enemy rifle pits and suffered only light casualties. The next day, after marching fifteen miles, the Regiment led the Sixth Corps in a general assault on rebel forces at Cold Harbor, Virginia....

From the Rapidan to Richmond

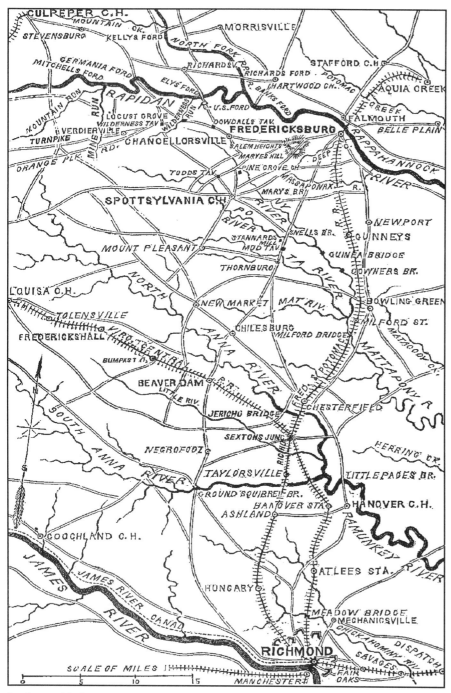

New Jersey and the Rebellion by John Y. Foster; Newark, N.J. — Martin R. Dennis & Co. — 1868

Vredenburgh

Hd Qrs. 3rd Army Corps
March 19, 1864

Dear Father

I received your letter dated "Trenton" all right. I am on excellent terms with the General and staff, without any apologies or compromises on my part. The General is a good hearted man and though I may be superseded, it will not be his fault. If the army is reorganized, of course, some regular appointee would be assigned. The Paymaster General at Washington remarked to a staff officer on this staff the other day, that we had a hell of an Inspector General in this Corps. That he stopped more officers pay than of any other two Corps in the army.

Our Corps was reviewed the other day and looked splendid. I overheard Gen'l Sedgwick remark to Gen'l French, "Why Gen'l, your corps appears elegant" Yes, says French, "it ought to be broken up though." Of course this was meant to be "sarcastic" As A. Ward would say, "The Irish" celebrated St. Patrick's Day in the morning & afternoon too, in an appropriate manner. Hundreds of ladies were present and a platform was erected for them and the Insp. Gen. on one side of a half mile track.

Hurdle races, mule races, and sack races without number interspersed with wrestling matches, boxing matches, and Lucifer matches were the order of the day while the exercises were occasionally oiled over, with a "greased pole" and a greased pig with a greasy tail, chased by greasy aspirants. Notwithstanding the primeval crudeness of the program, we there had lots of fun and whiskey. "I'll bet ye" — and none who had any fun or whiskey in him could help but laugh. Nearly every officer was mounted and such pushing, crowding, and cussing I never heard before, and never expect to hear again.

A telegram came yesterday to Gen'l French that the enemy were crossing at Raccoon Ford and our command was ordered to "fall in" immediately but in a few hours afterward the order was countermanded. Heavy firing was heard towards Warrenton. What does Ewell mean to do on the other side of the Blue Ridge? I shouldn't be much surprised if the rebels tried last year's maneuver again. Col. Hall returned yesterday — said he had seen you and that you looked well. If

Spotsylvania Court House

U.S. Army Military History Institute

*Carte de Visite of General
U.S. Grant USA*

you have the time and inclination to see the army, I will send
you a pass.

Your Affectionate Son
Peter

Vredenburgh

Hd. Qrs. where the 3rd AC used to be
March 25, 1864 10 1/2 pm

Dear Father

You will no doubt have heard by the time this reaches you
that the 3rd Army Corps is among the things that were. Yesterday afternoon the order was issued effecting the change, for
the details of which I refer to in the official order. General
French left this morning for Washington and I, with some of
the rest of the staff are still staying here on our own responsi-
bilities. Colonel Schriver Ins. Gen'l of the army told me yesterday that he had spoken for a position for me on Div. Inspector
in the 6th Corps to which our Division is now permanently
attached. The Q system of the Inspector General Dept, is to be
reorganized also; and hereafter Inspector of Divisions are
where the power of condemning public property be, the Inspector of the Army thinks very favorably of me and if it were not
that the corps have already officered in the Department already appointed by the President, I would have gotten in as
Corps Inspector. However, there will be only three Divisions in
the 6th Corps now while the others will have four in, and is
really more pleasant by far than at the Corps Qrs. My life here
has been a perfect succession of animosities, quarrels, and
investigations of charges. I was responsible for everything
reported in the corps and all reports returned from Washington
for investigation and were credited to me (name as Inspector of
the Corps) so the talk was, Major Vredenburgh said or reported
this and that or stopped furloughs and leaves on this regiment
and that and you can readily see that the position is not without disagreeable features. I have got my office business all up
some. The Inspector General told me that the reason he intended to allow Division Inspectors now to inspect and con-
demn public property was because nearly all the corps Inspectors had represented to him that they could not do the work. I
had between 3 & 4000 more troops to attend to than there were
in any other corps, and have never complained nor got behind
have I, because I worked every day. I still have the office record
papers and in charge and will wait here till I get express
orders. I suppose General Prince will command our old Division now as I see he is ordered to report for duty to General
Sedgwick, Carr has taken command of the 2nd Div (of this
corps) now the 4th of the 2nd corps.

General French looked very much dejected at his sudden
disnoblement and spoke very kindly to me. We have been on

the best of terms since our first (& last) set to. I understand the 11, 12 & 9th Corps are to come back to this army and that it will be 200,000 strong and take very active duty as soon as the season will permit but you have it on how I got it, I won't believe it hardly myself. There is no doubt though, but that we will have a sanguinary campaign, let us move how we will.

Your Affectionate Son
Peter

General Henry Prince USA

Stults

Camp of the 14th N.J. Vols
March 28, 1864

Dear Ma

A few lines to you but news is scarce. My health is good. Tell Grandma Symmes I'm well. General Grant is in Culpeper and we expect to be reviewed by him today. It is a splendid morning. We are now assigned to the 6th Corps. Address in future 1st Brigade 3rd Division 6th Corps.

Love
Marcus

Vredenburgh

Hd Qr's 3rd Div. 6th A. Corps
April 2, 1864 7 P.M.

My Dear Mother

I am very simply ensconced here in the elegant cabins left by General Birney & Staff. The day after Henry left, our command changed camps with what was originally the 1st Div. of the 3rd Corps but now the 3rd Div. of the 2nd Corps. I suppose Henry arrived home all right. Colonel Hall wants me very much to come back to the regiment and I am inclined to go there. I think it would look more honorable. I will keep an eye to the main chance though and be governed by circumstances. We expect to move in a very short time now and I for one am all ready and anxious to go.

Captain Alstrom and I mess together now and get along very well so far. Frank left me two days after Henry left, but when the time came for him to go, he looked very reflective and said he thought he would be back, "fore long," I wish I had

Photo: U.S. Army Military History Institute

shown Henry these Hd Qrs; they are really beautiful. I intend
to call on Ed Taylor tomorrow, I will hear the news from him.
We haven't been paid for the last three months, but as soon as
I am will send the money to Father.

Your Affectionate Son
Peter

Stults

April 8, 1864

Dear Ma

A few lines tonight duly. I wish you to hurry up that box.
There is a general order out that all sutlers must have their
goods and their persons out of the army by the 16th under
penalty of confiscation of the former and imprisonment at hard
labor of the latter should they not comply. It may not be that
the army is to move immediately after that but there is no
doubt the weather permitting, that it will move as soon there-
after as practicable. Should the weather continue as at present,
we won't move soon I think. It has rained about half of the
time the past couple weeks. It commenced raining last night
and has rained continually all day and so far at 8 P.M. is
raining very hard just now. There is no news, remember me to
all

Marcus

Stults

April 10, 1864

Dear Ma

Another letter in reference to that coat and now I have
concluded not to have it sent at all, as I think my dress coat
will answer this summer. It is a very nice coat but the set of it
never has suited me. I spoke last night of its storming severely.
This morning was a splendid sunshining morning but later in
the day it commenced raining again. In fact it rains half the
time. Not a favorable prospect of an early forward movement. I
think however it soon drys up this time of the year. There is no
doubt but what Old Grant has extensive preparations made for
a successful movement, but we fear he will not be as successful
as he formerly has been. We are not suited with his order
turning the sutlers adrift. We can live on pork and beans he
says. Well perhaps we can, and there is no doubt about what
we will be obliged to do. There is nothing in the country to be
had in the shape of victuals. Beef, pork, beans, coffee will be

the bill of fare, not much of a variety.

No important news that I am aware of. I hear the Lt. Col. is going to have us change camp again. The tents being greatly crowded. He thinks it is not as healthy as could be, we don't like the idea greatly. A detail from the regiment went out on picket this morning, Symmes included. I was out the last picket. Perhaps I have spoken of a concert saloon we have in this neighborhood. It has been largely attended all along. Now it is going to be converted to a church for our regiment and the 151st N.Y. My respects to all.

Marcus

Ross

Near Culpeper
April 14, 1864

Dear Mother

I am now back safe with the regiment but had a pretty rough time getting here. When we got to Washington we found no train running, so we went to Alexandria in a boat. We waited there four or five hours and found a trainload of hay going down so we jumped on and rode on that 70 miles. It was the roughest ride I ever had, but it is all over now and I feel all right. My cold is about gone now. I met Dr. Desbrow of our regiment at Freehold, who was going down the same day that I started so I had company all the way. Our camp now doesn't look quite as nice as it did when I left although I and the Adjt. have a very comfortable shanty. Nothing new is transpiring but it is expected we will soon move. I will send you some pictures in this for the friends you spoke about. Remember me to Miss Hanlin and give my love to Aunt Jane and Pop and write soon to

Your Affectionate Son
Burroughs

Vredenburgh

Hdqr's 3rd Div. 6 A Corps
April 22, 1864

Dear Mother

I am afraid you will think I treat you rather shabbily in not writing more punctually, but I have not had nothing very particular to observe and besides I think you owe me one. On the 18th we had a review of the 6th Corps and today the 2nd Corps was reviewed. I enjoyed the sight very much today. The

Major General Winfield S. Hancock USA

music was delightful, the day lovely and the troops looked superb. A Division of Cavalry and the artillery was reviewed also with the 2nd Corps. There was the time when Henry should have been present, nearly all the Generals in the army were on hand and one could have a perfect time gazing at them.

Grant is not taller than I am, round shoulders and a gross figure. If he is a very capable man, his appearance libels him. Hancock is an elegant officer.

Everything indicates an early movement. We had rations, have been issued baggage sent off, transportation reduced, and sutlers and women ordered beyond the lines, so that, Capt. Alstrom and I keep eight days rations ahead all the time. The sooner we move the better it will please me for we might as well face the music first as last. The inevitable battle must come off (somewhere). I saw Ed Taylor on the 21st. He was well and treated Col. Hall and me to ardent spirits.

Your Affectionate Son,
Peter

Ross

April 23, 1864

Dear Mother

Your kind letter reached me last evening and I write to answer. I feel as well as usual. My cold is entirely well. So Mrs. Vanderveer's son has been named after me. That is a great honor indeed. I wish him a long and prosperous life and hope he will make a better man than his namesake.

We are making great preparations for a move soon so you must not be surprised if you should hear in a few weeks of our being in Richmond. Everyone sems to think General Grant will take us through all right. I hope he will. We are expecting the Colonel and Quarter Master now every day. Our boys seem to think that unless Colonel is with them, the machine won't work, and I think myself they will do much better under him than any one else. For we all have confidence in his bravery and ability and when men have that feeling in regard to any one man, he is the only person that can lead them on to battle unflinchingly.

We are having some splendid weather here now, and if it continues long something must be done in the way of marching and fighting. The 10th New Jersey Regiment is in our Corps now, they came down here last week. Dr. Freeman is the surgeon of that regiment you remember. I have not seen them yet but Charlie went over yesterday and saw them. They have been lying up in Pennsylvania for a long time. There is a rumor that all mail communications northward is to be stopped. If that proves true, you will have to forfeit the pleasure of receiving my letters as often as usual. I will send you my picture

Colonel William S. Truex USA

with the addition of my name and rank as you wished. I believe my stock of news is about played out so I will close. Remember me to Miss Hanlin and give my love to Aunt Jane, Pop, Mimmie and all other inquiring friends and write soon to your

Affectionate Son
Burroughs

Ross

April 27, 1864

Dear Mother

As I have nothing special to do this afternoon I have concluded to employ a few spare moments by writing home as it may be in a few days I will not have an opportunity. Everything goes to show now that we will soon be on the move, for the splendid weather we have had lately has completely dried the roads so that great obstacle in the way of an army about to move, is done away with. We drill twice every day now and also practice target shooting a great deal. So that now some of the men think they can kill a rebel as far as they can see. Have you heard when the Colonel and Dr. intend coming down? We looked for them today but they did not make their appearance.

No more at present, love to all, write soon.

Your Affectionate Son
Burroughs

Stults

May 2, 1864

Dear Ma

I received yours of April 26th. I was on the picket line at the time, came in yesterday morning but felt too dull to write you. My eyes have been swelled nearly out of my head for a few days past. The doctor says it is the effects of a cold. I am getting better now. I see you are posted in military affairs but don't get down hearted too soon. We are not seriously fighting yet, of course there is a possibility of some fighting but perhaps not as seriously as you think. Burnside's Corps is on the way — part is already here. I think we will number as great as the rebel force.

We expected to be on the move before this. Now expect to move this week, some suppose we have not been ready to move sooner. The weather has been very fine for a long time back. The only rain we have had were thunder showers of an hour's duration-just sufficient to lay the dust. I suppose you are busy at home planting corn. How does Sam get along? I hear that Mary Ann is going to school this summer, but why doesn't she write me. I want to hear what she has to say. I don't encourage her to learn instrumental music, for I am sure she would never be satisfied by so doing. It would take at least four years practice to make it entertaining to company. She will find until sufficient talent is acquired, music of any sort is a nuisance.

The papers have it that mail communication from the Army of the Potomac is stopped but it is not credited here. It possibly may be stopped after the army moves. I received last night a package of envelopes and socks. Much obliged. Symmes is very well. Respect to all

Marcus

Ross

Sgt Major William Burroughs Ross
In the Wilderness near Chancellorsville
May 7, 1864

Dear Father

I write this as we lie behind our entrenchments expecting every moment a charge from the enemy. This is the third day we have been in the fight and everything seems to be going on all right. As yet, our regiment has been very fortunate having had only a few killed and wounded. None I believe from around Freehold. Captain Craig is among the missing. Some say he is captured but there is no certainty as to what has become of him. The rebs have been shelling us all day but they can't seem to get the proper range and therefore don't do much harm. The First New Jersey Brigade lost heavily yesterday. The First Regiment losing half their men and 11 officers. I will write more when I have an opportunity for I think trusting in God and General Grant we are sure to be successful. I saw Charlie Hall last night and also Dr. Freeman. They both look well. Also Jo Hulse. I don't now whether he is safe yet or not. His regiment was on the front line yesterday and lost very heavily. I saw him on the 5th inst.

May 9, 1864 10 A.M.

We are now three miles west of Spotsylvania Court House having advanced here on the night of the 7th after repulsing the enemy. We are entrenched here and think we can hold it against any force. None of our boys have slept any for three days and nights. The 10th New Jersey lost all but about 200 men yesterday having had 900 when they went in. Col. Ryerson is killed and their Lt. Col. prisoner. We have got 500 prisoners. We supported a battery yesterday and the way our battery mowed the rebs was awful.

11 A.M.

General Sedgwick commanding our Corps was killed about half an hour ago. He was standing right by our Regiment and was shot directly under the left eye, the blood flying on some of our boys. I saw him fall as he stood about 10 feet in advance of my position.

May 11, 1864

We are still in the entrenchments. Made a charge yesterday and captured two thousand prisoners. The artillery fire yesterday was awful. Kept up long after dark. The shells from our mortars and guns making a beautiful sight flying through the air.

[no signature]

General John Sedgwick USA

May 12, 1864

In the entrenchments near Spotsylvania Court House
9 A.M.

Dear Father

I will write a few lines as I have an opportunity to send them. This morning we received the glorious news that our cavalry has got in the rear of Lee and cut off his supplies and this morning Hancock of the 2nd Corps turned their right and is now driving them capturing 7000 prisoners. We are giving it to them here so that I can hardly write as the cannon shakes the ground all around us. I will sent you some notes I took down with this each day. You ought to hear the cheering along our lines this morning. The boys make everything sing. I will write more when I have a chance. All is well except a few killed and wounded yesterday. Write soon.

Hurrah for the Old Flag!

Burroughs

Vredenburgh

Hd. Qrs. 3 Div. 6 A.C.
On the North Bank of the
Nye or Po River about 3 miles
Northeast of Spotsylvania C.H.
May 15, 1864 10 A.M.

My Dear Father

I have had no opportunity of writing to you since the day we started till now, and I am not certain that this will reach you in several days. We started at 4 A.M. May 4th crossed the Rapidan at Germania Ford in the afternoon and bivouacked on the South Bank. The next day our whole army was engaged terrifically with Lee's army and at night our right was turned and our men were forced back a couple of miles, i.e., the 6th Corps — and I know that our side lost about 15,000. Our own Corps has lost 9000 men. Our 2nd. Brigade lost 1500 men the first two days and General and staff officers without number.

On the night of the 7th the army started at 9 P.M. and west to Chancellorsville thence to Aldrich thense short after right towards Spotsylvania C.H. We have been under fire every day till yesterday and I personally see who had narrow escapes every hour. Poor Sedgwick was shot in the face close by me. We had a terrible engagement on the 11th. The rebels were on our side of the breastworks and our men on the open ground.

The Rebels then charged and drove our forces back and then we fought all that day and all the next night till daylight when the rebs withdrew. The firing was incessant and hundreds of officers many of whom I knew were killed on our side. The next morning the entrenchments presented a most sickening sight, men were piled up on one another like sacks of grain at a depot — in every position, upside down, and here and there men with dead men on top of them would raise 2 arms only or turn their bodies showing they were still alive. It would be too much to give you matters in detail and it's about as embarrassing to have too much to say or not enough. All I can say is that we have lived in the most intense state of excitement for so long that now if we were certain the enemy would charge on us in five minutes I would go on to finish this letter without giving them a second thought. I think we are doing well on the whole and that we will eventually be successful if we keep on (as Abe says) "pegging away at them." Truex commands the 1st Brigade and though it has been under fire nearly all the time, has not been engaged. Now but 25,000 men, it is fearful to see how reduced the ranks are. I think from appearances that we still have heavy fighting as Lee is even now massing on our right and we are ordered to be in readiness to move at a moment's notice. With hopes for my safety and your health and love to all.

Your Affectionate Son,
Peter

Vredenburgh

Hd. Qrs. 3 Div 6th A.C.
May 19, 1864
6 P.M.

Dear Mother

I wrote last to father a day or two ago. The day after I wrote we were under very heavy fire, but only a few were injured. Today we have moved a little nearer Spotsylvania C.H. and am now throwing up entrenchments, while the booming of cannon seems to be continuous off to our right. I suppose there will be fighting tomorrow. This has been a terrible campaign and as Sam Miller says I hardly think it's worthwhile going through so much to get so little. We didn't see our wagon from the day we started till three or four days ago. I slept upon the ground every night without any shelter. I lost my India rubber coat yesterday so that now I am in a bad fix. I saw Cloke and Ed Taylor three days ago, they were both well. So many have been killed whom I know that, it makes it seem but a short step from this to the next world. You can have no idea with what perfect indifference everyone seems to regard life out here.

You hear the same jokes, songs and conversation when we are just on the eve of an engagement as in camp. Though as an army we do not advance. Yet in reality we are moving all the time, now charging front, now up all night expecting an attack, then attack the enemy's earthworks and finding ourselves baffled, are occurring daily. This is a slow way of getting to Richmond. If it were not for active combinations we never could get there. The enemy can retreat throwing up breastworks, one after another until our journey would prove as impossible as the feat of carrying out a stick, cut up in shavings. I think Lee's army is partially demoralized or he would have attacked us. The best account of the early stages of this campaign is in the "Army and Navy Journal" of the 14th inst. You can hardly believe any of the reports though and I even have no curiosity to see them any more. Quartermaster Cowart has not arrived yet and I am afraid he will get himself in trouble when he does come. Kerner has gone to the hospital — says he fell from his horse but he is such a white livered coward that I don't believe he is hurt at all. He has shirked every time there has been danger. This between ourselves. Write soon and send a few stamps.

Affectionately
Peter

Cold Harbor House, VA

Vredenburgh

Hd. Qrs. 1 Div. 6 A.C.
Under a tree
June 2, 1864

Dear Mother

I have a chance to send you word that I am well and uninjured though I have run great risks since I last wrote. I have been under severe fire every day.

My mare was shot the day before yesterday in the head but I think she will recover. Hitting her saved me as I was on her at the time. We are now 8 miles from Richmond near Cold Harbor and nothing but the wail of musketry and roar of artillery wrecks the ear from morning till night. Yesterday afternoon Our Division was arrayed in four lines and charged the rebel breastworks and took them with some prisoners. The 14th did splendidly but many men were lost. Col. Truex was wounded on the hand slightly. I am not with the Regiment but I was 25 yards in front of the 1st line till I got close to the pits mounted. Such terrible sights Mother as I have seen. Oh and how I wish this was over. Even now while I am writing men are being carried by on stretchers by the dozens, for the firing is very severe about 300 yards in front. I was up all night getting our regiment together out of the chaos they had got in yesterday.

Peter

Vredenburgh

Hd. Qrs. D Div. 6 A.C.
Between Gaines' Mill Va.
June 4, 1864 7 A.M.

I am still uninjured though yesterday was a very severe day upon our troops. Our Division lost 400 men and very heavily in officers. It was designed to attack along our whole line at once but it fizzled in some parts of it and that upset the design. We have now recd. orders saying that offensive operations for the present will be suspended and our advance made by regular approaches, though whether Grant means it or not I can't say. Just think what we have gone through with; for 30 days we have slept in the open air with no shelter, no change of diet from corn bread and hard tack and coffee, up four nights out of five and engaged nearly every day. The rebels are strong yet in front of us and I see no end to this matter without other combinations or perhaps and exhaustion of supplies at Richmond on the part of the enemy. All this stuff that you see in

the papers about our
brilliant victories, immense
losses of the enemy and
their full retreat from
Richmond are absurd.

We have killed a good
many of them as they have
of us but as we move to the
left and south so did they
until now they are between
us and Richmond as they
have ever been. If we
should move to the left
again so would they like-
wise move enough to keep
us at bay but the papers
would score it I suppose
another rebel retreat.

Gaines' Mill (VA)

There have of course been many brilliant charges and suc-
cesses at different parts of our line since the general engagement of the 12th but nothing that should force Lee to retreat.
The night before last Our Division charged the rebel earthworks and carried them. I have since been highly complemented by Gen'l Meade in orders. The troops were in four lines
and the 14th was in the front line of the 1st Brigade. We only
lost a little more than a hundred. It was a beautiful sight to see
the troops marching in steady lines across an open field in
direct range of the enemy's guns. I was selected by Ricketts to
lead them and I did so mounted and escaped unhurt while the
Regiment lost over a hundred. Don't say anything about this
for it don't sound well coming from me. I have just received a
note from Qr. Master telling me he has those things for me. My
bay mare that was shot in the head I think will recover in time.

Your Affectionate Son,
Peter

The Battle of Cold Harbor
June 1,2,3 — 1864

On June 1, 1864, the Battle of Cold Harbor began. Confederates
arrived and deployed their forces first. Grant planned to attack Lee
early in the morning, but delays postponed the offensive. Towards
evening, Federal Generals W.F. Smith and Wright ordered an assault,
gained ground, and fortified their positions. Again, delays postponed
events another day, and Lee solidified his defensive positions along
the Chickahominy. As the sun rose on June 3, 1864, Union "huzzas,"
drums, and rifle fire signaled a major Federal assault. Southern
commanders Anderson, Early, and Hill were opposed by Smith,
Wright, and Hancock. The Federal assault was met with murderous
volleys of "grape and canister" in a hell of "leaden hail." Losses at
Cold Harbor were frightful. Statistics differ but in about three quar-

Photos: U.S. Army Military History Institute

General U.S. Grant at Cold Harbor.

ters of an hour 7000 Federals fell. Confederate losses were relatively light in comparison. Both armies retired behind their defenses.

The 14th New Jersey Volunteers joined the main Federal assault over the open ground at Cold Harbor. In two hours of fighting, the Regiment lost two hundred and forty in killed and wounded. On June 3rd, additional Federal thrusts were turned back with heavy losses. It was here that Lieutenant Marcus Stults was killed. Captain John C. Patterson provided a vivid account of the fighting at Cold Harbor:

"We moved out from our position at Crump's Creek on the evening of May 31st, marching all the night in the direction of Cold Harbor, and reaching there a little past twelve o'clock on June 1st. We were immediately formed in line, and our corps (Sixth) ordered to get ready for a charge. The bugle sounded at about a quarter to five o'clock P.M. and we dashed forward, my company on the right. We suffered severely, but getting through a slough we were soon upon the enemy, leaping the works, and putting him to route. I being on the right directed the movement. We pursued the rebels some sixty paces beyond their works, when I ordered a halt, finding that we were alone. When I say alone, I mean companies D, F, and a part of A. I then formed the line, and passing to the left, found that we were broken from the rest of the regiment. I then faced left, and moved off obliquely to rejoin the rest of the regiment to the left and rear. In moving along the enemy's works, I found the cause of the break in the regiment to be a bend in the works. As we sprang on the works, just at the bend, we saw the enemy in pretty strong force just above the bend firing at the rest of my regiment. I immediately called to the men to follow me, but the noise of battle, I suppose, prevented my call being heard. I then called for volunteers, and in answer fourteen brave boys sprang over the works, led by young Rodman M. Clark. I ordered the boys to fire a volley into the rebels as they stood packed together, which they did, and the most of them threw down their arms. At this point young Clark displayed great gallantry, dashing in among the rebs and commencing to disarm them. Some of them still kept firing at us, but all the while we were disarming others. I ran up to the one I judged to be a superior officer, and placing my pistol at

Burying the dead at Cold Harbor.

his head, told him if he did not have his men stop firing I would shoot him, whereupon he ordered them to cease. Before they did so, however, one scamp fired at me so closely that I felt the heat of the explosion in my face. The rebel officer proved to be a major. I ordered him to pass to the rear, and then proceeded, assisted by young Clark and the other boys, to secure as many prisoners as possible — our time being short, as we were feeling the fire of rebel reinforcements. In about ten to fifteen minutes, I secured and turned over to the Provost Marshal one hundred and sixty-six men, including one major, three captains, and three lieutenants. I had one man killed and one badly wounded. We remained at Cold Harbor, with severe skirmishing, until June 7, when we moved and crossed the James River."

Vredenburgh

Hd. Qrs. 3Div. 6 A.C.
Near Cold Harbor Va.
June 5, 1864 11 A.M.

Dr. Mother,

I wrote you yesterday and soon after received your letter
of the 27th inst. of May. I have received but two or three letters
from you since I started. Our troops occupy the same ground
they did yesterday and we are digging trenches at night. In the
day time the men are in an exposed place as the rebel sharp
shooters can hit nearly every man who shows himself. Our
position now is Warren on the left (of the army). Hancock near
this way then our corps met Baldy Smith's 18th Corps and
Burnside on the extreme right. Fighting is occurring along the
lines all the time in some place or another. The enemy assaulted our (6th Corps) and the 2nd Corps the night before last
and last night they attacked us again. Of course when they
attack so near we all have to rush out to our horses and start
for the place immediately.

Your Affectionate Son
Peter

Vredenburgh

Hd. Qrs. 3 Div. 6th A.C.
South of Cold Harbor Va.
June 8, 1864   10 A.M.

My Dear Mother

I received yesterday the letter that Qr. Master had for me
and it shows how useless it is to bother persons with letters
when they can be sent by mail. We still hold our old position
and at night we run out zigzags thus the rebel line is concave
and ours convex that is the general line varied of course by the
necessary sinuosities that the ground and woods occasion. We
are now under fire from the sharp shooters of the enemy all the
time, that is if we do not take pains to keep behind trees or in
pits or behind the entrenchments we will be fired at and probably hit. A good many of our men are hit every day. Yesterday
there was a novel sight to see us talking pleasantly with each
other and exchanging papers and tobacco. We who but a short
time previously had been trying to take the lives of each other
and would soon again resume the unpleasant occupation. Our
lines are only 250 yards apart and an open field between.
There are incidents without number that would be interesting
to you but it seems hardly worthwhile to write them. I will tell
you of one that occurred to me about two weeks ago. I was on

Pontoon bridge across the Pamunkey River.

the bay mare then and riding out over a new position that we had taken on the bank of the Pamunkey by request of Gen'l Wright and Ricketts to see if we would have time to have the picketts regularly detailed or whether the skirmishers should be sent right out. There was a severe engagement between the cavalry going on at the time on our front and I went along a meadow on our right till I came to an open field. I saw no cavalry then and went on across the field looking sharp towards the left when the fighting was not indicating any danger in front. I looked fortunately at last towards my front and as I did so four rebel cavalrymen came suddenly over the crest of a hill in front of me not over two hundred yards off. I reigned up instantly and as I did so two or three of the four shot at me but as they were mounted missed me and the horse too. You would have laughed to have seen me cut across that field but I was afraid they would cut me off from a bridge I had to cross and so made lively time. My mare was shot in the head a day or two afterwards but she will be fit to ride in a month or so I think.

I see and know almost all the officers of repute in this army now and will be able to give you information that you can rely on I hope someday about them. I saw the Richmond Enquirer of yesterday's date and it acknowledges a defeat at Staunton by Hunter. I hope it is so as it seems to me that we will never get to Richmond this way without something to divert their attention in some other quarter. Tell Will that I did not get his letter till yesterday and that I am glad he has settled that Sherman estate satisfactorily.

With much love to all
Your Affectionate Son
Peter

Garthwright House at Cold Harbor, VA.

P.S. Give my love to Taylor if she is with you yet. Ed started for Washington a day or two ago. Don't mention what I may have said about Kerner to anyone.

Vredenburgh

Hd. Qrs. 3rd. Div. 6 A.C.
June 11, 1864
Near Cold Harbor Va.

My Dear Mother

Here we are yet you

see though our Division moved a short distance to the left from where we were last night. I don't see anything very encouraging in our case notwithstanding the press will have it, that Lee is retreating etc. I don't see how we are to get much nearer Richmond, though we may move by the left flank again further South or Southeasterly. In fact I have just heard that we are to move tonight. All our movements and all our work is now done at night and the day is occupied in lying quiet, drinking brandy punches and smoking. You would be surprised to spend a few hours in camp here and see how utterly oblivious everyone seems to be to his destiny. You could hear the same light conversation. The same songs and the same hopes of future prospect canvassed as if there were no more bloody fights for the Army of the Potomac to see. My opinion is that the hardest fighting is yet in store for us as the rebels seem to have their entrenchments everywhere in our front, and the only way we can advance is to assault their front, which as you may have observed is rather expensive.

The weather is delicious only a little too warm, and the numerous bands around afford us music from morning till night. We can also hear the rebel bands in front and on each side of us, but they are not so good as ours.

There is a Capt. Fisher from Philadelphia on our staff who is well acquainted with the Mortons. Capt. McClellan a brother to the General and Capt. Holmes son of Oliver Wendell Holmes are on the Corps staff with both of whom I am well acquainted. This is the poorest part of Virginia that I have seen yet and I long to get in a more pleasant place. I saw Ed Taylor a day or two before he started home and I suppose you have probably seen him by this time. Alstrom left as yesterday, having been mustered into the 3rd. N.J. Cavalry. I am now the ranking Inspector in the Corps and I think I will remain in the Department a while longer to see what may turn up. A number of the inspectors have been killed or wounded during this campaign. I could give you graphic descriptions of our engagements but you have seen so much of them in the papers that I will not attempt the last. Col. Truex is getting well and will only have one finger stiffened. I have lost many friends that I don't know for whom to grieve in particular and so look at the matter as inevitable destiny, and I don't grieve at all. I have seen four or five intimate acquaintances and warm friends shot down nearly at the same time around me and have hardly at the time stopped to give them a thought or much less, a tear of pity. You would be astonished to see how little noise or complaint the wounded make. They know that they have no weeping family near to soothe their anguish or lull their cries or take a personal interest in them, so it is a rare occurrence to hear a wounded man make any noise at all on the battlefield. The Sanitary and Christian Commissions have done much for the relief of the wounded and if there were not so many infernal rascals among their employees they would be much more effective. But still a certain proportion reaches the desired objects and many lives have been saved by them. Tell father that I have not written to him because I hardly get time or rather the facilities for writing a letter and you must consider

Captains McClellan (above) and Holmes (below).

Photos: U.S. Army Military History Institute

General W.F. "Baldy" Smith USA

a letter to one addressed to all. I received two letters with stamps in.

We expect to advance in a few moments, in fact we were ordered to move at 5 o'clock but we will not probably get off till 6. Our course is onward to Richmond but I cannot say which road. Do not believe half you see in the papers. The Rebels are not in retreat nor have we treated them in such a way as to cause them to retreat yet. They have killed more of our men than we have of them and my hope is in our superior numbers. We have a 100,000 men today and they only about 60,000 but with their knowledge of the country and the extraordinary natural advantage presented by the country may enable them to resist us for a long time. With much love to you and I am your Affectionate Son

Peter

P.S. I am just ordered to get ready to move. I have written 3 letters since I started. The General puts great confidence in me and never gives me any work to do till we get into a fight and then he gives me the most responsible part of it. Baldy Smith came up yesterday. I saw him. I have seen nearly every man of reputation in the Army. I sleep on the ground every night when I sleep at all, in boots and coat and sword.

After Cold Harbor

When General Grant broke off the action around Cold Harbor, he moved toward Richmond from the south. The Third Division was sent to Bermuda Hundred by transport after it had served as rear guard for the Army of the Potomac. From there it joined Butler's army before Petersburg. While destroying a large part of the Weldon Railroad, it was attacked and lost heavily in killed and wounded on June 23, 1864. There were Northern cavalry actions against the railroads around Petersburg. The Second and Sixth Corps were ordered to extend the siege lines south and west of Petersburg. In response, Lee ordered Hill to attack the Federal Second Corps now commanded by General Birney. The rebels drove Union forces near the Jerusalem Plank Road and, for the time being, thwarted Grant's plans.

Bermuda Hundred

While Grant was preoccupied around Petersburg, General Hunter was in command of Union forces moving up the Shenandoah Valley. They defeated rebel forces in their path and arrived near Lynchburg on June 15, 1864. General Lee considered the area strategically important and moved forces to challenge the Federal advance. He succeeded in checking Hunter's troops and forced them to retreat through the Kanawha Valley which left the Shenandoah at the mercy of the Confederates. Lee seized the opportunity and moved quickly. He wished to relieve pressure on Richmond by sending General Early on a flanking move into Maryland. If all went well, he hoped to capture Washington before Grant could reinforce the under-garrisoned Union defenses of the Capital. He sent General Jubal Early northward across the Potomac toward Frederick, Maryland. General Grant responded on July 6th, and detached the Third Division of the Sixth Corps from the army in front of Petersburg to strengthen Federal forces opposing Early. General Ricketts commanded this division of approximately 5000 and led it from Petersburg to Locust Point near Baltimore and then to Monocacy. The Fourteenth New Jersey Volunteers were the first to reach the area. They were opposed by perhaps 15,000 veteran Confederates...

Vredenburgh

Hd. Qrs 3rd. Div. 6th A.C.
2 miles North East of Petersburg Va.
June 20, 1864   11 A.M.

My Dear Mother

I have just recd. your letter of the 16th. The one that I spoke of the Haights calling on you. I wrote to you yesterday and in my letter stated that we expected to start for Petersburg soon and we did start in a very few minutes afterward. We are here now along the line of rifle pits. The rebels were driven some yesterday on their left, that is our right and now we can shell the city from this part of the line and prevent them from using the railroad. This part of Virginia is lovely — green fields and elegant houses meet the eye on every side. While we were waiting at Charles City the other day, I made the acquaintance of two very interesting young ladies, grandchildren of Chief Justice Marshall. They lived in an elegant house and had been in their day surrounded with every luxury. I rode up to their house one morning by accident and found the young ladies in great distress. Their father had been arrested, their servants mostly taken off and everything of value nearly destroyed or stolen. I immediately sent them a guard and saved some of their property — cows and corn etc. and they were very grateful and did their best to make my visit agreeable.

After that Col. Hall and I went there to see them without reserve and will only add that the more we communicated the more we affiliated. You see families left destitute so often here by the thieves that are more or less, in our army, that I never go near a house without expecting to hear a mournful tale from the occupants. I am glad to feel that I have not taken anything feloniously since I undertook this "job" (as Lincoln calls it) except it may have been a few vegetables. I don't know though but that I may become a "demoralized soldier" in time. I have seen very handsome places — as handsome as the Strong's, surrounded with everything the heart could wish for, completely demolished, obliterated, destroyed by our soldiers — directly gone — and this is about the way we have treated the

Major General David Hunter USA

neglected citizens of this forsaken country ever since we left Brandy Station. I have to hold this paper in my hand while I write so you must excuse the writing.

Your Affectionate Son
Peter

Vredenburgh

Hd. Qrs. 3 Div. 6 A.C.
6 miles south of Petersburg
near the Weldon Railroad
June 23, 1864   11 A.M.

My Dear Mother

I have not written or received a letter from you in some time, June 16 I believe I heard from you. We started from Bermuda Hundred about a week ago and since then have seen as hard times as we saw in the Wilderness. We were sent here on the entrenched left of the army three days ago and since then have been engaged off and on nearly every hour in the day. The night before last our Division charged the enemy and made a mile and a half towards the railroad, so that our pickets destroyed some of it yesterday, but last night we were attacked and in such force that we were forced to retire to where we started from. The rebels captured nearly the whole of a Division of the 2nd Corps yesterday. I have just left the division where the attack was made.

The rebels made a furious assault this morning on our right and the artillery was terrific but I am not informed yet what success has attended either side. We have just been ordered to get ready to move and things look unfavorable on our right. I haven't washed my face nor had my side arms or boots off in three days and many of the regimental officers might extend the time a week.

Its terrible Mother and I hope for God's sake we will finish this "job" up pretty soon. I've taken my sword belt in over 6 inches and I think from 145 lb. weight I have fallen to about 110 lbs. but I feel as well as ever. You find my letters rather personal but I know that all you want to know is about me and the public press gives better general information than I can give. They lie though like thunder and what you have heard about Petersburg being in our possession and our successful assaults is all false. The rebels got to Petersburg as soon as we got opposite to it and they hold it now. We are still extending our army down to the left to enable us to cut the Petersburg and Weldon Railroad and then they will have to attack us in our entrenchments or retreat from Richmond. Our army is now half managed — Generals trust too much to their subordinates instead of working for themselves and the most astonishing thing is that we get along as well as we do. Don't show these scraps to anyone.

Your Affectionate Son
Peter

Vredenburgh

Hd. Qrs. 3rd. Div. 6th A.C.
Six or Seven miles south of Petersburg
June 25, 1864 11 A.M.

Dear Doctor Kimball

I received your kind letter of the 16th inst. yesterday and hasten to answer. You must excuse me for not having written to you before, but if you were here you would immediately give me a quit-claim from all blame. This is only the second letter I have written since the first of April except to mother. I happen to have my valise up today and that is the reason I seize the opportunity. Well Doctor, what a devil of a time we have had of it — have we not? Nothing but fighting, starving, marching and cussing for 50 days with no cessation especially in the cussing. I don't see how we can end the trouble yet very soon though we will succeed in time. The papers publish so many lies that I hardly see how you can have any definite idea of the situation of affairs. Lee has never retreated a step since the opening of the campaign. He has ever been between us and Richmond and when we moved by the left flank he moved by the right. Of course he could not cover the sides of our army and therefore conducted his movements in such a way that we always found him in front of us when we started in the direction of our objective point. Grant has done just right I think and in the best manner but these stories that would lead you to believe that Lee has ever retreated are untrue.

Lee could not of course keep us from moving in any direction a hundred miles from Richmond nor did he want to. He attacked us in the Wilderness because he thought he had advantages (and he did) in his favor and he would have liked to have gotten in front of us, but, if he had stopped us from moving South by the left flank he would have been unable to have kept us from moving to the right and that is the way we have arrived to the James River. This is the true base and everybody feels the benefits of the water communications already. I don't see but that we can stay here till Richmond falls if it should not occur in a year. The beauty of our position is that we threaten so much of Lee's lines that he can't know where to expect us to strike. If we had come here in the first instance Lee would have started for Washington again and we would have been obliged to follow him as heretofore. We will have to whip his army before the rebellion can be crushed and the best that we can hope for is to have equal ground to do the fighting on. Our position at the present time reaches from the James River, a few miles above Bermuda Hundred where our right rests, and from thence to Points of Rock on the Appomattox, thence across the Richmond and Norfolk railroad, thence across the Jerusalem Plank Road and thence westerly to within a couple of miles of the Weldon Railroad distant about seven miles south of Petersburg. We hold this line by having men in pits or behind works of some sort, it may be dirt or rails, abatis or all three, anything to make a defense you know. The men are two ranks deep over most of the line and in the front of these entrenchments we have our skirmishers and pickets about five or ten yards apart and from 25 yards to a mile according to circumstances to the front. Now if we wished to advance and feel of the enemy we would order the skirmishers to go ahead which they would do till the enemy fired so sharply that they would have to stop and then if the general determined to go ahead anyhow he would order the line of battle forward, it might be in two lines or more (generally in four). Its astonishing how well our men stand the terrible work and exposure. We had no vegetables or any anti-scorbutic for thirty days after we started and yet there was very little more sickness than we had in camp. The rebels look fat and fine nowadays and are perfectly confident of success. Meade manages the army in detail and Grant does not interfere in anyway. This I know for I have been present attending to the (distribution) disposition of the troops of our corps and Meade asked the questions necessary and made the adjustments and gave the orders necessary without saying a word to Grant who stood directly behind him.

Though you may think that when the army is reported quiet we are doing nothing yet such is not the case. We are always shifting and moving about. Nearly every day our own division is moved and fighting is going on all the time on some point of the line. Yesterday afternoon our division was visited by Anderson's Division of Hill's Corps and we lost about eighty men out of the First Brigade. They drove our skirmishers back to the entrenchments and then it was so dark that they suspended operations. This morning nothing was to be seen of them, but as there has been much cannonading on our right I suppose it was a dodge to get us to move troops down here, and then they have moved back and are now attacking on our right.

There is nothing but the rattle of musketry and the booming of cannon all the time so that one scarcely notices it now without it on our immediate front. In the Wilderness at Spotsylvania and Cold Harbor we got pretty well broken in though for there they kept up the most terrific night attack every night. I should like you to hear one of these midnight roars. I can't imagine anything that could be more appalling to a person not used to it. It always comes on like a bellyache, all at once, and you would think from the sound that

Boats docked at Broadway Landing on the Appomattox River.

nothing could stand before the firing a moment. Of course we always get our horses ready as soon as possible, when the attack is near our front and hurry down to the line of battle. There are never many killed in such attacks and seldom pays the attacking party. Write to me again Doctor and give me the domestic news, nothing would be more acceptable. Give my respects to Mrs. Kimball and remember me to Will.

Yours truly
P.V. Jr.

Vredenburgh

Hd. Qrs. 3rd. Div. 6th A.C.
Near Petersburg Va.
June 28, 1864

Dear Mother

I have only time to write a few lines. A correspondent of the New York Herald came to our Hd. Qrs. yesterday and you may probably like to read his correspondence. His name is Hannan or something like it. I am perfectly well and I think we will have quiet times for a while now. We had a delightful orgy at Col. Truex's Hd. Qrs. last night and kept it up till 2 o'clock this morning. Woodward, Ross, Col. Hall, Alstrom and about fifteen others were there. We had any quantity of vocal music, whiskey, lobster, claret, pickles, salt, punch, cigars and fun. Yours of the 27th was recd. I am entirely out of stamps. Chaplain has given Kerner another thrust I see in the Democrat. Give my love to Helen.

Peter

General James H. Wilson, USA

Vredenburgh

Hd. Qrs. 3rd. Div. 6th A.C.
July 3, 1864
Near Petersburg, Va.

My Dear Mother

I received your letter of the 28th with the stamps in it. I was at Reams Station on the Weldon Railroad at the time. We left this place last Tuesday and went to Reams Station (about ten miles south of Petersburg) to help Wilson's cavalry out of a tight place they had gotten into. The Rebels had surrounded them, and we went down to open the way, but when we arrived there we found that Wilson had gone further southward after losing his sick and wounded, ambulances and batteries, and as the rebels had scattered too we occupied our leisure time in destroying the railroad and then returned here yesterday. We only destroyed about 3 miles of the road. Hannan, a correspondent of the New York Herald went with us and you had better read his dispatch.

You have a good deal more anxiety about me than there is any occasion for. As the fatigue that I undergo is not equal to that of any line officer or soldier of our large army. The private soldiers are the heroes of this war, and the mounted officers don't deserve a thought from the humane and charitable, while there is a soldier in the field. During an actual engagement the risk is a little greater for staff officers because they can't lie down as those on foot do, but we lose as many men who are marched to death as from the bullets of the enemy. (Don't send me any papers as I can get them here now.)

Chaplain Rose went home the other day and I suppose you have seen him by this time. You needn't believe more than half he tells you whether it is pro or con. He is a hypocritical rascal and I don't know hardly who is the best man, he or Kerner. I dare say he will give graphic descriptions of the fighting and he was never under fire in his life, whenever there has been an engagement he invariably went back to the hospital. I just write this that you may understand him thoroughly. You had better not say anything about it to anyone else. I am constantly hearing of the death of friends and last night I heard of the casualties in the 3rd. Delaware. This regiment was at Frederick while I was there and I was intimate with nearly all of the officers.

I had a young sergeant clerk for me in the Div. office by the name of Corson who was a very fine boy and I was strongly attached to him. I heard last night that he was killed a few days ago. I used to correspond with him and feel quite sad over his death.

I always thought Bill Spain to be what we call in the army a "dead beat" and it is well that he is out of the service. I wish you would send me by Rose or by letter a pen knife (for the nails). I have none now, also a good tooth brush, that one you sent by the Qr. Master is a miserable soft thing and the bristles came out the first time I used it. Tell Aunt Sarah that she can always tell whether an egg will hatch or not by holding it up to the light and looking severely at the butt end.

With love to Father and all
Peter

Ross

July 4, 1864
Petersburg, Virginia

Dear Father and Mother

I will again take the pleasure of writing home a few lines to keep you from thinking that I have become a victim of the

Johnnies. We are now lying on the extreme left of our line, about five miles from Petersburg. We have just got back from a raid we made on the Weldon and Petersburg Railroad. Wilson's cavalry needed reinforcements so the brave 6th Corps was sent to help him. We started from here about noon on the 29th of June with the thermometer standing at a hundred in the shade, and reached Reams Station by 8 o'clock the same evening. The next morning we went into the railroad iron, upsetting the length of a brigade at once and then piling the sleepers and rails together, and burned them and also the station, and then we started back, without having had the pleasure of a fight, as the Rebs had all skedadled before we got there.

Fortifications at Petersburg, VA.

Lt. George Mitchell of the 5th was here last evening and wished to be remembered to you when I wrote. We are having some awful warm weather here just at present. We expect to celebrate the fourth about five o'clock this afternoon by opening some batteries of hundred pounders on Petersburg. How is Mimmie and her little boy coming on? I suppose he is growing some by this time. I wrote to Let sometime since, but have not received an answer yet. I would like you to send me if convenient, a Herald. I see that order I sent home was published in the one you sent me. I believe I have nothing more of importance to communicate, so will close up hoping soon to hear from some of you. Remember me to Miss Hanlin and give my love to Aunt Jane and Mimmie.

Burroughs

Ross

On Board Steamer Enroute To Baltimore
July 7, 1864

Dear Mother

We started yesterday from Petersburg about five o'clock A.M. with orders to proceed to Harpers Ferry Md. (Virginia) We marched to City Point, a distance of about fifteen miles, and from there took a steamer for Baltimore, where we are going to take the cars and proceed to our destination. We have just now passed Annapolis on the Chesapeake Bay. Oh, I wish

Steamship "New Jersey"
on the James River.

you were here to enjoy our ride. It is splendid. We are on the Steamer Columbia which has been one day a splendid boat. Nice berths and state rooms and mattresses, all in the berths. Something we have not been used to. We have our Brigade Band on board which discourses some very sweet music. Some of the boys are dancing a cotillion on the upper deck now. We have got our flags flying although they look rather the worse for wear, the balls having torn them. Every vessel that passes us gives us three cheers when the boys give them the yell which we are so familiar with on making a charge at the Johnnies. Yesterday we passed an excursion boat full of ladies, when such a time as we had cheering and waving handkerchiefs you never saw. About tomorrow we will go past our old camp at Monocacy Bridge Md, on the cars. This has been so far, a delightful trip. The scenery has been beautiful all the way and the cool breeze delightful. Quite a contrast to the awful dust and hot weather of Petersburg. The boat shakes so much I can hardly write, so will close, write soon to

Your Affectionate Son
Burroughs

Vredenburgh

Hd. Qrs. 3rd Div. 6 A.C.
Baltimore
July 12, 1864

Dear Mother

I have not written to you since about the 5th of July near Petersburg. I recd. yours of the 6th and one from Will of the 5th. We took boats from City Point on the 6th and arrived in Baltimore the night of the 7th. We then started for Frederick in the afternoon and arrived at Monocacy Junction Friday morning at daylight. A line of battle was immediately formed facing the large wooden bridge near Thomas'. The rebels were there in Frederick in force and advancing towards us. I went to Thomas' and met Col. Hall there. We took breakfast with him a couple of drinks each, and then went back to the bridge, running across the turnpike leading to Thomas' — then up toward Thomas' front gate where the 14th rested. The rebels now came in force from behind Thomas' house over a little meadow (where Henry first saw me the day he brought Dash up). They advanced over the crest on a line with Thomas' house before the firing became brisk and then it opened as severely as I have ever heard from such a small force (say 4000) of ours actually engaged and 7 or 8000 of the rebels advancing. Their batteries enfiladed us and did excellent execution but our boys fought as if they were fighting for their own homes literally mowed down the first two lines of the rebels who thought they only had to fight 100 day men. Our men at Thomas' gate then charged up his yard and across his fields right up to his house and fought the rebels around the corner behind the trees and everywhere else till they retired behind his barn. Of course I only speak of the immediate front at this point for there was terrific firing along the whole line but I went with the charging party at this particular point. The rebels when we reached the house commenced shelling it and in less time than I write it had sent a half a dozen shells into it. I rushed into the house as soon as I got there to see what had become of Thomas and his family and found them in the cellar frightened to death.

He (Thomas) did not come out so I went through his home and locked the drawers — some of the doors and brought downstairs a basket of silver that they had packed up. They all hung on me and wanted me to stay but I couldn't do it as a rebel prisoner who was brought in wounded informed me that Lee with his army was on our left near Urbana and that Early's Corps was fighting our few troops so I had to go back to the General in order that we might get the orders to retire. I never saw such accurate firing — every one of our captains was killed or wounded except one and he did not stay up or he would have been too. Col. Hall was wounded in the arm. I paid the Thomas family a tender farewell and left them. We got the order to retire and did so in some confusion at first and struck for the Baltimore Pike. The rebels followed us closely and it was really magnificent to see how heroically they charged. I never saw such a bold move before. They evidently thought we were recruits and walked right up to us in this open field without skirmishing, dodging or running as soldiers usually do in the open on a charge. Our men never fought better and their loss of about 1400 in three hours shows how well they stood up in single line, without breastwork against the successive charges of the enemy. Capt. Conine was killed, Conover wounded. He had his wound dressed but the stretcher bearers were shot while carrying him off and he must have been captured. He will recover if attended to and they left him in Frederick.

Craig (Lt.) was wounded severely and captured. We only number 180 men in the regiment now and by request of the remaining officers I am to go back to it to take command. It is queer that I was not hit for I was right up to the front most all the time and though several shells exploded so close that many men said they saw me killed yet I didn't get a scratch. Our Adjutant General who was mounted also, came up by me and was shot almost instantly in the leg and arm. I have just been

General Lew Wallace USA

informed that our report of missing this morning was 1600 but four or five hundred more will likely come in and reduce our loss to about 1100. We marched all night and reached Ellicott's Mills near Chapville the next day noon making a distance of twenty-five miles after being up so many nights and undergoing so much fighting.

We came here from Ellicott's Mills last night and now the general has informed me that the rebels have surrounded Washington and I am to leave at daylight tomorrow morning to select a position for our command about 3 miles out of the city. It is all excitement here, and I am stopped quite frequently as I ride through the streets by refugees from Frederick City. They all seem glad to see me and I feel glad to think I have so many friends there. You may see us up in N. Jersey yet — but there will certainly be terrific engagements in this vicinity, or nearer Washington in a few days. Don't show this part of the letter where I seem to brag to anybody but Father. General Wallace who commands all the troops at Monocacy stood up on a hill where he could see everything and recognized me by my straw hat and the next day he told Gen'l Ricketts (who told me) that I was a most valuable officer, that he had seen me all the time. He complemented the Division very highly in his official report to Halleck.

Affectionately Good Bye
Peter

The Battle of Monocacy
July 9,10 — 1864

Early on July 9, 1864, the Battle of Monocacy began. It took place primarily on land owned by the Thomas and Worthington families. Confederate cavalry crossed the Monocacy, dismounted and assaulted the Federal lines on foot. Through the cornfields came the long gray lines only to be met with ferocious Federal fire. A second Confederate charge was also beaten back and the action slackened until afternoon.

General John B. Gordon's Confederates crossed the Monocacy River, formed in several battle lines and advanced all along the Federal positions. The two armies became locked in desperate close range combat. Union General Lew Wallace held his line until late afternoon until Confederate artillery fire from the Best farm made his position untenable. He ordered a retreat toward Baltimore and Federal forces retreated from the area.

The significance of the Battle of Monocacy might best be described as a delaying action. General Wallace was able to engage Confederate troops long enough to allow Grant precious time to rush reinforcements from the Petersburg theatre. Confederate General Early advanced on Washington but soon realized that he was too late. He crossed the Potomac which ended the South's third and final northern advance. There were about 3000 casualties on both sides.

The 14th New Jersey Volunteers were stationed on the extreme left of the Union line and absorbed enemy attacks for six hours. The Regiment suffered heavy casualties.

Lt. Col. Hall and Adjutant Buckalew were wounded, Captains Stults Conine, and Conover killed and all the other line officers were either killed or wounded with the exception of Captain J.J. Janeway, Company K. Janeway succeeded in supervising the withdrawal to a point some six miles to the rear at New Market. He too, was eventually wounded. The Regiment lost 14 killed and 105 wounded and 39 missing. The following is an eyewitness account from an officer of the 14th:

"When the enemy at Monocacy first struck us, three lines deep against our single line, his fire was terrific. Our Color-Sergeant (William B. Cottrell) while bravely waving his colors in front of his regiment, received a ball which before striking him passed through and severed the flagstaff just below his left hand. He fell forward and died upon the flag, his lifeblood staining its folds. Our colors were immediately raised by one of the color guards; he, also, was almost instantly shot down. Then another raised it up; he was badly wounded and turned it over to the next corporal, who was mortally wounded. These four were killed and disabled in almost the time it has taken me to write it, showing the terrible fire we were exposed to at the battle of Monocacy. Our Lieutenant-Colonel was at the first badly wounded, his arm being broken. Captain Conover, Company D, the next ranking officer, was mortally wounded. The command then devolved upon Captain Harris, who was shot through the lungs and carried from the field. The next in rank, Captain Stults, Company H, was shot a few minutes after and died almost instantly. The next in rank, Captain Janeway, Company K, was wounded and left the field, the command devolving on Captain John C. Patterson. In the meantime, Lieutenant Craig, Company D, was badly wounded and Captain Conine, Company A, was killed, leaving our regiment with only three officers, the Adjutant, Lemuel F. Buckalew, First Lieutenant Samuel C. Bailey, Company F. and Captain Patterson."

The Third Division regrouped at Ellicott's Mills picking up stragglers until July 11, 1864, when it marched to Baltimore, Maryland. It was then sent by rail to Washington in pursuit of General Early. By the 15th, it had crossed the Potomac from Edward's Ferry approximately 30,000 strong under the command of General Wright. By the 18th, the Division had reached the Shenandoah River and found the Confederates entrenched on the other side of the river. The command lost a number of men by sending out skirmishers to test Confederate defenses. The rebel army quietly moved off in the direction of Washington but was quickly pursued by General Wright who moved swiftly to Harpers Ferry and then to Bolivar Heights by July 29, 1864. Because of Confederate raiding parties and the uncertainties of their intentions, Wright's troops were ordered back to Frederick City and finally to Monocacy. By August 4th, Wright was joined by Generals Hunter and Grant. Grant then ordered Wright's troops to Harpers Ferry to become part of General Sheridan's command which numbered in the vicinity of 30,000 men.

Contemporary photo of part of the Monocacy Battlefield. The river is just beyond the trees in the background.

Major General J.B. Ricketts USA

Vredenburgh

Metropolitan Hotel Washington
July 24, 1864

I rec'd yours of the 18th inst. We left Baltimore the day after I wrote to you and came here then we went to Edward's Ferry, thence to Leesburg and finally overtook the rebels at Snickers Gap. Wright commanded the whole command comprised of the 6th Corps and the 19th Corps. 7000 men under Crook and about 4000 cavalry making in all about 27000. Crook's men were in the advance and fought the enemy on the west side of the Shenandoah and were driven back before the 6th Corps could cross. Ricketts commanded the 6th Corps and I was inspector of the corps and am yet. We could see the whole engagement as if it had been a picture. We were on a crest which overlooked the whole field with nothing to obstruct the view. It was a grand sight though heart rendering to see our men shot in the water. I crossed the river from Gen'l Ricketts and a good many were shot in the water near me and drowned. The water being about 4 feet deep. The rebels held us at bay here all the next day and retreated the following night. We followed them to near Perrysville and then marched back here. When we arrived yesterday completely worn out and used up and slightly depressed in spirits at the prospect of a speedy trip to Petersburg.

I applied to be relieved and went back to the regiment but Gen'l Ricketts would not let me go then. I mean to insist on it in a few days as soon as the organization is changed back to its original formation. I captured a very fine three year old colt and mean to sell my large gray as soon as I can. I wish I could send her home as she would be a capital horse for Henry or Will. We don't know what we are to do yet or where we are to go. I hope they will leave us here or somewhere in this vicinity.

Don't send me anything as I can purchase what I want. I hope Father will be inspired by the salutary values of the Richfield Springs.

Write soon
Affectionately
Peter

Ross

July 27, 1864
Near Hyattstown, Maryland

Dear Mother

I received your kind letter a few moments ago and will answer it immediately. We marched from Georgetown today a distance of 16 miles. We are now only 10 miles from Frederick which place we expect to reach tomorrow if nothing happens. And from there we expect to go after the Johnnies — up the valley.

We have two Corps here now so if we should meet them they will get rats. I had a pretty narrow escape after the Battle at Monocacy. I left the field among the last ones and as I was too mad to hurry any some of them cut me off so we had a race for it. I started for a piece of woods about two hundred yards off and they after me. But I think I could outrun them and got into a thick place in the woods and laid still there all night. The next day I started towards Baltimore but when I came to a house the gentleman told me that I could never get through. So I stayed at his house a day. When the rebs were driven out of Frederick and I went back there where I stayed until the railroad was replaced when I joined the regiment at Washington safe and sound and good for another fight. My love to all

Your Affectionate Son
Burroughs

Vredenburgh

Frederick City Md.
August 1, 1864

My Dear Father

I wrote Mother from Washington July 24th. Since then we have traveled from Washington to Frederick, thence to Harpers Ferry Va., via Harpers Ferry and then back here, where we arrived yesterday noon. The men are so nearly played out that we will likely remain here a day or two and then go either towards Harpers Ferry, or Hagerstown.

Your Affectionate Son,
Peter

Ross

Near Frederick Md.
August 5, 1864

Dear Mother

We are still near the favorite city of Frederick enjoying ourselves very much as we can now get anything, almost that, we want to eat, which is a very agreeable change to us. I heard today that Captain Conover was dead. We all feel very badly about it as he was a general favorite in the Regiment. There is a rumor in the Regiment that our Corps is going to stay in Maryland, which I hope will prove true. When Pop goes to

Jamesburg again tell him to ask Charlie Miller the telegraph operator, if there is a small carpetbag there for him which I ordered to be sent there as it belongs to me.

Captain Stults, late of our Regiment, who is from Prospect Plains was killed at Monocacy and our Quartermaster Sergeant sent his things home to his father, Mr. Isaac Stults. And by mistake, also sent a small red carpetbag of mine, thinking it belonged to Captain. It contained my dress coat, cap, and under clothes. I wrote to Mr. Stults about a week ago asking him if he would leave it at Jamesburg the next time he went there, for you to call for it, so if it is there the next time he goes to Jamesburg, let him bring it home until I call for it. Love to all, write soon

Your Affectionate
Burroughs

Vredenburgh

Hd Qrs. 3rd. Div 6th A.C.
August 5, 1864

I am sorry to inform you that Col. Truex has just been dismissed from the service for insubordination. He has been guilty of nothing reflecting upon his character and should be esteemed by the community as much as if the misfortune had not occurred. He left Frederick yesterday afternoon with his horses and will probably reach home the day after tomorrow. I sent a colt with him that was captured in Virginia by a man from whom I got it. There is so much risk here to horse flesh that I determined to send it to a safer locality. Ask Henry or someone to keep it for me and I will pay for it sometime or other. I have had a delightful time here in Frederick since I have been here this last time. Our camp is just out of the city — near Keefer Thomas' and I go to see him every day. Everybody seems cordial and glad to see me in Frederick and it was just like going home to come here.

Hundreds of persons speak to me whom I hardly recollect having ever seen and even the little children along the sidewalks sing out "there goes the Major." My position here made me known of course to many whom I would not know. I have called on the Ramsburgs every night and they are as clever as possible. I wish you treat the man that brings the colt to you kindly as he takes care of my horses and can tell you how we live and any particulars about me you may want to here. Capt. Conover died yesterday morning early and his body has been sent on. It is a terrible case and I have felt very sad over it, because he was a most noble fellow and very intimate with me. He acted as major for a long time and a braver or more high toned man never lived. He owed me $30 borrowed money but I forgive him the debt freely and should not mention it to anyone else.

The mail is about closing so I will have to stop. With much love to father and all

Your Affectionate son,
Peter

P.S. We recd. orders about midnight last night to be ready to move this morning at daylight — that the rebels were crossing in force at Shepherdstown — but it is now nine and as we have not been ordered out yet there may be some mistake about it.

Ross

We are encamped on Bolivar Heights
Harpers Ferry
August 9, 1864

Dear Father

Your kind letter I received a day or two since and will take this opportunity to answer it, as I hear we are going to move tomorrow morning. There are various rumors as to where we are going but judging from the preparations that are now making, we are going to make a bold strike somewhere. All of the Corps is now here, the 8th Corps, two divisions of the 19th Corps, Genls. Crooks, Sheridan, and Hunter. The whole amounting some say, to fifty thousand fighting men. Some say we are going on a grand raid, somewhere in rebeldom, for we are turning in all extra baggage, only one wagon now being allowed to a regiment. We have had quite a rest so far, and if they would only let us remain a few days longer, it would make us feel almost as good as new.

I suppose you have heard that Colonel Truex has been dismissed from the service. He had a quarrel with General Ricketts. The General not allowing him to put his horses on the cars after the Battle at Monocacy, while the General had all of his old pack horses and mules on board, which made Colonel mad, so he ripped out at him, and was put under arrest, and when we arrived at Frederick, General Hunter dismissed him for disobedience of orders and insubordination. But it don't make much difference now, there is only a few of us left, and it don't take a very talented man to command the remnant of the old 14th. When we go into a fight now, every man knows just what he has got to do, and needs not much telling, for what we have left are good and true and never turn their backs to the enemy, as long as a shade of success remains.

We had dress parade this afternoon, the first since the 1st. of May when we left our camp at Culpeper. It was a sad sight. Our line only being about one third as long as when we left our pleasant camp scarce three months ago. No captains now stand on the right of companies A & D, where the noble Conine and Conover once stood, and the old colors all tattered and torn are now guarded by but two corporals, out of eight which bore them in our first fight in the Wilderness. It is a sad sight to miss so many familiar faces, but perhaps it is all for the best. God grant that the rest of us may be spared to return to our homes. Write soon to your

Affectionate Son
Burroughs

Vredenburgh

Hd. Qrs. 3Div. 6A.C.
2 1/2 mi. North of Strasburg Va.
August 14, 1864

My Dear Mother

I forgot when I wrote to you last but I think it was at Frederick. We left Frederick about the 6th inst. and marched to Halltown thence down the Shenandoah Valley via Charlestown (near Winchester) Middletown, Newtown to this place which is about 2 1/2 miles north of Strasburg on the north bank of Cedar Creek. Yesterday morning we crossed the creek and followed the rebels as far as Strasburg where we saw them strongly fortified on the South side of the town. Their position was so strong that it would have been folly to have attacked them and so we looked at them all day and returned here last night with no other civilities than skirmish firing. The valley here narrows until at the place occupied by the rebels yesterday and it is only about six miles wide. On both sides the mountains are high and precipitous. Almost impossible of access. About 5 o'clock in the afternoon we discovered a rebel signal station on the top of a mountain on our left and not more than two miles off. Of course they could see every man we had and every movement, and could and did inform the rebels of them. It was a very humiliating to see these infernal rascals apparently right over our heads, thwarting every movement.

We therefore came back here last night and will I think return up the Valley in a day or two.

All you have ever heard about the beauties and fertility of the Shenandoah Valley have been true — for it is really lovely beyond conception. Suppose for instance some of the magnificent farms around Manalapan and imagine them extending for miles and miles with no cessation to the rich, rolling fields profuse with golden crops and luxuriant verdense and other natural concomitants as handsome houses, large barns, rich fields etc. and you

Cedar Creek, VA

U.S. Army Military History Institute

have the Shenandoah Valley. Tell Henry that it beats all places for game that either he or I ever saw. The woods are generally large open timber and I have scarcely seen any ground that would be bad cover. I hope we will winter somewhere here. I wrote to you in my last that I sent Bill Ayers home with a colt. I heard this morning that he had returned as far as Harpers Ferry and is waiting there for a chance to join me, which he can probably do in a day or two.

Affectionately your son,
Peter

Ross

Halltown Va.
August 24, 1864

Dear Mother

Today we are having a day of rest and I will improve it by writing home. We just finished making our breastworks last night, and as we have a splendid position here and now feel as safe as if we were home in Jersey. I saw Sergt. Fletcher last night. He was not hurt in the last battle. We have all kinds of rumors about the Johnnies making another raid into Maryland but I hardly think they will try it, as it is a pretty certain thing that if they cross the river again, they will never get back. I wish they would get up as far as Jersey once, just to let the people know that there is a war going on, and let you people see what an army looks like. I guess you would say you never saw such a ragged and dirty looking set of men in your life as we are.

How is Mimmie's little boy coming on? Does he grow much? I suppose he will be quite a young man by the time I get home. News is very scarce here now, so I cannot afford to write much, and as long as you know I am well, and contented, you are satisfied. I never felt better in my life than I do now. Give my love to all and write soon to

Your Affectionate Son
Burroughs

Ross

Bolivar Heights Va.
August 25, 1864

Dear Mother

Your kind letter reached me this afternoon and while I have a chance will answer it. We arrived here on the 23rd inst.

and have remained here ever since. We have a splendid position here and feel perfectly confident we can never be driven from it. The cavalry had some sharp fighting today in the direction of Martinsburg, the result of which I have not been able to learn. I met Alec Yard yesterday. He is on General Wilson's staff, a cavalry general. Alexander looks about as well as usual. The rumor tonight is that the Johnnies are going to invade Maryland again. If they do, I think they won't get off as easily as they did the last time they were there. Major Vredenburg has returned to the Regiment, which pleases the boys very much as they all like him. How is Colonel Truex coming on? Do you hear whether he says anything about coming back again or not. I received the paper you so kindly sent me and think the sermon of Mr. Chandler is excellent. I expect there were a great many persons at Captain Conover's funeral. We all miss him sadly. I should like to be home to help masticate some of the honey you spoke about in your letter, but I think I have had nearly my share of that precious stuff this summer, when we went down the valley. Every house our boys came to, they would make a search for the bee hives. At some houses there would be twenty or thirty hives and you must ought to see the work. Lots of them would get stung and such dancing around would beat all. But they generally came off victorious.

We burned all the grain we came across, and stole all the horses and cattle. I got one horse and sold him the same day for ten dollars, to one of our officers — for a pack horse. I would have had to turn him in to a Quarter Master if I had kept him so I sold him. We have been living on mutton ever since we started and looking at our drove today, I see we have two or three hundred head left of what we captured on our raid. I should like to spend today at Long Branch or some other seaport town, to get cooled off once more. It is awful warm here. I suppose you feel rather lonesome sometimes do you not? Now that we are all away. How is Jacob getting on, is he well yet? I met Capt. Cloke the other day. You remember the young lawyer who went out in the fancy cavalry regiment. Lieutenant Kerner has been discharged from the service so he is no longer a member of the old 14th. How is Mimmie's little Willie coming on? Remember me to Jacob, Mrs. Wikoff, Mr. and Mrs. Manning and Maria and write soon to your

Affectionate Son
Burroughs

Vredenburgh

Hd. Qrs. 14th N. Jersey Vols.
Near Bolivar Heights Va.
August 25, 1864

Dear Father

It is so long since I have written to you that I forget where or when it was. I think I wrote to you last from Frederick and enclosed some money which you received. The boys call us the "Harpers Weekly" and most appropriately too, for it seems as if the ferry was the grand central magnate about which the forces of the upper Potomac revolve. You see I have taken command of the regiment again and I send you herewith the application I made last July and returned to me about a week ago. I then, after seeing that it was disapproved, went personally to the General and insisted upon being relieved, so it was done. I joined last Saturday at Charlestown and on Sunday the rebels attacked our lines very suddenly and we were ordered out on the double quick. Our regiment did not get into the fight, but two regiments of this Brigade did. We were in the front line, but the engagement was between the skirmishers pretty much, particularly in our front, and they were taken from the troop in the rear line. Our two regiments charged up a small hill upon the rebels but as they reached the crest a line of battle was discovered behind a low stone fence, which opened terrifically upon our skirmishers and they fell hastily back. At night we fell back to this place.

Gen'l Wright came to where I was looking with my glasses and talked considerably. He said the cavalry had deceived him in not reporting the advance in time and that he was doubtful about the enemy towards Martinsburg and Shepherdstown. We took position here Monday morning and the rebels were close up on us. Our pickets have been firing at each other incessantly ever since we halted here, and the air is filled all the time with the pounding of artillery both on our right and left. I shouldn't be much surprised if we were in Maryland in 24 hours. I am most comfortably fixed here and they all seem glad to see me in the Regiment.

I wrote to Gov. Parker today and recommended several promotions in this Regiment. If Col. Hall comes to Freehold, Mother should show him every attention for he is an elegant gentleman and has a remarkable intellect. His judgement is always right about everything that he gives a decision upon and if he wasn't so easy and luxurious in his habits, would make his mark. I met a good many persons here who recollect me at Frederick as they had to come to my office there to get passes. The Col. commanding the Brigade is "Corps Officer of the Day" today and tomorrow and that throws me in command of the Brigade till he is relieved. There are several officers who rank me in the Brigade but they are either sick or on some special duty.

Your Aff Son,
Peter

General George Armstrong Custer USA

Vredenburgh

Hd. Qrs. 14th N.J.V.
August 26, 1864
9 A.M.

Dear Mother

I have just received your letter of the 21st dated Richfield Springs. Our affairs here look rather dusty and I shouldn't be much surprised if this was the last letter you receive from me for a few days. Our cavalry were driven back on our right flank and Custer's Brigade was cut off entirely from the rest of the command. They have not been heard from since. The rebels are reported in immense force in the neighborhood of Shepherdstown and yet still they are attacking us on the left. The air is resonant with the firing of artillery and musketry — all the time. The mail agent is waiting for me. I command the Brigade temporarily. I wrote yesterday to father. Give my love to him and tell him I am very much obliged for his letter.

Peter

Ross

Bolivar Heights Md.
August 27, 1864

Dear Sister

I have concluded to wile away a leisure hour by writing to you, so here goes. It has been sometime since you have heard from me directly, although I suppose Mother tells you when she receives a letter from me. This has been a very rough campaign and one long to be remembered by us. Since the 4th day of May we haven't remained stationary in one place longer than two days until now. We are having quite a resting spell, not having had to move our camp in the long space of four days. How is your little Willie coming on? I suppose he is flourishing and will soon be as big a man as his mother. I should like to see him very much, as soon as he grows old enough to understand matters and things. You must inform the young gentleman that he has an Uncle Will in existence. How does Garrett like his new farm? And you the responsibility of having the sole charge of a farmer's house. I suppose by the time I see you again you will be quite settled down in your notions. I received a letter from Let, a short time since. In it she mentioned of having been down home on a visit and Mother's letters also stated that you had company in the persons of Miss Fringer.

We have been down the Valley as far as Strasburg some eighty miles, and burned all the grain and stole all the horses, cattle, sheep and the like that we could find, living meanwhile splendidly on everything good in the shape of apples, green corn, peaches, and honey. Of the last mentioned article every house we came to had an abundance of and the way our boys confiscated it was a caution. I suppose you heard of our fight at Monocacy, where we lost so heavily. It was a hard struggle but they overpowered us by numbers and I came within one of spending a few days at Richmond. But by good luck, I came off first rate.

Remember me to Mother, also brother Garrett and when you have a few leisure moments on hand, that you don't know how to dispose of, nothing better would suit me than to have you occupy them by writing to your incomparable brother. I expect in a few days, to wear the straps of a 1st Lieutenant now, by meritorious conduct on the field.

Your Brother.
Will

Vredenburgh

Hd. Qrs. 14th N.J. Vols.
September 1, 1864
5 miles S.W. of Charlestown Va.

Dr. Mother,

I received your letter with the stamps in it and the bundle of stockings and handkerchiefs. I am very sorry to hear that Father is only a little better. I was in hope he would be fully recovered. I think I wrote to you last from Halltown. Since then we have come to this place. The rebels attacked us very suddenly the other day and our Division marched in line of battle over three miles. The rebels all the time falling back, till we arrived near Smithfield where we halted and after dark returned to this place. Leetown where you said Apaelid Wilson lives is only about two miles from here but no one seems to know her or her father. I wish you would tell me again as near as you can find out, where she lives for I should like to see her. Mosby hangs all the Yankees he catches now prowling around the country so that I will be careful of him.

I live very pleasantly with Adjt. Buckelew. I have five horses and he has two. We therefore pack everything except valises. They are all good horses picked up along the road. There are thousands of horses changing hands all the time. Many horses are abandoned for want of shoes or a sore back, and with good treatment they recuperate soon and some of the finest horses in the army have been often picked up horses. The cavalry are destroying a great deal of property here and burn dwellings and farms, wheat stacks etc. indiscriminately. It is a shame that we stoop to such vindictive means which cannot affect the great issue and I hope the rebels will catch and hang every man engaged in it.

Affectionately,
Peter

Ross

Charlestown Va.
September 2, 1864

Dear Mother

We are now encamped at Charlestown. We charged the Johnnies day before yesterday and drove them two miles when we halted and let the cavalry keep it up. Nothing of interest is occurring. I saw where John Brown was hung and also the place where he kept his arms etc. There is a rumor of us being sent home to recruit our regiment. I hope it proves true. Nothing would suit me better at this time. What do the people think of the draft that is to take place soon? Has Freehold filled her quota yet? I saw Fletcher a day or two since and he said he had received a letter from Pop. Charlie Bartruff sends his compliments to you all.

Lt. Woodward, Col. Truex's brother in law, was dishonorably dismissed a day or two since for cowardice. I pity the poor fellow but he couldn't stand and hear the bullets whistle past him. I don't know anything more of importance to write so will close my long letter, remaining still in excellent health and hoping you are the same. Love to all from

Your Affectionate Son
Burroughs

Ross

September 11, 1864

Dear Mother

Your kind and welcome letter reached me a few days since, and as we have plenty of spare time just now, will write you a few lines in return. We are now encamped about eight miles from Barryville, on the Winchester turnpike. The Johnnies are no nearer to us than five miles, although they may pay us a visit at any moment. If they do, they can rely on a warm reception from us. Captain Cloke, and Major Alstrom from the 3rd Cavalry were over to see us yesterday. They both look in very good health. How do you think the election will go in Jersey this time? I suppose Monmouth County will go for McClellan. Of course I wish they would give the 14th a chance to vote. I would cast my first one for Uncle Abe, as would nearly all of our regiment. We have had plenty of rain here lately, but I would rather have that than so much dust. Nothing much of interest is happening around here just now. I would like to come home at election if possible, but don't think I can get off. All the rest I can tell you is that I am well and hope you are enjoying the same blessing. Remember me to all and accept much love from

Your Affectionate Son
Burroughs

Jones

Near Berryville Va.
September 15, 1864

Dear Father

As I understood there was a mail going out and feeling pretty sure I would have a letter from you to answer I will begin now so as to get it off with today's mail. Everything remains in the same condition as were I wrote you last. There was quite a sharp fight on the 13th close to our picket line in which the 3rd New Jersey Cavalry were engaged. They captured one whole regiment of infantry and some cavalry. The movement was a complete success on our part. We have to make a jump upon them once in awhile to see if they are not sending some of their force away and we seem to find some of them "every time." Everything appears to be favorable in regard to military matters all over the country, more so than they did six weeks ago when it looked rather the other way and I think the stinging blow to the Rebellion will be the reelection of Lincoln — although not in favor of it myself. I reason it in this way. If Lincoln be reelected they know exactly what they have to put up with if McClellan should. They would hardly know how to take him and would stick out still longer hoping to get back by some dishonorable terms which I think they would never get under Gen'l McClellan.

Politics are running pretty high here with us although the poor Jersey thieves are not allowed to vote. There was a vote taken in the Regiment this morning and stood as follows — officers and all.

Lincoln	143
McClellan	75
Scattering	30
Total	248

Majority for Lincoln — 38

So you can see Lincoln has the choice. The scattering consists of men who have not made up their minds but I think most of them are McClellan.

There has been a great change in the men. Co. C when we lay at Camp Hooker the vote stood 60 for Lincoln and 21 for McClellan and 3 scattering. So you see there has been a change in Co. C and those that are away in hosp'l will be about the same.

I spoke in my last about their being some wire pulling going on in the company in regard to the vacancy of the 2nd. Lieut. I being around Head Quarters continually, found out that there was a man fishing for it that would not suit the Company at all and I let the boys know of it. I also found out that Lieut. Muddel was in favor of him. He immediately set to work to report the whole thing. He and I will draw up a petition signed by all the company to have a Sergt. in the camp commissioned. This we sent to the Major and done very well. We done it so that he could see how the Company went. The Sergt. we propose being our 2nd. Lieut. was our old First Sergt. when we came out. You will find his name on my roll at home (Henning) and being a married man with considerable of a family and a competent man with all the rest. I do not know as I ever mentioned it to you that our First and Second Sergts. were reduced to the ranks for absence without leave at the Battle of Monocacy (Wardell and Hand).

I see I have a lot of stuff mixed up. They may be of no interest to you at all but it helped to fill up and its about all that is going on at present. I think I had done pretty well in the way of writing this week so you see my will is good everywhere I have time.

Remember me to all
From Your Son
Edward C. Jones

Inside of a Union officer's tent.

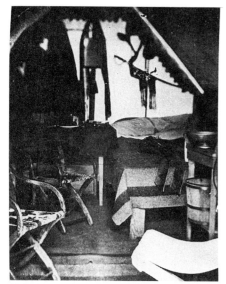

Ross

September 16, 1864

Dear Mother

I will make use of some of my spare time and answer your questions continued in your last welcome letter to me. We are still encamped in our old place near Berryville and with every prospect of remaining sometime longer. Nothing of interest is transpiring here now and time hangs heavy on our hands, but by drilling and shooting squirrels we manage to pass the time without getting the blues very bad.

You wished to know what I had to sleep in and how we fared in the eating line etc. The Adjutant and I have what we call, a wall tent about ten by six feet square, just the same as we had at Camp Vredenburgh. Perhaps you remember those, and as for our food we have, potatoes sometimes, flour once in a while, soft bread, ham, beef, hard tack, coffee & sugar, and pork. But of course we don't have all of those things every day, all except coffee, sugar, hard tack and pork we buy off the commissary.

As for my duties, the first thing after breakfast, I make a detail of men to clean up the camp. Then at 10 o'clock we have Battalion drill at which I have to assist and then I have nothing to do until 5 o'clock P.M. when we have dress parades, that is my regular duties every day. But sometimes I have to get pickets ready and then again send off a squad as guard at Hd. Qrs.

When we are in a fight, I keep the men in as straight a line of battle as possible and carry any orders to the companies that the Colonel may wish to send.

How is the excitement about election coming on? I suppose that is all the talk nowadays. I am going to try and get home at Christmas, if I can. Charlie Bartruff wished me to remember him to you all when I wrote. How is Aunt Jane? Have you heard from her lately? Remember me to her when you write and also to Mimmie and tell her to answer my letter or I will

General Sheridan USA (standing in the center) and staff.

give her a rousing up. Remember me to Miss Hanlin and write soon to your

Affectionate Son
Burroughs

The Shenandoah Campaign Continues...

On August 10, 1864, Sheridan detected Confederate troops strongly entrenched on Fisher's Hill and quickly moved off. He did this hoping to lure Early's Confederates after him. The Union forces took up positions at Charlestown while the Southern troops occupied the west bank of Opequon Creek, covering Winchester. The Fourteenth New Jersey Volunteers had picked up some new recruits and participated in reconnoitering maneuvers until mid-September. Then on September 19, 1864, General Sheridan ordered a full-scale attack. The geographical conditions were not favorable as the troops had to advance through a narrow ravine and across a broad open field. The Battle of Opequon raged for three hours culminating in a Union victory. It was a costly victory, particularly for the 14th Regiment....

Peter Vredenburgh, Jr.

U.S. Army Military History Institute/Monmouth County Historical Association

Tuesday September 27th 1864
Frederick, MD

My Dear Mrs. Vredenburgh,

Although almost a stranger my Dear Mrs. Vredenburgh, I hope you will not deem it an intrusion that in this your time of sorrow I write to express our sympathy in the deep affliction of your bereavement.

We would scarcely realize the sad tidings, and you will believe, there are mourning hearts who have felt stricken by the sad news, far beyond the home circle of your well beloved son.

I have felt impelled to write you, thinking it might afford some gratification as we saw him last — late on the ere, before the departure of the army for the Valley of Virginia.

We were in the country, at the residence of my brother-in-law Mr. R., and as ever, bright and cheerful he parted from us and little dreaming we should see his face no more. But even now in recalling that evening, I remember, that in the midst of his cheerful talk a sober grave thought seemed to come over him, perhaps a premonition of the fate that awaited him — a fate we had never thought of in connection with him. He was a great favorite with them both. My sister Mrs. R. says of herself, "I could think of nothing else — the bright sunshining day was all gloom after the sad tidings that paper revealed.

The ballijah of victory was all lost, in the veil of mourning, when we read the list of our "killed in battle." And turning to Mr. R, "I could have better borne to have heard of the loss of any other than the Major." He seemed so glad to get back to Frederick, and you should have seen his welcome here, to know how he was appreciated. The sad news of his death has passed from lip to lip of those who knew him, and many hearts have mourned his untimely loss. Even among the children he had made himself known and loved, and I know, their childish hearts were filled with grief when we learned the fate of one who had always shown such an interest in them.

My heart bled most for the mother, to whom he was so dear, and while our eyes filled with tears my heart turned to you and trembled for the anguish you have been brought to suffer. He talked often of you to us, of the mother, whom he so reverenced, and for whom he cherished so deep an affection. I kept for him a while, his Bible, which you had given him, but when I put it into his hands again he promised to remember your wishes and to notice the passages you had marked for his benefit.

It was the heart so noble and true, beneath his often gay and light interior, that was for him our affection — his kindness to those around him — his forgiveness of those who had done him injury, that made him beloved wherever known. All his comrades attested to his bravery even to rashness, and his, was the pure patriotism which nobly sacrificed his life in defense of his country. In our midst, no hero has fallen among our brave ones whose loss has been more deeply deplored. In our home we could not, would not, realize it — hoped there might be some mistake till the sad news was confirmed, that the body of our friend had arrived no. B — on its passage homeward.

My Dear Mrs. Vredenburgh, my words do not convey to you our grief. I could not refrain an expression of our sympathy, for our hearts have known sorrow the severing of homes' dearest ties, and we can well believe in the depth of your affliction in the loss of your well beloved son. May we hope at some future day, when time has somewhat relieved the poignancy of your sorrow, to learn what you may have heard about the circumstances of his death? It would be to us a melancholy satisfaction to learn the sad particulars. My brother and sister Mary write with me in telling to you our deepest sympathy. We cannot restrain our tears when we think of our friend as no more on earth — but hope with purified spirits to meet him in that better Land where the battle cry is heard no more and the word of parting shall never again be spoken.

In Sorrow Yours,
Charlie Ramsburg

Letter from Quartermaster Enoch Cowart to his wife:

Camp near Strasburg, Virginia
Wednesday, September 21, 1864

My Dear Wife

I sent you a letter on the 18th in reply to your two last date 4th & 7th which I hope you will get. On the 19th at 2 o'clock A.M. we received orders to advance and attack the enemy who were lying near Winchester. About 12 o'clock the fight opened with brisk musketry and severe cannonading. I rode up where the signal station was placed on a high bluff commanding a fine view of the valley, and the scene of battle, and with the aid of two good glasses we could see distinctly the movements of the two armies engaged. We watched the Union Banners and Colors as they waved to and fro and the day being cool and fine and clear the prospect was truly grand and imposing. The 6th, 8th and 19th Corps were in the hottest of it, and during the hardest struggle the 19th wavered and were in part flanked by the enemy and compelled our whole line to fall back a short distance. This struck a thrill of doubt in our minds but our forces soon rallied and drove back the rebel forces. The rebel batteries worked finely and made sad havoc in our ranks being in open range. General Sheridan then resolved to charge them and the order was made.

Major Vredenburgh was at the head of the 14th on horseback. His remark last to them was, "Boys, we are the guide on the left of the line in this charge, advance on double quick, keep your ears open to the orders, and I will do the best I can for you." The words were just uttered when a shell or some say a solid shot struck him, tearing away the left side of his neck and passing out through his shoulder. The ball glazed the left ear of his horse. He threw up both arms and fell back, his head striking first on the hard ground of the turnpike road. Lt. B. Ross was near him and fell back to the rear with two other men to render him assistance. He, the Major, covered his face after he fell with both hands and with a little heaving of the breast expired. Four men brought him back to the hospital on a stretcher where I was and you may imagine my feelings at the sight. The gash was an awful one. Poor fellow, only on Saturday evening he, Captain Cloak and myself were together talking over old times in his tent. Afterwards we went over to Colonel Emerson's Brigade Headquarters and stayed two or three hours, and I never saw him more lively and cheerful. Captain Cloak then left for his quarters, and Major and I returned to ours. He then invited me to sleep with him, but I declined as I was near my own. As he rode out with the regiment early on Monday morning he called out, "Quartermaster, you will attend to taking care of the Regimental Property I suppose." I answered, "All will be right." Those were his last words to me. Poor fellow. I believe he had no idea of his fate. He is greatly lamented by our officers and men and all who know him, and I shall miss him very much, for I considered him a good confidential friend and the life of the Regiment.

Very soon after this sad event, Lieutenant Green of Trenton in command of Company I, was brought in dead. He was shot through the body, lived about one hour but never spoke. Lt. Green was a patriot, a Christian and a prompt good officer and he is greatly lamented. I proposed to Chaplain Rose to write or see General Rickets and get him to make provision for getting Major's and Lt. Green's bodies sent to Harpers Ferry to be embalmed and sent home. I then went out in search of boards to make boxes to put their bodies in, which in that region was extremely scarce as well as nails. General Russell of Massachusetts commanding the 1st Division, was killed and they made him a box of oak fencing lath which was very uncouth and rough. I was not satisfied with such material and rode out in search of something better. I found at some distance in a barn some new inch boards and had then brought in and made two nice clean boxes for Major and Lt. Green. They were nicely washed off and placed in their boxes and after grasping the cold hand of each. I started with the train for this place where we are now encamped. This morning orders were read from President Lincoln and General Grant congratulating our army on this single victory, and each ordered 100 guns fired in honor of it. We were unable at this exciting time to get transportation for the bodies of Major and Green and were compelled to bury them and will forward them on by the trains which come up with rations etc. as it is necessary to have a strong guard with them. Chaplain Rose has applied and got permission for a 7 day leave to go home with the bodies. I would very much like to have had this mission, but it is impossible to leave now, he will bring home his watch and clothing etc. but the two horses will remain here for the present. About 60 of our Regiment were wounded, 12 killed as yet known. It is rumored our loss is about 2000, the enemy much greater. Major Dillingham of the 10th Vermont in our Brigade was killed also with many others. General McIntosh, 3rd New Jersey Cavalry lost a leg, the one Captain Cloak and Major Alstrom are under. We drove the rebels pell mell through Winchester charging them at every jump, and the roads are strewn with dead horses. The battlefield presents an awful sight of dead and wounded on both sides. The enemy has fallen back in the region of Strasburg and we expect to get orders at any moment to advance for another attack. Although we lament the loss of so many noble men, the success of our army in this case is most cheering and just what I have been ardently desiring for, as this will form a line of victories to each army department and tend to discourage our foes very much.

General Sheridan displayed great bravery, riding along the lines waving his hat and cheering on our men. All our officers in fact deserve great praise. After Major fell, Captain Janeway took command of the 14th and behaved credibly. Lieutenant Ross is all right. Wm. Clayton and others. Adjt. L. Buckelew was slightly wounded on his right hip, also Lieutenant Muddell of Co. C. Captain Craig Co. B, Captain William Conover Co. G more seriously among these. We captured several pieces of artillery, near 1000 guns and some 3000 prisoners. General Grant was at our army headquarters a few

Lieutenant Theodore Green

days before we moved out and his orders were to drive General Early and his forces out of this valley, which I think we will not fail to do. A man named Haley from about Englishtown in Co. G, 14th N.J. died in his tent very suddenly last night. He is said to have fought in the battle of the 19th.

We are now skirmishing with the enemy and firing is heard nearby and we may soon expect hot work again.

Give my dear wife my warmest sympathies to Mrs. Vredenburgh and the family for the loss they have sustained.

Your Ever Affectionate Husband
E.L. Cowart
Lt. Q.M. — 14 N.J. Vols.

Ross

September 21, 1864

Dear Father

Photos below are of the Opequon battlefield; the second photo is a view looking west across the Opequon River (circa 1875).

I have a few moments to spare and will write a few lines home. I suppose you have heard of our great victory. It was a hard fight but the right triumphed. I am now acting adjutant of the Regiment. Buckelew being wounded but not seriously. Major Vredenburgh was killed by a solid shot through the neck. I raised him up in my arms and he breathed only once and died. We all feel the loss greatly. Our boys thought more of him than any other officer we had. Our Regiment lost about 60 killed and wounded. We drove them 18 miles when we stopped taking any quantity of prisoners. I did not get a scratch and have come to the conclusion that our army can whip anything of equal numbers they can bring before us.

Love to all, Your Son
Burroughs

Jones

Near Strasburg, Virginia
September 21, 1864

Dear Father

We have had an awful fight and have given the Johnnies tar. Our loss is heavy. Maj. Vredenburgh and Lieut. Green were killed. Lieut. Muddel was wounded but only slight. I hurt my shoulder last night and that accounts for the writing. I think there is something out of place and am going to the surgeon and have it put back. The Chaplain is going home and I send this to Harpers Ferry with him. I will write you again in a few days.

Remember me to all,
Ed. J.

Ross

Sept 23, 1864

Woodstock Va.
September 23, 1864

Dear Mother

I suppose you have heard of our great fight at Winchester the other day when we whipped the Johnnies so handsomely. Yesterday we met them again and it was just the same way. We drove them from a position that they boasted could not be taken. I haven't heard how many prisoners we took but I saw four pieces of artillery which our division captured. We started after the rebs the same night and expected to take the whole possession of them before we stopped. I am acting adjutant. I haven't time to write more now. Tell Mrs. Clayton that Bill is all right and in good spirits and is a first rate soldier. Chaplain will take this to you as he is going home with Major's body.

Your Affectionate Son
Burroughs

Ross

Harrisonburg
September 25, 1864

Dear Mother

We have just got back from a raid we made to a place called Mount Cranford about two miles from here. We are living splendidly and having everything good to eat you can think of, such as sheep, chicken, turkeys, milk, apples, peaches, and flour to make cakes. We destroyed about fifty mills and as many more barns filled with grain

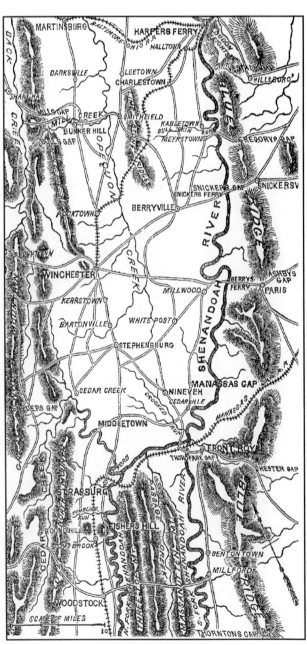

The Shenandoah Campaign

Source: New Jersey and the Rebellion by John Y. Foster, Newark NJ — Martin R. Dennis & Co. (1868)

and came back loaded with enough provisions to keep us a month. Early's Army is all broken up into squads so we have nothing to fight but quite likely Mr. Lee will send some of his force over this way. I am now acting Adjutant of the Regt. but is a very hard berth, you hardly have time to eat, so many reports to make out and everything to see to generally.

How does the Major's folks take his death? They must feel very badly about it. Our boys can't seem to get over it. They thought so much of him. When we charged up Fisher's Hill, they all commenced shouting, "Give it to them for killing the Major," and we did give it to them. Our Brigade charging clear over a battery of five pieces and capturing it.

We expect to go back towards Winchester soon, as there is nothing to fight up here. We have just received news of Grant's operations at Petersburg. We seem to be giving it to them from all quarters just now.

Nothing more of importance to communicate at this time. Write to your

Affectionate Son
Burroughs

Jones

Harrisonburg Va.
September 26, 1864

Dear Father

As we are laying still this morning I guess I had better drop you a few lines as I may not have time when the mail goes out and the Dean only knows when that will be. We have quite a lively time since we left Winchester. At Strasburg we had a pretty sharp time with them, but we drove them out of a place that was always considered impregnable to any attacking party. I was close to the charge and a prettier sight I never saw. I would not have missed it for anything and what made it still better was that we lost little or nothing in taking the place. What I make reference to is the celebrated Fisher's Hill. Our Division flanked them and captured 4 pieces of artillery.

Such a time as there was among the Johns never was seen before. We followed them sharp until we arrived at Woodstock, where we had to stop and get rations. We then started on and travelled until

Fisher's Hill, circa 1885.

U.S. Army Military History Institute

night halting up in a woods at Edenburg Mills.

The next morning we started on after them without any breakfast, coming upon them at Mount Jackson. Here we deployed our whole army in line of Battle with a skirmish line of infantry and cavalry driving them before us like the wind. I saw the cavalry charges upon them and a person would hardly think a man could get up and get as they did. We kept on driving them this way until dark when we had to stop for something to eat. We came to a halt about three miles this side of New Market. The next morning we started marching in line of Battle but the Johns had gone. We came to this place yesterday afternoon and as our rations are nearly out I think we shall lay here until they come up to us. The Rebels worked out a gap close to us which leads to Culpeper and my impression is that we will take that route again. Our loss at Winchester was very heavy. We lost one of the best officers we ever had. Maj. Vredenburgh. He was killed instantly, as was also Lieut. Green. Adj. Buckelew and Lieut. Muddell were wounded but only slightly.

I have just been appointed Regimental mail carrier, something which I have been looking after for some time. Our former mail carrier has been appointed Brigade mail carrier. Remember me to all

From Your Son,
Edward C. Jones

Harrison

Camp Near City Point
September 27, 1864

Friend P.C.

Don't you think Uncle Abe will be selected and don't you think he is the man that ought to have the chair for the next four years. All is quiet along the lines this morning, there was some cannonading on the left early this morning but it has ceased and all is again quiet.

What do you think of the campaign in the valley? Don't you think Old Sheridan is doing the thing right.

That's what we want, that is worth more votes to Uncle Abe than Wood can gain for McClellan. That's what we call properly speaking, putting down the Rebellion & before a great while friend P.C., you will hear good news from the army at present before Petersburg.

The weather is delightful and the roads good as a general thing. My health could not be better than at the present time. We are laying off, nothing to do and plenty to eat, good health and good spirits. Just keep up good courage. Gen'l Grant is with us yet never give up to think that this matter of subduing

Admiral David G. Farragut seated on the left.

the South is an impossibility for it will be done. Write soon. Give my kind regards to P.J. and all friends who may enquire.

Yours Truly,
A.C. Harrison

Harrison

Camp Near City Point, Va.
October 4, 1864

Dear Father and Mother,

The mosquitoes are so troublesome I cannot rest in peace if I go to bed. So I will try and pen you a few lines while I sit awhile & smoke my pipe which is one of the great comforts the soldier enjoys besides eating game dinners.

I feel that this War is near its close. We have every manifestation of the same. Our Army is meeting success at every point. The right of our Lines is within eight miles of Richmond. Old Lee has his army divided and the first thing we know Grant will have an Army before Richmond. Old Early's Army [General Jubal A. Early, C.S.A.] is scattered here & there through the mountains, & Sheridan will soon be cooperating with this Army.

Admiral Farragut [Rear Admiral David G. Farragut, U.S.N.] is relieved from the South Atlantic Squadron & will assume command of the North Squadron & then down goes Fort Dasling. The Key to the doomed city.

We have been quite busy for a few days drawing wounded. Our train is out tonight but as luck would have it I got clear from going as my Saddle was broke and of course I didn't like to borrow one that wouldn't be military. Not at all.

Give my best respects to friends & may God bless you. Write soon.

Sergeant A.C. Harrison

Harrison

Camp Near City Point, Va.
October 10, 1864

Dear Mother and Father,

Having a good chance to write this afternoon. I will pen you a few lines, for I may not have another opportunity for several days, as we are going to change camp tomorrow and get a little closer to Army Hospitals, about two miles from our

Hospital at City Point, VA.

present camp. We move on the morrow if nothing hinders & will put up winter quarters. We will also be a little nearer to the Point. The season for changing camp is this. They have been building works around City Point and we have got to get inside.

For there will be a big move pretty soon which may throw City Point open to the enemy but a Force will be left in the works to defend them and it will take but a small force for the works are as strong as we often see and in case of an attack our Gunboats would have a fair sweep also.

City Point, VA

The weather is cold and clear. There was a very heavy frost last night for the first, and I guess it put an end to all the mosquitoes for I have not felt but one since.

There has been somewhat of firing in the direction of the James River today. Old Butler [Major General Benjamin Franklin Butler] will not let the Johnnies rest but just keeps them on the lookout all the while.

But I must now close with the best respects to any stray friends of sympathy. I don't get any letters from Red Bank. I hope you are all in good health as this leaves you your loving Son,

Albert
City Point, Va.

Ross

Headquarters 14th N.J. Vols
October 16, 1864

Dear Mother

Once more we are in a quiet state and I will take advantage of it and write you a letter. We started last Monday the 10th inst. for Front Royal, stayed there one day, and then started for Alexandria, there to take transports for Petersburg. Alexandria was about one hundred miles from Front Royal. We marched all one day and got as far as Ashby's Gap, when our Aid ordered us to "about face" and march back to Strasburg, as fast as possible. We marched all that night and about 5 o'clock

Photo: U.S. Army Military History Institute

the next afternoon arrived safely back. The Rebels attacking our position but were repulsed. So we did not get to Petersburg after all, and I hope we won't, for I have had enough of that place. Captain Cloke was over to see us today, he looks as well as usual. We have sent in a petition signed by every man in the Regiment, to allow us to go home to vote. I would like to make a charge down Main Street, against all the "copperheads" in Monmouth County, with our regiment, and in about two minutes you wouldn't see nary a Copper. Let them talk about resisting the laws by force of arms. Just one regiment of veterans like the 14th, can go through all the Copperheads in Monmouth, and if Uncle Abe will send us home when anything of that kind comes to pass, we will give them a practicable illustration. I haven't heard from Trenton in sometime, and it strikes me that my adorable sister is indebted to me a letter also.

By the way, I am now the owner of a beautiful piece of horse-flesh and when we come home will bring him with me. He is a sorrel colt, four years old, gay as they make them, and cost fifty dollars. Has Pop received that money yet from the state treasurer? I suppose you will receive it in due season to buy your cloak. I would like you to send my cap to me through the mail, small articles like that can be sent very easily by that way.

Everything goes on seemingly here, plenty to do, but I suppose that keeps me out of bad company. Colonel Truex is here awaiting trial, which will take place about the last of the month. How are all the girls coming on in Freehold? Will there be any left for us soldiers by the time we come home again? For my part, I don't think I will trouble them much again as I can find my ideal of beauty, farther south.

Remember me to Miss Maria Manning and Miss Hanlin and all enquiring friends. My love to Aunt Jane, Mimmie, Pop, and yourself and write soon to

Your Affectionate Son
Burroughs

The Hailstorm Continues ....

Following the costly campaign that led to the fateful battle of Opequon, and eventually the charge up Fisher's Hill, there was a brief lull in the fighting and the 14th encamped at Harrisonburg until October 6, 1864. It was not long however, before General Early regrouped his forces at Cedar Creek. Taken completely by surprise on the morning of October 19, 1864, the Federals lost some 1200 prisoners, 24 guns and an enormous stock of equipment. It was here that the 14th suffered another terrible loss as Lieutenant William Burroughs Ross was fatally wounded.

General Sheridan, away in Washington, rushed back to Winchester. While the Sixth Corps were making their stand against the Confederates, Sheridan made his famous ride, rallied the Northern troops and counterattacked. General Early's forces were routed and the Federals recaptured lost arms and provisions as well as significant amounts of Confederate munitions.

Letter of sympathy to Mrs. Ross:

Philadelphia
November 22, 1864

Dear Mrs. Ross

I feel deeply and painfully about my inability to address you as the occasion requires. To say I sympathize with you in this hour of bereavement is true for I also suffer and I feel how utterly vain are words to express the desolation and loneliness of heart.

Lonely, yes I am lonely for though absent in the flesh our spirits often went out to meet each other and it was a comforting assurance in those days to know that although separated so far apart we were thinking of each other at the same time. I can not look calmly upon the present.

I little dreamed at our last parting as his cheering voice breathed the soul's harmony, what shadowy form then rose between us and with icy darth wrote, ye shall meet no more. I little dreamed that death's darkened veil would tread before me. At times I feel as though I could not be comforted and then I try oh so hard to banish these wicked thoughts for whom the Lord loveth he is sure to chasen and we know that it was God's will that we should suffer thus and that though afflicting us, he yearns over us for He has promised. "I will sustain thee, not remove the load but help ye to bear it.. I will pray the Father shall give you another comforter that He may abide with you forever again. I will not leave you comfortless I will come to you."

These seasons of darkness when my grief seems to overwhelm me are frequent but I pray for strength.

Please accept this picture as a token of love. I knew of nothing that would give you more satisfaction. It is but a small return for all your kindness to me. I appreciate it. Though a person of few words my heart has been touched by both yours and Mr. Ross' kindness, and I feel more than I can express. It was always an expressed wish of our loved and departed one to have one of these for himself.

In concluding this painful epistle I would add that when you feel as though you can I would love to hear from you. Do not forget me either of you for I have nothing to interest me now. It was his love that made life happy and earth beautiful to me.

Yours Respectfully
Fannie

William Burroughs Ross

Jones

Near Strasburg Va.
October 20, 1864

Dear Father

Yours of the 8th came to hand today. Yesterday was an awful day for us and came near being disastrous to us. The Johns attacked us about daylight coming in on our left flank, completely surprising the 8th & 19th A. Corps. The Rebs played a smart game on us as they had men that relieved our pickets on a portion of the line. They were dressed in our clothes which accounted for our not knowing them from some of our own men and instead of their coming in front of the breastworks they came at our flank.

The 19th & 8th Corps came down on us like sheep and for the first time since I have been in the service I was in an almighty tight place. The Rebs were close on my heels but I have got a little quick that the Devil himself cannot catch. The whole concern fell back until we came to a woods where the Gallant Sixth Corps came into line and was the means of saving the army from destruction. The 19th & 8th are not worth powder to blow them up. All of the artillery of the 8th Army Corps and some from the 19th. Oh I tell you things looked bad but Sheridan made his appearance on the ground about noon.

His presence seemed to put a different heart in the boys and to use his own words, "Boys By God you must go back to where you came from by four o'clock." We charged the Johns and were successful and away we went (I say we but I was about 6 miles in the rear) driving them to where they came from in the meantime the cavalry came in their rear and captured 9 pieces of artillery, 2800 prisoners and lots of wagons. After all proved to be a defeat to them and a gain to us. In the morning we lost 24 pieces of artillery and in the P.M. we captured them all back. All of them and 25 pieces besides and the Sixth Corps saved the whole concern. Now then I suppose they will want to send us to Petersburg but as soon as they do, away go the Rebels to Pennsylvania.

I would like to say more and will some other time about yesterday's proceedings. We lost our acting Adjutant, Lieut. W.B. Ross, a warm friend of mine he was in our mess. He rose to his present position from a private. We had one captain wounded — 23 men wounded & 3 killed. Our company lost only 4 wounded. We have three officers left — "heavy losses."

I went to the first Jersey today

Cedar Creek, VA, circa 1875. Hill occupied by Sheridan's left, October 19, 1864, from Kershaw's Ford.

and Caleb Martin is missing
since Sept 19. The Winchester
fight — whether he is killed or
captured they do not know.

From Your Son
Edward Jones

Harrison

Camp Near City Point, Va.
October 23, 1864

Dear Mother and Father,

*Winchester Township near Middletown
looking northwest to Winchester
(Sheridan's Road).*

It is the Sabbath and all is quiet in Camp and at the front.
I have heard but two or three reports of Artillery this morning
and they were on the extreme Right of the Lines in the direction of Richmond.

I am sorry Uncle Henry is in ill health. By the way you
write, he and Aunt must be strong McClellan men. I for my
part cannot imagine why any man or woman can preach up
little Mac who has any mind of their own. I am young to be
sure, but for all that, I am a Democrat but because I am a
Democrat is no reason I should vote for the democratic candidate. I cannot chew that Chicago Platform fine enough to
swallow it. After enduring privation and difficulties which
none but the soldier can imagine, for upwards of two years
then vote for a man who says the South cannot be conquered. If
elected he will bring peace on any terms and furthermore one
who dreads to hear of a Union victory. No sooner will I die
under the old Stars and Stripes. Don't talk about Mc to the
Soldiers in the field. We have a better chance here of knowing
the vast difference between the two men. Take the majority of
the soldiers in the field, they would sooner vote for Jeff Davis
himself. Then again look to the Rebel Authorities and what say
they to our men whom they hold prisoners of war, why this,
that they will give them a furlough for 30 and 60 days if they
will go home and vote for McClellan. Here but a few days since
the enemy in front of Butler was heard to give three times
three cheers for McClellan. I tell you it don't go down with the
blue bellies.

Uncle Abe, the soldiers friend, retains the chair for the
next four years, if the Good Lord spares his life.

The weather is delightful today, but it was cold last night.
We have good quarters. Better than ever before. If we can only
remain in them. The prospects are good at the present time.
We are still at work at our stables and will get them done by
the last of this week if nothing turns up to hinder.

Your ever loving and affectionate son,
Albert

[Chicago Platform — Democratic Party Platform
that had a peace clause in it.]

Harrison

Hd Qrs Amb. Corps
3rd Division 6th A.C.
Near City Point Va.
October 31, 1864

Dear Mother & Father

Having an amount of leisure time this evening I will devote a few moments to penning you a few lines, to assure you that your Boy is safe & sound.

The letters come through all right as you now address. You can still continue to address the same until I write otherwise. There is some talk of our going to the Corps. but I cannot see it yet awhile the movement of the Army has taken place and we are successful having gained all that was intended with but slight loss.

The weather is beautiful, pretty cold nights and warm days. It is very healthy with us at present. There are some cases of the chills & fever in the Army hospitals. But they are mostly new recruits. The old Soldiers have become accustomed to the climate and get along as well as if they all belong to the 14th but one. A. Stoddard he belongs to the 10th Vermont, and a good Boy he is. We have made a Jerseyman of him though, and that isn't much honor to him.

There is somewhat of noise over in Butler's department

Engine House — City Point, VA.

tonight. I guess he is going to keep the Johnnies awake by the sound of the Big Guns. I tell you they sound good. I don't know how it would seem at home.

I haven't heard from the Regiment since the last fight. I don't know where Eseck is or any of the Boys in the Company. You see I am the only one from my company belonging to the Train. There are several from the Regiment. There are Seven of us who tent together. I will give you the names — Sergt Kent, Jim Bowers, Wm Sarge, Albert Stoddard, Wm Ross [no relation to Lt. W.B. Ross] & myself. John Imlay.

But I must now close or I guess you will get tired for my pen is poor and I am getting sleepy.

Your loving son
Albert

SHERIDAN'S RIDE

Up from the South at break of day
Bringing to Winchester fresh dismay,
The affrighted air with a shudder bore,
Like a herald in haste, to the chieftain's door,
The terrible grumble, and rumble, and roar,
Telling the battle was on once more,
And Sheridan twenty miles away.

And wider still those billows of war
Thundered along the horizon's bar;
And louder yet into Winchester rolled
The roar of that red sea uncontrolled,
Making the blood of the listener cold,
As he thought of the stake in that fiery fray,
And Sheridan twenty miles away.

But there is a road from Winchester town,
A good, broad highway leading down;
And there through the flush of the morning lig',
A steed as black as the steeds of night
Was seen to pass, as with eagle flight.
As if he knew the terrible need,
He stretched away with his utmost speed;
Hills rose and fell; but his heart was gay,
With Sheridan fifteen miles away.

Still sprung from those swift hoofs, thundering South
The dust, like smoke from the cannon's mouth,
Or the trail of a comet, sweeping faster and faster,
Foreboding to traitors the doom of disaster.
The heart of the steed and the heart of the master
Were beating like prisoners assaulting their walls,
Impatient to be where the battlefield calls;
Every nerve of the charger was strained to full play
With Sheridan only ten miles away.

Under his spurning feet, the road
Like an arrowy Alpine river flowed,
And the landscape sped away behind
Like an ocean flying before the wind,
And the steed, like a bark fed with furnace ire,
Swept on, with his wild eye full of fire.
But lo! he is nearing his heart's desire;
He is snuffing the smoke of the roaring fray,
With Sheridan only five miles away.

The first that the General saw were the groups
Of stragglers, and then the retreating troops;
What was done,—what to do,—a glance told him both,
And striking his spurs, with a terrible oath,
He dashed down the line, 'mid a storm of huzzas,
And the wave of retreat checked its course there because
The sight of the master compelled it to pause.
With foam and with dust the black charger was gray;
By the flash of his eye, and his red nostril's play,
He seemed to the whole great army to say,
"I have brought you Sheridan all the way
From Winchester down to save the day."

Hurrah, hurrah for Sheridan!
Hurrah, hurrah for horse and man!
And when their statues are placed on high,
Under the dome of the Union sky,—
The American soldiers' Temple of Fame,—
There with the glorious General's name
Be it said in letters both bold and bright:
"Here is the steed that saved the day
By carrying Sheridan into the fight,
From Winchester,—twenty miles away!"

THOMAS BUCHANAN READ

Sheridan's Ride

Photo: U.S. Army Military History Institute

BATTLE HYMN OF THE REPUBLIC

mf

Mine eyes have seen the glo-ry of the com-ing of the Lord: He is
I have seen Him in the watch-fires of a hun-dred cir-cling camps, They have

tram-pling out the vin-tage where the grapes of wrath are stored; He hath
build-ed Him an al-tar in the eve-ning dews and damps; I can

loosed the fate-ful light-ning of His ter-ri-ble swift sword; His truth is march-ing on.
read His right-eous sen-tence by the dim and flar-ing lamps; His day is march-ing on.

From the Music of "John Brown's Body," Julia Ward Howe wrote the words to "Battle Hymn of the Republic" in November, 1861. Source: The Free Library of Philadelphia, Music Department.

6 The End is Near

November 1864 — early April 1865

The Third Division of the Sixth Corps, Army of the Potomac encamped in winter quarters until late March, 1865, when it received orders to move with other Union forces against Richmond. The Confederate forces attacked the Ninth Corps on March 25th in sufficient strength to convince General Meade that such a force could only have been gathered at the expense of the rebel defensive line. Accordingly, General Meade ordered a Federal advance along the front of the Sixth and Second Corps to the left of Fort Steadman before Petersburg. This marked the final advance of the Army of the Potomac, an advance that would continue until the ultimate surrender of the Confederacy.

As the winter of 1865 approached, Sergeant Harrison remained with the Division ambulance train at City Point, VA, but his situation would soon change. He would receive orders to rejoin his regimental ambulance train in the Shenandoah Valley, and the eventual reunion with his comrades would create an uneasy stir within him. Upon observing the devastation of his regiment after the brutal Shenandoah Campaign, Sergeant Harrison would once again pick up his weapons in the service of his country as the 14th prepared for the final days of the Civil War.

Union Railroad Mortar at Petersburg, VA — circa 1865.

Harrison

Headquarters, Ambulance Park
3rd Division 6th Army Corps
November 8, 1864

Dear Mother & Father

I believe I will pen you a few lines this morning as it has been nearly a week since I last wrote you. I have been waiting to get the box before I wrote, but it has not arrived yet.

I wrote to the express agent at Fortress Monroe this morning requesting him to

U.S. Army Military History Institute

Fortress Monroe

forward the box to me in case it has been received there. If I don't get it this week I will try to get a pass from the Provost Martial and take a trip down and inquire into the matter.

The weather has been warm — it was uncomfortably hot last night. It has rained off and on for the two days past & I think we will have more. The roads are awfully muddy. Today is the Great Election. I will be glad when the returns come in. I am anxious. I haven't heard a gun fired at the Front this morning. I expect the Johns are as anxious as we are, and trembling in their shoes for fear that Uncle Abe will retain his prosit. But I must close for this time as I have to draw bread this morning. I will write you soon if I am spared. God be with you all, & protect you & I remain your

loving son,
Albert

Harrison

Near City Point, Va.
November 10, 1864

My Dear Mother

As I have a few moments left after writing to Aunt and Uncle, I will drop you a few lines to inform you that the Box has arrived safe and the contents in good order. It came last night and the boots fit as neat as a pin. I haven't had better fitting boots or ones to feel any easier. The cake tasted very much like home. I fancy those neck ties.

I am anxious to hear from you, I fear John is very sick. Do write as soon as chance offers. I always feel contented if I know you are both well, but I get the blues as soon as I hear you are sick. I hope he is better. God grant and I hope you are as well as can be expected. I have work on hand this morning and I cannot write you a long letter besides I wrote you the day before yesterday. Our Camp has got to be cleaned up and the manure carted away from the stables. The weather continues uncomfortably warm — I slept last night with no covering it was so warm.

About dark last night there was some lively cannonading. I could hear no musketry as the wind was unfavorable. I like the handkerchief and in fact everything was nice. I must fill my pipe and take a smoke this morning. The clouds look wild and rainy. The wind keeps to the south.

Give my love to John and tell him to trust in God. He is my only friend in sickness. I am glad he is at Home where he can get a good woman's care. I tell you dear mother if there is anything in this world that will make the boy value his parents, it is to come out here and soldier three years. It will learn him a lesson which will not leave him through life and a good one if he will but take it. But I have written you quite a long letter after all. It begins to rain and I will have a chance to wet my boots, I guess. Do write soon and the Good Lord be with and bless you in sickness and health.

Your loving son,
Albert

Harrison

Camp Near City Point, Va.
Friday, November 18, 1864

Dear Mother & Father

     I must pen you a few lines to inform you that affairs have changed considerable since I last wrote. But I must tell you that it is some time since I have heard from you.
     I do earnestly hope John is not seriously ill. We are up at an early hour this morning for at six o'clock we hitch up & turn in our Train, and about tomorrow we will be on board a

Practice drill conducted by a Union Ambulance Corps.

transport enroute to the Shenandoah Valley to join our respective detachments. And if the thing be really necessary — to fight with the General Phil Sheridan. But as I stated above, we go to our old Train, which is under the command of a Lieutenant by the name of Tabor. He is a good boy and thinks considerable of this chap, and of course I will retain my old position in the Train. It is true we had everything arranged here comfortable, but none of the boys seem at all sorry that we are going to our old Corps to see the old boys once more. It is four months and over since our Corps left here, and we can afford to build winter quarters once more. But the order has come to hitch up and I must close. It is a little rough to leave this good Train, for we had some of the best of Teams. Our Division Train has the name of being the finest in the Army of the Potomac. But they say our Train in the Valley isn't so bad. We will soon have a good Train again. God bless you dear Mother & Father.

Your true son,
Albert

Harrison

Headquarters Amb. Corps
3 Div. 6th A.C.
Friday, December 2, 1864

My Dear Mother and Father

Before retiring for the night I must drop you a few lines to inform you that we have at last reached the old Sixth Corps. We left Bolivar Heights early yesterday morning, took the cars at Harpers Ferry and reached the old Train early last evening. We had about ten miles to march from the station and consequently were pretty tired and slept well. But I felt first rate this morning and never felt any better than I do tonight for I have seen the old 14th once more and found all the old boys well and hearty. That is the few who are still alive. I can tell you there have been many changes. The boys are delighted enough to see me back once more and I was glad enough to see them.

Foster and the Chaplain were over here to the train bright and early this morning to see me. We had a good long talk. Sergeant Foster is now first Lieutenant and is acting Adjt. He has walked right up in the military. He is a good boy and well was he deserving. All the old Sergeants have been promoted. It didn't seem like the same regiment. There were a great many new men that I never saw. Captain William Conover is in command of Company G. G.W. Robbins is 1st Lieutenant but is not with the company. He just came from home a few days since and he stays at Brigade Headquarters, in command of the Sharp Shooters.

The old Colonel came back a few days since and he has

command of the Brigade. Eseck is all right. He is the cook for some officer. I forget now who it was. I tell you the old chap gave me a hearty shake. He wished to be remembered to you. I am anxious to hear from you. I do hope John is better. God grant it. I hope you have received my letter ere this, and answered it. I intended to make application for a furlough as soon as I arrived here, but there is no use at present, for our Corps is under marching orders and expects to move at any moment. Some think we are going down to North Carolina and some think to East Tennessee. But there is nothing positive. I hope we will get down with old Sherman for a change. I hardly know what to do. I am in sort of a stew. I don't know whether to stay in the train or go to the Regiment. The boys are crazy to get me back. It seems in my absence from the Regiment, I have not been forgotten by either officers or men. They had everything arranged for my promotion when I returned, if I would accept of it in a short time, by going to the Regiment, I could get a commission. I haven't fully made up my mind as to what I shall do.

I will have a talk with the Chaplain if I am spared until the morrow and then I can form a conclusion. Hartshorne and Charlie White have not returned to the company as yet. The Chaplain had a letter from Charlie this morning. He said he was going to start for the Regiment next Monday. If John is only better I will feel better contented, but I cannot feel at rest until I hear from you. May the Good Father bless you dear Mother and Father. I know he will, God is good. I don't think I can write you anything more interesting. I will write again soon, if we do not move. Do write soon.

[no signature]

Harrison

Washington D.C.
Sunday, December 4, 1864

Dear Mother

I wrote you a letter night before last when I was in Shenandoah Valley near Winchester and now I am in Washington. I had no opportunity of mailing my letter so I thought I would enclose a few more lines to inform you that our Corps is again on the move, and that your dear letter was received. I am so sorry that John gets no better, and it is in just the time I cannot possibly gain a furlough. I have tried three times but it's no use, while we are on the move.

The Chaplain has been good to me. He has tried his best for me but of no avail. We arrived in Washington this morning and it is the Sabbath or I should go to General Halleck. I can only pray for you. The Chaplain prays for you and Father that he may recover. I don't know where they are going to send us. The most of the troops are on board Transports. I will write again the first Port we land. God bless you and John. May the Lord spare his life. I hope you can read this.

Your Son,
Albert

Harrison

Camp Near City Point, Va.
December 6, 1864

Dear Mother and Father,

I stated in my last that I would write you as soon as we arrived in Port. So as the opportunity offers this afternoon, I will make good my promise by penning a few lines to inform you that we left Washington Sunday afternoon and yesterday morning found us at City Point again. It was the least of my thoughts that we would come back here. The Corps has not all arrived yet, the second division is still to come. The lst and 3rd have gone to the Front to the left of Petersburg. It is said they relieve the Fifth Corps.

We are waiting back here to get our train. We will probably get it tomorrow morning. As soon as we received it, I am going to make application again for a furlough. The Chaplain told me he would have my papers made out and ready for me by the time I called for them. I hear that they have stopped granting any furloughs for the present, but it don't make any difference. I will try it again and stick to the old rule. If at first you don't succeed, try, try again.

I do hope John is better. I know there must have been a change before this and I hope for the best. God grant it for your sake dear Mother. The Lord is good. I feel to thank Him for the preservation of our lives thus far. I have passed through many dangers, which to look back, seem impossibilities. But nothing is impossible with our Heavenly Father. Let us love Him more and serve Him better. I will now close. Everything is the same here, as when we left. May the Lord preserve you and bless you and allow us the privilege of meeting once again on earth.

Remember me to the neighbors and friends and receive the love and sympathy of your son Albert and his many comrades.

Sergt. Albert C. Harrison

Jones

Camp of the 14 New Jersey Vols.
Warren Station Va. near Petersburg Va.
December 15, 1864

I sometimes think I would like
Father or someone down here just about five
minutes. Tonight "Old Fort Hell" is roaring
away at a furious rate giving the Rebels
some of General Meade's compliments and
the Johnnies are replying musketry in one
continued roar. If there is any Hell on Earth
it is here at Petersburg. This "Fort Hell" is
no fictitious name ...

EJ

*Interior of Fort Sedgwick ("Fort Hell")
at Petersburg, VA.*

Harrison

Headquarters, Ambulance Corps.
3rd Division, 6th Army Corps.
Yellow House, Va.
Christmas Day 1864

My Dear Mother

I will try this morning to drop you a few lines in answer to yours, which was most thankfully received and my joy
knew no bounds when I found that John was a little better. I
do earnestly hope and pray that God will be still more merciful
and that he may fully recover from his illness and enjoy better
health than ever before.

I tell you Mother, the trouble is just here. We are busy
and have been for the past two weeks, getting our trains in
condition for the winter. Building quarters, etc. and the Medical Director of the Corps is in my opinion about as mean as can
be brought along and we belonging to the Ambulance Corps
who send in furloughs. These furloughs have to be approved by
him and its just as the notion takes him, whether he signs or
not. If I could have sent one through the Regiment, I would
have received one without doubt, as some have been granted
through that source and not as urgent cases as mine. But my
chance comes first for one and I will probably get it in the
course of a month, if the Army don't move.

All remains quiet at the present time. It is true mother
it would be hard to part if I came home. But then it would only
be for eight months or such a matter. I thank God that I have
been permitted to live 2 years and 4 months, striving with the
many thousands to crush this Rebellion and with the help of
God we will do it. Sherman and the fighting Thomas are doing
great things and here we lay, at the gates of Richmond. The

Major General George H. Thomas USA

Photos: U.S. Army Military History Institute

South must come to their right minds soon and cry Peace. But I must now close and scratch a few lines to Aunt C and two or three other correspondents, for I am getting behind in my writing. Write soon or get some one to scratch a few lines. May God bless you Dear Mother and Father. Look unto Him. He will comfort you.

Your loving son,
Albert

Harrison

Ambulance Park, 3rd Div. 6th AC
To the Left of Petersburg, Virginia
January 1, 1865

My Dear Mother and Father,

A Happy New Year Greeting

I hope you are today enjoying yourselves and most earnestly hope John has more fully recovered from his illness. But I hope to hear from you soon and to hear you are both in health once more. It is a very quiet New Year in Camp and being the Sabbath and the major portion of the men in comfortable shanties no work is being done outside of their regular line of Duty such as caring for their Teams etc, etc. Although there is enough work yet to be done to our stables and policing our Camp to keep us busy two weeks, and we Sergeants haven't finished our dwelling house yet, as the door is yet to be hung and one gable end to be put in. Also a floor is to be laid and bunks to be put up.

At present I am putting up with my old mess. Comprising the 14th Jersey, that is I sleep with them and mess with the noncommissioned staff. We had oysters for our New Years' Dinner and as a matter of course I had a poor appetite for them.

The weather is clear but very cold. All is now quiet along the front, but yesterday morning the enemy surprised our pickets, driving a portion of the line back and capturing a number of Prisoners killing two and wound-

Winter Quarters — 6th Corps at Yellow Tavern (1864-65).

U.S. Army Military History Institute

ing two belonging to the 9th New York heavy artillery attached to the 2nd Brigade of our Division. But our men rallied and drove them back capturing four. Those taken said the reason they charged was to get hard tack and some overcoats and blankets, etc., for they were cold and hungry over there. They are hoping to get about 60 coats and blankets.

I was at the Regiment day before yesterday, and found the Boys well. I didn't see anything of Eseck. I shall try for a furlough some time this month. I wish you would send me a few stamps as soon as you write again. Give my regards to all the neighbors and friends.

Now I close with love. Do write soon and believe me truly Your Dear Boy in the Army,

Albert C. Harrison

Harrison

Camp at Warren Station, Va.
February 6, 1865

Home Again

Dear Mother and Father,

"Time and tide waits for no man." Here I am once more upon the Sacred soil of old Virginia to await the result of coming time be it good or evil. Let us pray for the former.

But now to my passage which could not have been more pleasant. We arrived safe in the City of Frederick and went to Aunt C's instantly. Went out a while in the afternoon. I called at Mr. Dorr's office (old happy Dorr you know), and he asked me about a hundred questions in one breath. He stuttered terribly but I couldn't tarry with him a great while.

I then started up town again and called at Mrs. Brehant's but she was not in so I hadn't the pleasure of receiving a kiss from that married lady. At night I was out a while then went to bed on the sofa bed in the parlor until Aunty C sung out that it was time we was on the move. She got out breakfast and off we went.

About the boots, Uncle Henry told me they were $14.00. I paid Aunt Clemmy part of it and left. Told her I would settle the balance at some future time. She said she didn't have the least idea that he would charge me anything, but it's all right, I don't wish to be beholding upon them for anything. I'm satisfied and am glad its the way it is. I will be independent one of these days, I hope, if the Good Lord prospers me.

I find the weather quite cold here. But I must tell you when I arrived I came in last night and found the boys all well and glad to see me back. After arriving in Washington I had to get transportation to Annapolis as the Potomac was frozen up tight as a jug. The boats were running from Annapolis altogether, but I came through all right at last. I tell you I did murder the grub.

There's a movement afoot of some sort. The Fifth Corps and the first division of our Corps has moved to the left of the lines. I guess nothing more then a raid. They have captured several wagons and several prisoners and 25 went down to Army headquarters about half an hour since.

I guess we will have peace soon...as soon as 25 more come in. I think I shall try now for a pass to go down to Fort Powhattan with Charlie White. I was over to the Regiment this morning and saw all the boys. Eseck wished to be remembered. I hope to hear from you soon. Try and make this out and I will write you better next time. Give my love to Grandma and remember me to all friends. I must get this in the mail tonight. May God bless you.

Your loving son,
Albert

Harrison

Camp of the 14th N.J. Vols.
Near Warren Station, Va.
February 21, 1865

Dear Parents,

I must scratch you a few lines this morning as I am at leisure for the present, and inform you of the many changes which have transpired since I last wrote you.

I expect you will wonder some, if not more, at the heading of this so I will explain the change. Instead of being in the Ambulance train I am home again, with the Gallant 14th, having been relieved from the train, through the extreme kindness of the Corps Medical Director. There being two sergeants from my Regiment and he sent an order to the Chief of the Train to have one of us relieved. I had the oldest right to remain if I had chosen but I thought I would leave as I would be better off at the Regiment since matters and things became so mixed up in the Train and entirely too many bosses to live with anyway pleasantly. I might have received a new detail if I had wanted it, but after coming to the Regiment and finding myself so much better contented that I thought I would remain.

And the old boys were glad enough to see me back with them after being away from the Regiment over a year. At the present I am not with the Company but Acting Sergt. Major of the Regiment which is a splendid position. All the Duty I have to perform is in the mornings generally. I have the Regimental details to make our Guard Duty fatigue, etc. Charlie has just come in. He is Regimental officer of the day, today. Sends best respects to you. The boys in the company are all lively as crickets. In fact, the weather makes everyone feel full of life. Eseck wishes to be remembered. Charlie Conrow is fatter than he was when he called to see us that day. He had just come in from Fort Fisher, having been on fatigue duty with a detail of forty men from the Regiment.

Foster is with the Regt. but Capt. Conover has not returned as yet. I don't believe his intention is to return. If he remains away sixty days he will be mustered out of Service.

Fort Fisher — Petersburg, VA.

Nothing new has or is transpiring along the lines of the two armies. General Sherman still gladdens our hearts by his successful movements.

I don't think we will move far away from here before our term expires. It is dinner time. I must see if the boys have the grub prepared. Give my kindest regards to your near neighbors and don't forget me to Aunt Elizabeth and all relatives.

Sergt. Albert C. Harrison
14th N.J. Vols.

PS, There is a salute of 100 guns being fired for the fall of Charleston and Columbia

Harrison

Near Petersburg, Va.
March 8, 1865

My Dear Parents,

It seems to me almost a week has glided by since last I wrote you, but I have been very busy writing for the company that I have been unable to spare a moment when I felt like writing.

But now as I have time before darkness closes over the face of Virginia I will drop you a few lines in acknowledgment of your kind and loving epistle dated Feb. 28th which came duly to hand. Yes I am perfectly well contented at the Regiment and expect to remain so.

It has stormed about twice every other day for two weeks and in consequence a fellow stirring around outdoors much goes shoe deep in mud, which is not very agreeable. There are no ladies around so it don't make any difference if a fellow's boots don't shine with blacking instead of mud.

The boys are all in good health and lively as crickets as the spring opens. The frogs all croaking ready to split their throats. I guess the winter is over in this part of the world and I must say I'll be glad of it if such is the case, but I must now go to supper and try to finish this during the evening.

The news of the day still continues to make our hearts glad. It's truly rich to think how Phil Sheridan slipped up on old Early. So it goes, it seems as if we can only be successful of late in any of our undertakings. God is aiding us in crushing this Rebellion. Slowly the Angel of Peace is descending to visit the American People once again. Slowly but surely is old Lee being entrapped and he will one of these days find the trap sprung.

There is nothing new for me to write you. We have meetings nearly every night during the week and there is a meeting held by the Christian Commission at Warren Station. Very many have been hopefully converted and among them are some of my old comrades in the Train.

I must close now for this time. Give my kind regards to your loving neighbors and I remain your loving and affectionate son,

Al

Harrison

Camp of the Fourteenth, N.J. Vols.
March 14, 1865

Dear Parents

In answer to your kind letter which came to hand last night I take my pen to scratch you a few lines but I cannot write you as long a letter as I could wish as we have orders to pack up and be ready to move at a moment's notice. Whether we will move or not remains alone with time to be told. The probabilities are that we will as the weather is fair and favorable for a movement at the present time.

Another thing we are expecting is the arrival of Phil Sheridan and his Army on our left in consequence somebody must be out there to help him form a Junction. Still we may not move as we have often received similar orders and not moved. It is always the best policy to be in readiness, whether or not. So after I conclude I will repair immediately to my tent and pack my knapsack. I am now in Charlie's tent penning these few lines hoping they may find you all in the enjoyment of good health. If we do not move I will write again soon. If we do, the probability is I will not have the opportunity for three or four days. My best regards to friends.

Your son,
Al

Harrison

Camp of the 14th New Jersey Volunteers
Near Petersburg, Va.
March 19, 1865

Dear Parents,

I was much delighted last evening to receive a couple of newspapers from you, one printed and the other written through the kindness of Dan Thompson, who arrived safe at Camp.

I was surprised to receive such a long letter. Really, you must have been tired after you had done writing. I could not tire of reading from home, dear Mother.

We received orders to be ready to move, which have since been countermanded and from present appearances I don't think we will move in a fortnight or such a matter. It has seemed very dull about Camp today as the greater part of the Regt. is on Picket. I haven't been on guard of Picket since I came to the Regiment and for the present am doing no Duty.

Captain Jeff Thompson, Dan's brother was over to see us today. He looks finely with his new bars. The weather is lovely. The air so pure it seems there cannot be any such thing as sickness and in fact there is but very few cases if any. If any odds, it's more healthy here than at home. There is much Fever raging about the country and in the cities.

I see gold has fallen to $1.65. This is good news indeed. I am in hope we may yet live to see gold and U.S. Greenbacks on a par.

The news for Sherman, Sheridan and Schofield continues good. I am in hopes they will drop in and see us one of these days and visit Jefferson Davis and R.E. Lee with some big guns.

The boys are in good spirits each one thinking he will see the end of this War before many more months.

I hope to hear from you again soon and remain your loving son,

Albert C.

Union Artillery before Petersburg, VA.

Major General J.M. Schofield USA

The Assault at Petersburg

The 14th New Jersey Volunteers bravely participated in the assault on enemy lines at Petersburg in late March and early April, 1865, with the 10th Vermont Volunteers and supported by two Ohio regiments. These units captured part of the enemy's outer works and were temporarily placed on picket, while they awaited orders to assist in other advances.

On April 2, 1865, General Sheridan drove the rebels from their works at Five Forks which destroyed the right wing of General Lee's army. At about the same time, General Grant ordered the three corps which held the Union line to advance all along the front. At dawn the assault began. The Sixth Corps drove hard to the Boydton Road and pivoted to the left towards Hatcher's Run, thus sweeping through the rear of the rebel lines. Thousands of prisoners were captured along with artillery pieces and great quantities of supplies. The other corps captured Petersburg's main defenses. Among the five regiments of Colonel Truex's brigade, the 14th N.J. was placed in the second line of battle and instructed to deploy upon entering the enemy's works and drive them out. General Park's Ninth Corps was held in reserve and General Sheridan attacked the rebel flank. At about 4 o'clock the signal guns opened the engagement and the entire line became locked in desperate combat. Later in the same day, Colonel Truex and Keifer's brigades attacked the Southside Railroad and destroyed ten miles of track. The Division continued to move toward the Confederate left and fought a desperate skirmish with a rebel gun battery. With the fall of this position, the enemy was in full retreat. During the entire struggle the 14th N.J. Volunteers demonstrated the highest standards of courage under fire and contributed as much as any other unit to the Union victory. Colonel Truex's report sheds light on the brave deeds of this day. [April 2, 1865].

The following is an extract from Colonel Truex's report:

"I have the honor to submit the following report of the operations of this brigade at the assault on the works in front of Petersburg, April 2, 1865, which resulted in the capture of the entire line and evacuation of the above-mentioned city. In accordance with

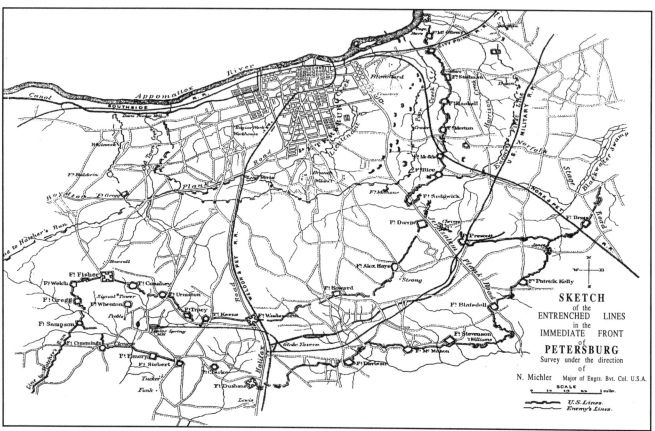

Source: New Jersey and the Rebellion by John Y. Foster, Newark, NJ — Martin R. Dennis & Co. (1868)

instructions received from Brigadier General Seymour, commanding the division, I moved the brigade at twelve o'clock, P.M., April 1, 1865, to the position which had previously been designated for it to occupy, viz: In the rear of our picket-line in front of Fort Welch, and on the extreme left of this corps. At about half-past twelve o'clock, I reached the ground and formed my brigade in three lines of battle, as follows: Left line, composed of the Tenth Vermont Volunteers, Lieutenant-Colonel George B. Damon commanding, on the right, and the One Hundred and Sixth New York Volunteers, Lieutenant-Colonel Alvah W. Briggs commanding, on the left, distant about twenty paces from the picket line. Second line, composed of the Fourteenth New Jersey Volunteers, Lieutenant-Colonel J.J. Janeway commanding, on the right, and the One Hundred and Fifty-First New York volunteers, Lieutenant-Colonel Charles Bogardus commanding, on the left. Third line, the Eighty Seventh Pennsylvania volunteers, Captain James Tearney commanding. This latter regiment was composed almost entirely of raw troops, five companies having joined it within two weeks of this movement, and most of whom had never before been under fire. The troops were placed in position without attracting the attention of the enemy, although within one hundred and fifty yards of his picket line. About half an hour later, the enemy on their extreme left opened, suddenly, a very severe and galling picket fire which ran down the line to my front, which continued for nearly one hour. Under this fire my brigade remained quiet, not answering with a single shot or otherwise betraying our presence to the enemy, although a number were killed and wounded. Too much praise cannot be given to my officers for the splendid manner in which they moved their men into position, and afterwards controlling their commands under this severe picket fire. At about one half past four o'clock, A.M., the signal gun to advance was fired from Fort Fisher, when I ordered the brigade to advance. Instantly a terrible fire of musketry and artillery was opened upon us by the enemy, but my men gallantly and bravely advanced at a double quick and in a few moments scaled the breastworks, which at this place were from twelve to fifteen feet high; driving the enemy before them and holding the position. I must here state that then the order to advance was given and the enemy opened on us, the Eighty-Seventh Pennsylvania Volunteers broke to the front, passing through the second and first lines and becoming temporarily the first line. The first colors inside the works were those of the Tenth Vermont Volunteers and Fourteenth New Jersey Volunteers. We here captured three hundred prisoners and either five or six guns. The first line, composed of the Tenth Vermont and One Hundred and Sixth New York Volunteers, were instantly reformed inside the works, wheeled to the left and charged down the line at a double quick, the balance of the command following as they entered the works, driving and doubling up the enemy as they advanced. The next fort was seized with but little opposition, my troops capturing about one hundred and fifty prisoners and two guns. Again advancing, I ordered the brigade to charge on the next fort. The enemy here endeavored to make a stand, but my command pushed forward and compelled him to evacuate it, when the fort was instantly occupied by my brigade, the first colors to enter being those of the Fourteenth New Jersey Volunteers. Here my command was joined by a small portion of the Second Brigade, which remained with me until I fell back temporarily to the second fort, where they were ordered to the right and joined their proper commands. We here captured about one hundred prisoners and seized twenty guns. This fort we held about twenty-five minutes when the enemy advanced in two lines of battle, one in front of the fort and the other from the woods on the right, compelling us to fall back temporarily to the second fort above mentioned. On this charge of the enemy we lost heavily in killed and wounded, besides many prisoners, my men falling back reluctantly and contesting the ground inch by inch; but were overpowered by superior numbers. The enemy was enabled to hold this fort for some length of time, and it was not until the arrival of a battery to our aid that we were successful in dislodging him, capturing forty prisoners and two pieces of cannon. In the capture of this fort the sharpshooters of the brigade deserved a special mention in silencing the rebel guns by picking off the gunners wherever they made their appearance. For this purpose a number of them were deployed on the left of the works in the direction of a house facing the fort.

The brigade was formed in column of regiments and advancing on the left flank of the fort, compelled its surrender. Without halting we advanced on the next fort, which was evacuated almost without a struggle, leaving in our possession four guns, caissons and horses. Still pressing on about half a mile, we met the Twenty-Fourth Corps, when a halt was ordered.

At this point I was ordered to countermarch my brigade and proceed in the direction of Petersburg.

At the 'Brick Chimneys,' in front of Petersburg, and on the extreme left of the Ninth Corps, we remained until Four o'clock, P.M., when I was ordered to move my brigade and occupy a line which in the morning had been occupied by the enemy's pickets. Earthworks were thrown up, a picket line established and the troops bivouacked for the night. The results of the next day's operations may be summed up as follows: Five hundred and ninety prisoners and fifteen cannons.

I have every reason to be proud of the regiments composing my brigade, the Tenth Vermont, One Hundred and Sixth New York, the Fourteenth New Jersey, Fifteenth New York and Eighty-Seventh Pennsylvania, and the coolness, judgement and gallantry of their commanding officers, Lieutenant-Colonel George B. Damon, Lieutenant-Colonel A.W. Briggs, Lieutenant-Colonel J.J. Janeway, Lieutenant-Colonel Charles Bogardus and Captain James Tearney. My thanks are also due to the field and line officers for their efficient manner in which they discharged their duties during the eventful day. I also mention with pleasure members of my staff, who were throughout the whole day conspicuous for prompt action, courage and personal exposure:

Captain and Brevet-Major Charles K. Leonard, A.A.G.; Captain and Brevet Major Hiram W. Day, Brigade Inspector; Captain and Brevet-Major Charles M. Bartruff, A.A.D.C.; Captain Benjamin F. Miller, A.A.D.C."

On April 3, 1865, news came that the rebels had abandoned Petersburg and were in full retreat. The 14th New Jersey Volunteers together with other units pursued the enemy through Sutherland Station piercing the Confederate flank at Sailor's Creek. The Brigade was forced to ford a stream some seventy-five yards wide and storm a hill under severe fire before it was successful in dislodging the Confederates from their positions and forcing them to surrender. Intermittent volleys were sustained by the Federals from pockets of Confederate defenders, until Major Pegram appeared with a flag of truce. This Confederate Inspector General surrendered the Southern forces with the following words, "I surrender Lieutenant General Ewell and staff and his command." At this point all firing came to a halt.

Harrison

Major John Pegram CSA

Camp of the 14th N.J.Vols.
Near Petersburg, Va.
March 26, 1865

My Dear Parents,

No doubt 'ere you receive this the Papers will have informed you that we have had the first Battle of Spring and it will be glorious news for you to learn that your boy is by the blessing and kind mercies of God still spared without a scratch and in good health.

It is needless for me to give you a very lengthy detail of the engagement which commenced on yesterday morning.

Gen. U.S. Grant and company set a trap for the enemy in front of the 3rd Division 9th A.C. and the enemy took advantage of the opening which was made in our lines, and after they marched into this Yankee Trap, our troops kept falling back until we could bring our batteries to bear fully upon their advancing columns, Then gave them particular fits in the shape of Grape and Canister. They went back howling but not without leaving a large number of prisoners in our hands. Not long after this transpired in the centre, the Second Corps attacked the enemy on the left but I am not positive with what success they have met with.

Fort Fisher — Petersburg, VA.

Soon after the Second Corps engaged, our Corps charged the left centre after charging twice in which we lost but one man wounded out of our Regiment, we captured the enemy's first line of Works. Capturing their entire Picket Line and still hold the Line. The most part of the Rebel Pickets never fired a gun but stood in their works until they were taken by the Shoulder and led back to our Provost Guards, and taken off to the rear. Some ran into our line soon after we started on the second charge.

Every Regiment but ours seemed to suffer pretty hard. I expect if the weather continues fair we will give them another turn in a few days. Phil Sheridan is somewhere around these parts, but he don't show himself. He will turn up where the Johns least expect him and give them a little of Phil and they will get their fill, if they don't give up this war pretty soon.

I can assure you this Rebellion is getting squeezed down to a mere nothing and it fills our hearts with Thanksgiving to the God of Battles for our great and lasting Victories over our National Enemy. May God bless us all and prepare us for the glorious end. The boys are all joyful and ready at all times to do their duty like men, remembering our old Revolutionary Fathers, of the hardships, privations and difficulties they encountered before they accomplished their Just and Glorious Cause.

I will bring this to a close hoping soon to hear from you. My kind regards to friends and your neighbors and I remain your loving son, with a happy wish for your well being and a Blessing from on High.

Your dear son,
Al

Harrison

Camp of the 14th N.J.Vols
Before Petersburg, Va.
March 31, 1865

Petersburg, VA

Dear Parents

Your kind and loving letter of March 26th came into eager hands last night and it is with pleasure I take my pen this morning to scratch a reply. I cannot seem to realize that poor Dear Amos is gone. But so it is. May God bless and comfort the bereaved and sorrowing friends. When I hear of a death in the Army, I scarcely give it a thought, but when the sad news comes from home I cannot seem to free my mind of it. I hope Amos was fully prepared for the sudden change from life unto Death. I loved that boy as I would love a brother, but he is gone from me. I trust we may meet him in Heaven. He is only gone before. I was sorry to learn of my cousin's death but that seemed not so strange as Amos'. But we know not how soon we may be called to bid adieu to earth and those most dear. It matters not if we are prepared, if we are clothed with the preparation of the Gospel. Sooner or later we must all pass away and give place to unborn generations. May God guard over and protect us through the struggle of life and fit our spirits for eternity in the presence of our Maker and our Redeemed Jesus Christ.

It is storming today and it has been the means of delaying a Heavy Battle on our Left, and one which would have a telling effect upon the rebellion. But it is all for the best.

Phil Sheridan is down on the left with his thirty thousand Cavalry supported by the fifth Corps. We moved from our old Camp yesterday morning, came down about three miles to the left where we now hold

Petersburg, VA

the works of the Second Corps which has moved farther to the left. We have good shelter from the storm. Still it is not a cold one as it would be at home.

Gen. Sherman has been here and is holding a council of War with Gen. Grant, and his Army is still pressing its way through North Carolina. I suppose this storm will hinder its progress some, but they will be up inside of two weeks at the farthest if they meet not with too many obstacles on the road. Whoever lives to see the 4th of July will see a happy one in my opinion.

The Rebels do not fight with the courage and determination they once did. They seem to be utterly beaten. They know their cause to be hopeless and they don't care. There has been some firing on the left this morning but it amounted to nothing.

Last night about ten o'clock we heard a heavy musketry firing on the right of the lines but very little artillery was used. We now have a powerful Army and trusting in the God of Battles, we will whip the Rebel foe. He will not forsake us upon the eve of battle. My earnest prayer is that God will bless you all in churches and give you a spirit of prayers that you go forth with a prayer upon your lips for the welfare of our armies and the sudden downfall of the Confederacy. May God bless you Dear Parents and keep you within the hollow of His hand and comfort you in sorrow.

I must draw to a close hoping again to hear from you. I don't need any money. For the present I thank you, the ten cents will buy me a paper some time. The boys are all hearty and in good spirits for whatever may come. I now bid good bye for this time. Bear me in remembrance to friends and relatives and I remain your loving and affectionate son,

Albert

Union dead at Petersburg VA.

Confederate Dead at Petersburg, VA.

Jones

"Victory" "Victory" "Victory"

Camp of the 14th New Jersey Vols
Near Petersburg, Virginia
2 1/2 P.M. April 2, 1865

Dear Father

When you are in Rebel land do as Rebels do - write on their paper. We have had one of the noisiest times here last night and today, was known about one of the Greatest Victories.

The Johnnies were attacked last night about midnight and before daylight the 3rd Div of the 6th Corps occupied the works of their front. They were the first troops to enter at the same time the attack was made above and below us and the whole left swung around. The boys are now driving them into the City of Petersburg - which will be in our possession by night. The 9th Corps lying directly in front of the city have drove them some but we are coming up in the rear. Our loss I can tell nothing about but it is small in comparison to the work they had to do. The last I heard from the Regiment they were within 1 1/2 miles of Petersburg and pushing them on. I have remained in camp with my horses but I feel so good "Oh My."

This paper was picked up in the camps directly opposite. You will hear from me everyday and will get the news of the day. Sheridan is in between them and Richmond.

From Your Son
Edward C. Jones

Harrison

Camp in the Field
April 2, 1865

Dearest Parents

I must scratch a few lines to inform you that after going through a leaden and war hail storm, thanks to the God of Battles, I am alive and happy.

Our Corps charged the enemy's lines last night, broke their

line and drove them out of sight, driving them right down their works. I never felt more like fighting than I have today and I kept my shooting iron hot for about an hour and a half, and with prayer all the time. I felt as if I was willing to give my life up freely and I felt assured I would be received in Heaven.

Two men in my company were wounded. Those are the only two that have as yet been heard from. There are three we cannot find as yet, but I guess they will turn up in a day or so. We are now before Petersburg and are going to have the Fort the Rebels hold, which is directly in front of the City.

The Confederacy is gone up.

I lost part of a third finger, right hand. Boys bound it up — am all right and doing well — a few more days and the grays will go down...

[no signature]

First Union forces moving into Petersburg, VA — April, 1865.

Library of Congress

When Johnny Comes Marching Home by Louis Lambert; Published by Henry Tolman & Co., 1863.
Source: The Free Library of Philadelphia, Music Department.

7 Victory....at Long Last

early April 1865 — June 1865

Camp of the 14th N.J. Vols.
7 Miles from Appomattox C.H.
April 10, 1865

Dear Father

The "Gig" is "up." Old Lee surrendered yesterday here. We have had no chance of sending a line since leaving Petersburg until today and have received none. We have marched like devils but it has paid us "Big." Be home in a month. I am well and can hardly hold myself.

Lee surrendered the entire army of the Confederacy. Such a time was never known in the army as this. I wrote the day we started but we were not allowed to send out any mail.

Ed

Harrison

Camp of the 14th — N.J. Vols.
Near Burke's Station, Burke's Co. Va.
April 17, 1865

Dear Parents

I might as well be penning you a few lines as I am at leisure and our accommodations being quite good for after the past short, but decisive campaign we find ourselves encamped in a perfect wilderness of Pines, and it is quite a pleasant place for a Camp. Good water and plenty of it. We are beginning to get enough to eat once more, for I tell you it was rather slim dodging for a couple three or four days. Our Haversacks didn't hurt our shoulders any for they were full of empty sugar and coffee bags.

The McLean House at Appomattox Court House, VA, where Lee surrendered the Army of Northern Virginia.

But we were doing a Union's work and could afford to go hungry as long as there was an enemy, and kept in good spirits and fought just as hard as if we went in with a full belly. Excitement would keep us alive for two days or even longer. But the war is over in this state. She will no longer suffer from the ravages of war.

But the worst news which was received in any army came to us night before last. A dispatch came to us stating that our President, Secretary and son had been murdered. It is horrible. Today the news came official stating the Pres. was dead and the Secretary's son could not survive but that the Father there was very faint hope entertained of his recovery. God grant he may yet live to see the end of this Wicked Rebellion. The best friend we soldiers had on earth was Uncle Abe. He done all the good that lay in the power of man to do and offered the enemy every inducement to come back to the old union. But they would not now may the sword never be sheathed until the blood of every traitor North and South is spilled to atone for the crime. No quarters should ever more be shown to them if they still persist they should wear the halter.

May God still sustain us through this our greatest National Calamity. We know it is all for the best. But it fills every soldier's heart with the most bitter hatred against a Rebel. If it is our lot to get in another engagement before the expiration of our term of service, the old double Six will not show any mercy or take many prisoners and that is the best way to serve them, kill all we catch.

I wonder how the Copperheads view the war now. Whether they still think old Lee and his invincible Army cannot be whipped into surrender. Time works wonders. But we worked wonders in a short time. We fully appreciate the bounteous praise the worthy editor of the Herald heaps upon the gallant sixth Corps. Mr. Bennett did not view things a year or two ago, in the same true light that he now does.

I will never be sorry that I left the Ambulance Corps. and rejoined my company so long as my life has been spared for which I

John Wilkes Booth (above), Lincoln (at right) and Ford's Theatre (pictured below).

thank God. I have been fully repaid.

I have not as yet received any letter from you in fact I have received no letters from Jersey in two weeks. I am anxious to hear from you. I hope you have before this become settled down in your new home. I hope John is fast improving and that you are all in good health as this leaves me for since we came here three days ago I have had a good rest.

I don't know what they intend to do with us. We don't get any papers so we hear nothing but rumors, and being in a Pine woods we see nothing but Pine trees and soldiers.

The weather is lovely. Give my love to Grandma and bear me in remembrance to any friends and now I will close. The boys are all well. May God bless and protect you. I remain your loving and affectionate son,

Albert

P.S. I don't think I shall attempt to write another letter on Rebel paper.

Execution of the Lincoln assassination conspirators pictured above. Lincoln's funeral is pictured below.

Photos: Ford's Theatre, Lincoln's Funeral — National Archives; John Wilkes Booth, Abraham Lincoln, Execution of conspirators — U.S. Army Military History Institute.

Harrison

Camp of the 14th N.J. Vols.
Near Danville, Va.
April 28, 1865

Dear Parents and Sister

I have but few moments to write as the mail goes out at half past eight and it is nearly the time now. I merely wish to state that I am still in good health but pretty well tired out for we have been on the Tramp since last Sunday morning having marched 90 miles in the past five days and now find ourselves nearly on the North Carolina line being about 5 miles from the line. We marched through Danville yesterday afternoon about 3 o'clock. The situation of the town is beautiful. It being on a side hill with the river Dan running along past the town. All the country we have passed through since leaving Burkesville is in a state of cultivation and the most splendid part of Virginia for I have now been from one end of state to the other and know pretty nearly as much as about the state as I ever wanted to know.

There is but our Corps down here and it is said we will remain here for a time, but how long I cannot say. But I will write to sister if we stay any length of time, and there should be any mails leaving. We are laying in an oak woods about 3 miles south of the town. A splendid situation, plenty of wood and good water. The weather is hot and sultry but it has been splendid for marching. The bottom of my feet are all a blister. I tell you it is rough. But it's all right. The citizens of Danville sent to Gen. Grant for protection and he sent the Sixth Corps.

If they can't kill us all off by fighting they try to in marching, sometimes making 25 miles a day. You must try to make this poor writing out, for I am hurrying things and will soon have to close. Some of the boys became so foot sore that they are not up yet, but those who are up are feeling pretty good after the past night's rest. I received two letters from you and was glad enough to hear from you. Tell sister I am going to write her soon. I received her letter night before last and it helped me along wonderfully yesterday on the march. I cannot say enough if I say I am glad she has come to live with you and that I have a dear sister. But I now close for I must scratch a few lines for one of my boys. Good Bye and May God bless you.

I remain affectionately your son,

Al

Railroad bridge at Danville, VA.

P.S. There is no prospect of our getting home before our time expires unless Johnston surrenders pretty soon. [General Joseph E. Johnston C.S.A.]

Harrison

Robert E. Lee and Joseph E. Johnston.

Camp of the 14th N.J. Vol
Danville, Va.
May 6, 1865

Dear Parents

It is a very warm day but as it will be but little exertion I will pen you a few lines. I don't know whether I will ever be content to settle down to hard labor again or not, such as Clerking. I imagine it would nearly kill me to be shut up in a store for a couple of weeks weighing out family groceries. But I must begin to study up some plan for making the cents, and I suppose the dollars will take care of themselves as they always have. But I have made up my mind that my friends have got to keep me for a while if not, I have another plan to work upon. I will put up my canvas on Sandy Hook and make a living from the River. Fishing, clamming, etc. and that is just what would suit me for a while. I think I would sooner recruit up.

But to the news of the day, there is nothing current of any importance. I hear the Army is to be discharged by the first of June. I expect the old sixth will be the last Corps to be mustered out of service. It is also reported that we are to march through to Washington. If that should prove to be fact, I think I would about reach the famous Capitol next winter some time and it looks very much like it for they are going to discharge several out of our Regt. for Disability — three out of my company.

There are about thirty recruits in one of the companies that have never been armed yet. They came to the Regiment at Burkesville and I don't believe they will ever carry a gun. Some of them got their $1400. I tell you it looks mean to me to think that we should come out here and do all the fighting and somebody that never fired a gun gets all the pay for it. But so goes the World. It is one satisfaction to know that the men who came out in 62 came not for money, but I am going to have it out of the State of New Jersey, if the Good Father spares my life.

It was reported here in the Regiment some time ago, that Judge Vredenburg and several prominent citizens of Freehold were making efforts to raise a bounty for survivors. But now that the war is over, I don't suppose they will give us a thought. I don't ask any odds of them anyhow. I'm poor but I am independent.

We don't have anything much to do here but Picket Duty and that is nothing for there is no enemy in our front anymore. They have been swept away and thanks be unto God

Union camp scene.

for bringing a stronger and I trust a better people. The great curse of slavery no longer hangs above the heads of the American People. It now may be called a Free Nation. Capt. Conover came to the company day before yesterday. He is settling up his company business and goes back home next Monday. I have been writing for him. Give my love to Grandma. Tell her to have a sugar cake ready for me by the time I get home. My love to sister Addie and best respects to any friends.

Hoping soon to hear from you, I remain your loving and affec. son,

Al

Harrison

Camp of the 14th N.J. Volunteers
Danville, Virginia
May 15, 1865

Dear Cousin Clemmy,

Perhaps a few lines from your coz in the old 6th will come acceptable so I will try to scratch you a few lines upon this monstrous sheet of paper. But it looks almost discouraging to begin yet it's not my intention by any means to fill the sheet for I imagine it would take me a week of Sundays to complete it especially as dull as times are now hereabouts.

Without doubt you have heard of the whereabouts of our Corps 'ere this, as the Herald gave full account of our movement after leaving Burkesville. Our hard march to Danville, etc. and it is two weeks since we came. Yes it was two weeks last Thursday that we marched in and through the town. But meeting with a very cool reception by the citizens and inhabitants in and about Danville, but the Darks were glad to see us come. They would jump and sing for joy and as soon as the Brass band would strike up with some old National Air the Niggers would commence dancing their old fashioned hoe down.

Our camps were alive with them for two or three days, until they began to be a nuisance and the boys floured everyone that came in. They haven't troubled us much of late. It is awful lonesome here. We lay about a mile and a half from town in an oak woods and there is nothing to be seen to cause the least excitement or disturb the quiet monotony of Camp life. But so long as this cruel war is over we should be content and happy. But it is hard to satisfy man. I presume if we were at home, we would eventually grow tired of home comforts and long to be upon the tented field once more.

Many in the Regiment now have expressed a desire to enlist to fight under the Republican flag in Mexico and I see by the papers that very many are enlisting in Philadelphia and receiving large bounties and so much land in the Sonora Valley. I would like very well to have the gold, but I will wait awhile before I sell myself to Mexico. My own country may need my service again and then I would be on hand for the emergency. We may all be in our graves before there is another War in this country, but it is my opinion the Country will not enjoy peace as long as she did before this war. Yet, I never wish to pass through the same ordeal again, as that of the past two years. And still I cannot seem to fully realize that the Rebellion is crushed, that the fighting is done, so long as we remain in camp. But when I get home and get inside of a suit of citizen's rig then I can fully realize it and two or three years from now, I can better recall to memory what I have endured and the many changing scenes I have witnessed than I can at the present time.

A soldier does not care to look back over the many bloody battlefields if he expects to get in another engagement, for if he does, he is apt to think of some of his comrades who's hopes one day were as bright as his own. But they were gone and he might go in the same way. It don't do for a man to go to battle thinking that he is going to be killed. I have noticed many a time that the ones who were most reckless of their lives, always came out first best.

But I must say that I felt a little frightened when we charged the 2nd day of April in front of Fort Fisher. I had supposed the Rebels had stronger works and had a stronger force in the works opposing us, than they actually had. I had a sort of a feeling that I was going to get hurt, but I came out safe. I was struck on the foot with a spent Ball, while laying down while the sharp shooters opened the engagement, but I thought nothing of that, any more than I think I was lucky. I was hit almost the same way with a spent Ball at Locust Grove, Nov. 27th, 1863, only that took me fair on the heel while I was lying upon my face behind the fence. My ammunition being all expended, poor Elliot Fields lay beside me dead. I crawled behind him, and lay down again, and just as I done so a ball went in his breast, which no doubt would have killed me. So my life was spared through the body of a dead man. He was struck several times after he was killed.

Upon going into that fight, he told me he would be killed. I talked with him and told him to try and shake off such a feeling as that. But it was no use and sure enough he was killed and never spoke a word after he was struck, scarcely breathed. And he wore almost a smile, for he had been laughing at a Rebel that was wounded to see him run a ways and fall down, get up and start again and fall down until he got out of range, behind a stack of corn stalks. The weather today is beautiful but for a few days it was uncomfortably hot.

Dead Confederate soldier in trench at Petersburg.

U.S. Army Military History Institute

We are about two miles from the North Carolina line. I have been across the line once since we came here, but I didn't get far in the state, for I saw nothing but woods.

When I last received any tidings from home, John was sick again, but not seriously. I hope we will get out of this before a great while, but I don't suppose there is any chance for me to get a job dropping potatoes down your way. But I would dearly love to be at home this time of the year. But God willing we will get there sometime between this and next August. I am daily expecting a Captain's commission. My papers went through to the Governor nearly two weeks since I took command of my own company if I agreed to get mustered. That will depend upon the time we will remain in service, if we stay until our time expires. I would be mustered so I would have a chance to pay for the outfit, for you know I would have to be decently clothed, etc. But now I must close. If you cannot read this in one day, why lay it aside until you have time.

Give my love to all the family,
I remain your affec. cousin,
Al

[The reference to soldiers signing up for duty in Mexico refers to American outrage at French intervention in Mexico in violation of the Monroe Doctrine. France withdrew its support of the puppet dictator Maximillan who was ultimately executed by Mexican nationalists.]

Harrison

Camp of the 14th N.J. Vols.
Manchester, Va.
May 19, 1865

Dear Parents

Being at leisure for the present, I will drop you a few lines to inform you that I am still blessed with good health. Trusting in the gracious mercies of God you are enjoying the same privilege.

As time rolls onward so does the 6th Corps toward our National Capitol, but we are not moving very fast at the present time. But we bid adieu to the fair town of Danville day before yesterday and arrived at Manchester yesterday morning having taken the train along the bank of the James, opposite Richmond for four or five hours. Then went into Camp outside the City of Manchester where we are to remain until our Wagon Train comes up, when we will push on for Washington, I think.

You must excuse this poor writing for my pen I guess has served in the Rebellion for the past four years. If we remain here for a few days, I shall procure a pass to visit the great city of Sodom [referring to Richmond]. Although we will

have to pass through the town before we leave here, but I want
to go over on Belle Isle, and around to the principal places
which will long be remembered by those of our brave boys who
were so unfortunate as to be prisoners of war and survive their
imprisonment. But from what I have already seen of the city, it
is a splendid place and much superior to our National Capitol.
The streets are better laid out, but the nicest part of the city
was burned. Also, the Rail Road bridge across the river was
destroyed and I saw the Confederate Capitol and the Statue of
Washington in front. Those I saw from across the river. We
have free access to the town of Manchester, also to the river.

I must go down tonight and take a swim. I should have
gone last night, but as we had been in camp but a short time.
My duties would not allow me to leave. I am Acting Sergt.
Major. I am daily expecting my commission as Captain, Company G. I was recommended some time ago. I will get it I guess
about the time we are mustered out. Then I don't want it.
Charlie is well and wishes to be remembered to all.

May God bless you. I pray this may find you in good
health.

Your loving son,
Albert

Harrison

Camp of the 14th N.J. Vols.
Near Manchester, Virginia
May 21, 1865

Dear Parents

I may not have the opportunity of writing you many
more letters in Virginia, so I will pen you few lines again and I
presume it will be the last one I will write while in the vicinity
of Richmond, at any rate, as we leave here next Tuesday,
unless we receive new orders in the meantime. But how we will
go to Washington, yet remains to be seen. Some are of the
opinion that we will march and others think transportation
will be furnished us from City Point. I as a matter of course am
in favor of the last. We will know by tomorrow night so there is
no use thinking over the matter, as it will only make it the
harder if it should chance to be our evil luck to march one
hundred and thirty miles. But I can live through it, if the rest
can. I always have.

When Charlie wrote home, I did think something of
taking my discharge, as it was freely offered me. But I refused
to accept it and the same night the Colonel recommended me
for the captaincy of my own company. My commission has not
arrived as yet, but I am daily expecting it.

It has been an extremely hot day and this afternoon,
we had a severe thunder storm. The lightning struck a tree
about forty yards from Headquarters where I now reside as I

am still acting Sergt. Major of the Regiment during the furloughed absence of the S.M.

I have not fully made up my mind as yet whether I will get mustered on my commission or not. There is an opportunity for all those who wish to remain in service to do so and there is nothing in this world that I would like better than soldiering in time of peace, especially if I held the commission of Captain, but not as a private soldier. No not any more carrying gun for me, I thank you. But about my getting my discharge, that need not worry you in the least, for I assure you I'll come out all right without any discharge even had I been sick, I should not have taken a discharge. After remaining two years and nine months with the Regiment and going through what I have and lived, for which I thank God. No I could not see leaving my old comrades until I am obliged to, when the time is so short. If I came home I would not be doing anything.

You and I cannot afford to lose much time. I must be doing something. Had I been one of those who have grown rich from this war, it would be well enough for me to lay down the shovel and the hoe, but that is not the case, and when the soldiers all get home, it is going to be slim dodging to gain a situation [employment] and you know mother, I cannot feel content to longer look for support, but instead to lend a helping hand toward making you comfortable in your old days. So, here's the chap that's going to pitch in. I have nothing else to work for in this world. But to see you both comfortably situated, and trusting in God who has preserved my life, as I believe for that purpose I shall one day be successful.

It has ceased raining and is now quite cool. But I have been sitting all evening with my sleeves turned up as far as I could conveniently get them and my shirt turned down around the neck. It cannot be possible that the weather is as hot with you as it is and has been for the past month down here. While we were at Danville, I was out in the country and I noticed the corn was turning yellow from the long absence of any rain. While I am informed it has been right the reverse up North. The grain crops hereabouts are looking splendidly. There is a field of wheat before our camp which contains one hundred and seventy five acres. Quite a wheat field, don't you think so. It continues to lighten up in the Northeast and I think we shall be blest with more rain before the morrow. It did awfully come down this afternoon after the hard clap of thunder. It reminded me very much of the thunder of artillery we used to be accustomed to hearing not many miles from here, in a southeasterly direction from our camp.

Our Corps has to march through what I once told you was the doomed City (Richmond) that the citizens may see the old Sixth Corps, who have figured well in the past rebellion and which will ever retain a name in the History of the Great Rebellion of '61.

Paper Mill — Richmond, VA (1865).

God grant there never may be another such cruel war in this country or in any country upon the face of the globe. So Addie has left you. She didn't make a very long stay, but about as long as I anticipated. Yet I hoped she would remain for I supposed she would be a great help to you. But I suppose it is as you say. She has had her own way too long. The boys are well and anxiously looking ahead to home and the comfort of a quiet life once more. But one half of them will never be content to remain at home. After a due course of time they will become tired and leading a civil life and will long for a life more exciting unless it is some of the old men. They of course, who have survived this Grand struggle for the maintenance of the old Union, will be glad to live in quietude the remaining days of their life. But to the young man, the past seems but a dream for the hardship tells not so much upon his constitution as it will in after years. The Chaplain gave us a good sermon today, but I think it is now time I close so I will now bid you good night and may God watch over and bless you and I remain your loving and affec. son,

Downtown Richmond, VA (1865).

Albert

Harrison

Camp of the 14th N.J. Vols. Infty.
Near Washington D.C.
June 3, 1865

Dear Parents

I feel to thank God that I am still spared to pen you a few lines after our severe and trying march from Richmond, which place we passed through in review on the 24th of last month and continued the march for our National Capitol three days, when we were caught in a severe storm and the consequence was, we were stuck in the mud and had to lay by for days. During this time the storm abated and the roads dried up somewhat and we moved on making Fredericksburg where we encamped for one night and crossed the river the next morning. It seemed for the first time we were gaining ground. We came in camp here yesterday just in the heat of the day and now our marching days are over. If there was one among us who felt sorry we would tie him to a stump and whip him, but happily there are none but what are glad the days work's done. We will soon pass onward to new scenes.

I am unable to form the least idea as to how long we shall remain here, but I don't think it will be many days before our old Corps will be broken up and we shall go home rejoicing. Next Monday we are to pass in review through Washington and then return to camp. It will occupy nearly a day. But we can afford it, as it will be the last time I trust.

I was made glad last night by receiving a letter from you and exceeding glad that John was doing well. He had better not be in any hurry to go to work. I shall have to get a new suit of clothes I suppose and I will have enough left to keep us for a couple of months.

I owe considerable for grub for Uncle Sam could not give us enough sometimes and I am not one to hate good victuals for the sake of a few dollars. But most of us soldiers like to eat as well as anybody and we are bound to have it if money will buy it. So we borrow and lend. I have two old pennies I have carried along on the march and I take them out and look at them once in a while and wish for more that I might buy a pie or some bread or something besides tack.

But we have not long to gnaw our tack now. I believe we are to draw soft bread this afternoon, then we will feast on bread and pork and coffee. We will not be paid until we arrive in our state. I shall go by the way of New York from Trenton if I can, then settle with Aunt Clemmy for those boots the first thing, get my suit of Cits, give Aunt a polite invitation to accompany me to R.B. and off we will start to surprise you. So look out for the returned Soldier Boy.

I have shaved off my whiskers and you may not know me. They make such a change, but they may have time to grow out again before I arrive as I have marked them out again. It is a very hot day and I am truly thankful that our destination was reached yesterday. Do not think because I am free that I shall do as I please. That I did not mean, when I wrote it. I know Mother, I have always been free. But you know there are so many who long for that day to come and they are no better off afterward.

But I see you have no taste as to my remaining in service, as you shall have your way this time, as I had mine before. But holding the position of Captain I could command more wages than I could at anything I can find to employ time elsewhere. Still I have no particular liking to the service. So I shall follow your precepts and come home to enjoy a few days or weeks in peace and harmony with all men. Johnny Ingling stated in a letter I received from him that he was preparing to keep one a week and I received a polite invitation from Freehold, New Brunswick, and Eatontown. Miss Edna Wolcott invited me to give them a call and said they were very much disappointed at my not giving them a call when home last winter. She wrote me a splendid letter. I shall call upon them most assuredly and take dinner.

How like old times it will seem. They used to think so much of me. I must try and establish myself again in their good graces for I may get an acre. But, I cannot longer waste my time joking. I hope to hear from you again soon and please send me a couple of stamps and give my best respects to friends and relatives.

I remain fondly your loving son,
Albert

Harrison

Camp of the 14th, N.J. Vols. Infantry
Bailey's Cross Roads, Near Washington, D.C.
June 7, 1865

Dear Cousin Clemmy

I am at leisure this evening and I cannot better devote a few moments than by penning you a few lines and this may be the last letter I may ever write as a soldier for I expect before many days have passed away, I will lay aside my suit of blue and become a peaceable citizen of the United States. I had some time since a strong notion of remaining in the service, but mother is not willing that I should remain and I must obey her this time, for I believe I have done my duty and should rest from my labors. Well, we had a very tedious march from Richmond, leaving there on the 24th of last month and upon the third day's march we were caught in a severe storm and the consequences were we were stuck in the mud and were obliged to lay aside for two days during which time the storm abated and the roads became passable for our trains and we moved onward to Fredericksburg. But the weather became very warm and many poor boys dropped by the roadside from sun stroke. Very few recovered.

We arrived here on the 2nd day of June and we have been preparing to be reviewed tomorrow in the City, prior to being mustered out. But I will not take part in the performance as I have enough writing to keep me busy a week. I am at work on our Muster out Rolls at present. The sooner we get them done, the sooner we will get home. We could go day after tomorrow if we had our papers finished, for there is plenty of transportation now. The more I think of coming home, the more anxious I am to get there. I really have not been so home sick since I have been in service.

Still we have a very pleasant camp. Good water and plenty to eat. But it isn't home yet. I had a letter from home since I came here. Mother is quite well and John expected to go to work in a few days. I fear he will never be strong enough to stand any amount of exposure or hard labor. It is a splendid evening. I should love to be at the shore tonight. I think I could fully realize God's mercies to us poor weak creatures who are not worthy, the least of them. But I will now lay aside my letter and try to finish tomorrow before the mail goes out.

One day has passed away and here my letter remains yet unfinished. But I will now write a few more lines before I retire. I have been busily engaged writing all of the past day during which time our Corps was being reviewed in the City, and they had a hot day for it. But thank the Lord it is over, but not without the loss of a few lives from sun stroke. But they cannot have the opportunity much longer of marching us to death. I was very glad that I was considered out of the performance, for I came near biting the dust last night soon after I stopped writing. I looked out of my tent and saw the night so beautiful. I thought I must take a stroll down the Washington Pike, so I asked the Sergeant if he would accompany me. He assented and off we started down the Pike. We got about 100 yards from Camp, before that old familiar sound which accompanies a bullet brought us to a stand still. The ball passed through the rim of my hat, upon the left side of my head. I took off my hat and gazed at the rent the ball made. My comrade asked me if I was hit for I never said a word, but kept my eye on my hat and thinking it was a pretty good shot. While we were thus standing, along came another token of respect passing to the left of us both. I then decamped closely followed by my comrade. I made up my mind if there was a shooting to be done I must have a hand in. But I was foiled for all our ammunition was taken from us yesterday. But I did reach to send a ball back in the direction they came from. Someone in the Fifth Corps fired the shots at a crowd of our boys, who it happened were about thirty yards from us sitting by the roadside and throwing out insinuations at each other, about fighting, etc. I tell you Clemmy, there is a hard set of men in this army. I give them credit for coming so close to me, without hitting. But it wouldn't have set very well on my stomach if I had been shot after the war was ended.

Had I been in battle, I should not have given it more than a passing thought, but truly God is good in sparing my life and to Him only am I indebted for the preservation of my life. I have thought over the matter seriously several times today and just came to the conclusion finally that I wasn't born to be shot.

Before next week this time, I think we will be in Trenton. I will have our company account all in order by Saturday night, if I am spared. I hope this may find you all in good health. I wish I had time to write more, but I must now go to bed on Mother Earth, for a few more nights. My love to all and hoping soon to see you. I remain with many kind wishes, your loving Coz,

Al

Harrison

Camp of the 14th N.J. Volunteers Infantry
Bailey's Cross Roads Near Washington, D.C.
June 10, 1865

Dear Parents

Your loving missive of June 6th came most welcome to hand last night and as I am at leisure this afternoon, I will be penning you a reply. Although I wrote but a short time since and you will not be looking for a letter, but it will do no harm to write at any rate. But for the past three days, I have done nothing scarcely but write and my fingers are actually sore from holding the pen. But I am through at last, having com-

pleted our muster out Rolls, Pay
Rolls and Discharges this morning. I expect we will start for the
Capitol of Jersey in the course of
two or three days, today being
Saturday. I think there will be
transportation for so small a
band as we will be. Not many
over two hundred and 25 out of
one thousand men nearly three
years ago. Only a remnant of our
former strength.

It has been raining some
this afternoon and still continues which makes it quite comfortable. I hope you are not
having such a warm spell of
weather at home. If it is, I don't
think I can put up in the House.
I shall have to pitch my tent in
the yard or in the garden under

The Grand Review in Washington, D.C.

a gooseberry bush. You must have quite a garden I should
think. You ought to have plenty of peas by this time. I think
you said some time ago you had some planted, but I guess I
will be in time for them if I am too late for my strawberries and
cream. I expect they will be played out before we get to Trenton. But I have picked quite a good many wild ones along the
road from Richmond. I picked a cup full two days before we
arrived here. But they were so sour it took two days rations of
sugar to sweeten them then I had to drink my coffee without
sugar. But, that was nothing new, for almost always on the
march I take my sugar on my tack instead of keeping it to
sweeten my coffee.

I didn't see that it made any material difference after I
became used to it, and a soldier can get used to almost anything but fighting. That hardly ever came natural to me to tell
the truth if there was fun in it, I saw it but seldom. But there
was a stern reality, when a man was expecting every minute
would be the last. The sun is coming out again. I guess the rain
is nearly over. I suppose you have seen by this time the full
account of yesterday's review in the New York papers.

It was a big thing in the dust and hot sun and some of
the boys who have been through thick and thin for nearly three
long years fell from the effects of the heat and dust, which
comprises the City of Washington.

I believe there is nothing more for me to write. I wrote
to Clemmy last night. That will be one more kiss. I now close.
May Heavens richest blessing crown you all and I remain
affectionately your loving son,

Al

Epilogue

The great political questions that had plagued the United States during the mid-century were finally settled on the battlefields of the Civil War. General Joseph E. Johnston surrendered Confederate forces shortly after Appomattox, and isolated pockets of Confederate resistance followed suit. President Lincoln instructed his military commanders to "let em up easy" and had the military band in Washington D.C. strike up "Dixie" as it was then "contraband of war." He intended on implementing a liberal reconstruction plan that would have "bound up the nation's wounds." The bullet fired by John Wilkes Booth killed not only the President but also any hope that the nation might have been reconciled on a smooth and liberal basis. It is generally conceded that Lincoln would have been better suited to preside over Reconstruction than his successor. To what extent he would have been successful, given the nature of Congress in 1865, will never be known. It is clear, however, that the "Radical Republicans" were determined to treat the South as conquered provinces and to readmit them gradually and conditionally.

The ensuing decade saw the nation grapple with the two momentous problems that came out of the war: how and on what terms

Albert C. Harrison, circa 1905.

would the Confederate states be readmitted, and what would be the status of the newly emancipated freedmen. Reconstruction was to become a tumultuous episode in the Republic's history wrought with problems that would persist well into the next century.

There was a conspicuous lack of retribution, notwithstanding the bitterness generated by the war. With the exception of Henry Wirtz, commandant of the infamous Confederate prison at Andersonville, Georgia, there was no execution of rebels which has been typical in unsuccessful revolutions worldwide—before and since. Americans as far back as the Revolution of 1776 refrained from the ghastly extermination of political opponents.

The 14th New Jersey Volunteers were sent to the Virginia/North Carolina border on occupation duty for a short time after the war. After securing the Danville, Virginia area, it marched with the 6th Corps to Bailey's Cross Roads and was reviewed in the nation's capital. It returned to Trenton, New Jersey where it was mustered out of Federal service in June, 1865.

Major Peter Vredenburgh Jr., Lieutenant Marcus Stults, Lieutenant William Ross and Private Jacob Wolcott sacrificed their lives for their country. Sergeant Harrison and Private Jones survived. Together, these six men comprised a group whose sacrifice has ennobled them for all time. Contemporary commentary proves inadequate to eulogize them beyond what Abraham Lincoln expressed when he wrote . . . "We

Civil War veterans, probably members of the local Arrowsmith Post, posed for this picture sometime around 1885 in Red Bank, NJ. Sergeant Albert C. Harrison is second from the right in the second row from the top.

cannot dedicate—we cannot consecrate—we cannot hallow . . . the brave men . . . who struggled here, have consecrated it, far above our poor power to add or detract . . ."

Edward Jones moved west to Ellsworth, Kansas, and Albert Harrison returned to Red Bank, New Jersey. They would both experience the profound changes industrialization would bring to America. Transcontinental railroads would erase the frontier line by 1890; the telephone, the automobile, and the airplane would catapult the nation forward within a few short decades after the close of the Civil War so that men like Harrison and Jones would see their world as it existed during the "Great Rebellion" fade quickly into the past.

Albert C. Harrison returned to his home in Red Bank, New Jersey and married Eliza Chadwick. They had six children. He became involved in a number of business enterprises, joining thousands who turned to free enterprise capitalism as America became industrialized. He started a butcher's business in Red Bank and later moved to New York, where for six years he carried on a carpet business. In 1882, he moved back to Red Bank and started a wallpaper business with his son John, under the name of "Harrison & Son." He retired from business about 1915.

Albert put in thirty-one years of service as town clerk of Shrewsbury Township and Red Bank, New Jersey. Red Bank at that time was part of the township, but it was governed by a town board of commissioners. He resigned as clerk in 1919 and received a pension from the town as a reward for his long and faithful service.

Albert became a member of Arrowsmith Post of Civil War Veterans. He held every office of the organization, and at the time of his death he was the chaplain. He was a member of the Baptist Church and enjoyed a ten year retirement until his death, which occurred on September 10, 1925 at the age of 81. He was buried at the Embury Methodist Church in Little Silver, New Jersey.

Private Edward C. Jones returned to his home in Plainfield, New Jersey immediately following the war. He had been born in

The 14th N.J. Volunteers pictured here and opposite at a reunion at Monocacy (Frederick, MD), where a monument stands commemorating their integral role in that key battle in July, 1864, circa 1905.

Rochester, New York on September 9, 1844, moved to New Jersey at an early age and enlisted in the 14th New Jersey Volunteer Infantry in August, 1862. He was promoted to musician on October 16, 1862, and saw continuous service with the Regiment throughout the rebellion.

Edward moved to Ellsworth, Kansas in May, 1884, no doubt following Horace Greeley's maxim, "Go West Young Man, Go West." He married and raised three children. Ed was employed by E.W. Wellington and was regarded as a dedicated and faithful worker. He was a highly regarded citizen of the community and became an enthusiastic member of the veteran's group — the Grand Army of the Republic (G.A.R.).

Jones died at his home in Ellsworth, Kansas on February 17, 1910 at the age of sixty-five.

In those years following the war, both men would remain active in the G.A.R. veterans organization. No doubt, as they took a nostalgic glance at the past, they would, as Sergeant Harrison reminisced — long to be *UPON THE TENTED FIELD ONCE MORE.*

ACKNOWLEDGEMENTS

As with all research projects, there are a number of institutions and individuals that prove to be indispensable sources of background information. The following list are the ones that proved most helpful and contributed greatly to this project. Special thanks to James M. McPherson for his encouraging words and review of the letters.

Alexander Library — Special Collections
Rutgers University
New Brunswick, NJ

Frederick Historical Society
Frederick, MD

Maryland Historical Society
Baltimore, MD

Monmouth County Historical Society
Freehold, NJ

New Jersey Historical Society
Newark, NJ

Shrewsbury Historical Society
Shrewsbury, NJ

The National Archives
Washington, DC

The U.S. Army Military History Institute
Carlisle, PA

U.S. Military Academy Archives
West Point, NY

Freehold Public Library
Freehold, NJ

Free Public Library of Philadelphia
Philadelphia, PA

Guggenheim Library
Monmouth College
West Long Branch, NJ

Handley Library
Winchester, VA

J.H. Robbins Memorial Library
Ellsworth, KS

National Park Service
Washington, DC

Princeton University Libraries
Princeton, NJ

Red Bank Public Library
Red Bank, NJ

State Library of New Jersey
Trenton, NJ

The Library of Congress
Washington, DC

T.J. McMahon, Fair Haven, NJ

Dr. John Olsen
Eastern New Mexico University

Dr. Richard Sommers, Archivist-Historian
Library at the
The U.S. Army Military History Institute,
Carlisle, PA

Mr. James O. Libby, Neptune, NJ

Mr. John Kuhl, Pittstown, NJ

Edward J. McKenna, Jr. ESQ., Red Bank, NJ

SELECTED BIBLIOGRAPHY

As noted historian James M. McPherson points out in the Foreword to Upon the Tented Field, there have been some 50,000 publications about the Civil War published in the last 130 years. The following works were invaluable references as this book was put together, and each of these is highly recommended for further study.

Aman, William Frayne, ed., *Personnel Of The Civil War,* New York & London, Thomas Yoseloff Publishers, A.S. Barnes & Company, Inc., Vols I & II, 1961.

Barber, John W., Howe, Henry, *Historical Collections Of The State Of New Jersey,* New York, S. Tuttle, 1844.

Boatner, Mark Mayo III, *The Civil War Dictionary,* New York, David McKay Company, Inc., 1959.

Bradford, Ned, ed., *Battles And Leaders Of The Civil War*, New York Appleton-Century-Crofts, Inc., 1956.

Catton, Bruce, *A Stillness At Appomattox,* New York, Doubleday & Company, 1953.

_____, *The Army Of The Potomac, Glory Road,* New York, Doubleday & Company, 1952.

_____, *The Army Of The Potomac, Mr. Lincoln's Army,* New York, Doubleday & Company, 1951, 1962.

_____, *This Hallowed Ground, The Story Of The Union Side Of The Civil War,* New York, Doubleday & Company, 1956.

Commager, Henry Steele, ed., *Documents Of American History,* New York, 7th edition, Meredith Publishing Company, 1963.

Denny, Robert E., *The Civil War Years, A Day-By-Day Chronicle Of The Life Of A Nation,* New York, Sterling Publishing Company, 1992.

Donald, David, *Charles Sumner And The Coming Of The Civil War,* Norwalk, Connecticut, Easton Press, 1960.

Dyer, Freederick H., *A Compendium Of The War Of The Rebellion,* New York-London, Thomas Yoseloff, Sagamore Press, 1959.

Ellis, Frank, *History Of Monmouth County, New Jersey,* Philadelphia, R.T. Peck & Company, 1885.

Foster, John Y., *New Jersey And The Rebellion: A History Of The Services Of The Troops And People Of New Jersey In Aid Off The Union Cause,* Martin R. Dennis & Company, 1868.

Ketcham, Wilbur B., *The Royal Gallery Of Poetry And Art, An Illustrated Book Of The Poetic Gems Of The English Language,* N.D. Thompson Publishing Company, 1886.

Lewis, A.S., *My Dear Parents: The Civil War Seen By An English Union Soldier-James Horrocks,* San Diego-New York-London, Harcourt Brace Jovanovich, 1982.

Long, E.B., Long, Barbara, *The Civil War Day By Day-An Almanac 1861-1865,* New York, DaCapo Press, 1971.

McPherson, James M., *Battle Cry Of Freedom, The Civil War Era,* Norwalk, Connecticut, Easton Press (MBI, Inc.) 1989.

Rawls, Walton ed., *Great Civil War Heroes And Their Battles,* New York, Abbeville Press, 1985.

Sifakis, Stewart, *Who Was Who In The Civil War,* New York, Facts On File, Inc., 1988.

Stevenson, William G., *Thirteen Months In The Rebel Army,* New York, A.S. Barnes & Company, 1959.

Stryker, William S., *Record Of Officers And Men Of New Jersey In The Civil War 1861-1865,* Trenton, New Jersey, John L. Murphy-Steam Book & Job Printer, 1876.

Underwood, Robert J., Buel, Clarence C., ed., *Battles And Leaders Of The Civil War, Being For The Most Part Contributions By Union And Confederate Officers-Based On "Century War Series.",* New York, Century Magazine, 1884.

Vandiver, Frank E., *Their Tattered Flags, The Epic Of The Confederacy,* New York, Harper & Row, 1970.

INDEX